HARDPRESS.NET

ISBN: 9781313372800

Published by:
HardPress Publishing
8345 NW 66TH ST #2561
MIAMI FL 33166-2626

Email: info@hardpress.net
Web: http://www.hardpress.net

evidently means birds bred from pure-bred parents on each side, and which are generally known as birds of a first cross. As a rule, the author seems to have used Cochin instead of Brahma crosses; but in his introductory remarks upon crossing he says that if it is more convenient such substitutions as Minorca for Spanish, or Creve Cœur for Houdan, or Brahma for Cochin, may be made. We cannot, of course, do more than select for mention one or two of the many crosses instanced:—Hamburgh-Cochins are described as very good table birds, and enormous layers, averaging 240 to 250 eggs per annum. They do well in confinement, or a large run. Houdan-Cochins are described as very hardy and easily reared, good table birds and layers of large brown eggs. Six hens of this cross averaged in the winter of their first and second years 26 eggs per week, and the author considers 240 eggs per annum about a fair statement of their laying powers. For table purposes the author recommends Game Dorkings and Houdan Dorkings, the latter being spoken of as good all round birds, where there is an ample run. We can safely advise a careful perusal of the entire work to such of our readers as take up poultry-keeping with a view to the return in eggs or table fowls, and those who already do something in this line will also gain much useful information from the author's narrative of his experience.—*Journal of Horticulture*, October 19th, 1882.

Practical Poultry Breeder; or, How to make Poultry Pay. By William Cook. Published by the author, Tower House, Orpington, Kent.—Seeing that over £3,000,000 a year are paid away by this country for foreign eggs and poultry, it does seem extraordinary (as Mr. Cook remarks) that English farmers pay so little attention to poultry. With corn and land to be had cheap, surely the only thing wanting to make the business remunerative is proper management. Mr. Cook's suggestion is that poultry farmers should have three crops growing at once—fruit, sheep, and poultry. He admits the risk of working on a large scale, but shows conclusively how profitable fowls may be made under the owner's personal supervision. The work, which is of the most practical kind, has reached a third edition.—*Lloyd's News.*

Mr. W. Cook, of Orpington, has just published a third edition of his poultry-book, re-written and greatly enlarged, wherein the author has recorded the results of an extensive series of cross-breeding between the different varieties of pure-bred poultry. Without for one moment admitting that a cross-bred bird is better for any one purpose than a pure fowl, I none the less cordially recommend this manual as a useful and practical guide, by following which poultry keeping can be made to pay.—*Bromley Telegraph.*

The Practical Poultry Breeder and Feeder. By W. Cook.—We have received a copy of the third edition of this poultry-keeper's *vade mecum*, which has been re-written and revised to date, and we can recommend it to the careful attention of those who keep, or are about to keep, poultry. Mr. Cook has added about 170 pages to the previous edition, and the book now abounds with a fund of useful information requisite for the management of poultry with a view to profit as well as pleasure, the information being explained in a thoroughly practical and simple manner. Commencing with a few general remarks, Mr. Cook goes on to explain the proper mode of constructing houses, runs, &c., and then gives his opinion as to the best fowls to keep. Next follow chapters on feeding, how to breed and what to breed from, incubation, sitting and hatching, chicken rearing, descriptions of the various pure-bred and cross-bred fowls, poultry farming and keeping, fattening fowls, preparing birds for the show-pen, how to preserve eggs, &c. Ducks, geese, and turkeys are also touched upon, and several pages are devoted to the treatment of the various diseases poultry are subject to. This valuable book may be obtained of the author, Tower House, Orpington.—*Norwood Review.*

Cook's Poultry Breeder and Feeder.—Books upon poultry are very numerous, but we are always glad to welcome one which comes as the result of practical experience, as there is sure to be something new therein, or, if old, put in a new way. And in this work, a third edition of which has just been issued by the author, Mr. W. Cook, of Orpington, Kent, there is much to learn, especially in the direction of crosses. There are upwards of 40 crosses recorded, and each one of these the author says he has personally tried, and the results here given are what he has himself seen. For this section of the work alone it would be a decided acquisition to poultry literature, as our knowledge of the effect of crossing is comparatively limited. The chapter on diseases is also a very useful one, and these form the best sections of the work. In spite of the fact that throughout the pages references are constantly made to the business of the author, it is a useful handbook on poultry keeping for amateurs. A hint as to how best the want of a grass run can be met may be useful to some of our readers. When fowls are deprived of a grass run and fed liberally, and at the same time are rather short of green food, their blood gets very hot, especially in the spring months. It is well to use a little flour of sulphur (sometimes called brimstone). There are two sorts, the dark and the yellow; the latter is the best; one heaped-up teaspoonful for 10 fowls is the quantity to be used. Sulphur, unfortunately, causes the eggs to have a strong taste. This is partly counteracted by using the same quantity of common salt as sulphur. It is not well to use this medicine too early in the spring, as it opens the pores of the skin too much if it is given in cold weather, or when the cold wind is blowing.—*Live Stock Journal.*

Practical Poultry Breeder and Feeder; or, How to Make Poultry Pay. (By William Cook).—We have long thought that poultry and egg farming must become a great industry in this country; but we have also the conviction that it must be intelligently carried on and scientifically systematised. These things Mr. Cook's admirable volume will help to do. Meanwhile, it gives to the immense number of amateur and professional breeders of poultry a cyclopædia of the most reliable information. It is specially offered to those who require elementary instruction; but the simple fact is that the keeping of cocks and hens can never pass beyond a certain simple and measurable sphere of knowledge, having mastered the facts and data of which, the rest depends upon the usual qualities and qualifications, more or less common to human nature itself—aptitude, intelligence, care, diligence, persistence, cleanliness, and thrift. The author does not waste space and labour upon the exhibition of poultry, but everything is done to assist in the increase of the useful and profitable qualities of fowls. He is himself an experienced and competent teacher, and chiefly sets himself to show how any one may keep fowls with profit.—*Manchester Weekly Post.*

BOOK TESTIMONIALS.

Forest School, Guernsey, C.I., September, 1885.

DEAR SIR,—I wish to add my testimony to the excellence of your little hand-work, the POULTRY BREEDER AND FEEDER, which I purchased some time since. Although I had had a good experience in poultry-keeping, I have gathered a vast amount of information from it. All who keep poultry should purchase it.

Believe me, yours faithfully,
WELLINGTON CORBETT.

Eagley Lodge, Blackburn Road, nr. Bolton,
March, 1885.

DEAR SIR,—Have received your poultry book, and am very pleased with it. I consider it the best I ever read. Yours truly,
A. HOLT.

Didbrook Vicarage, Winchcombe, Cheltenham,
July, 1885.

DEAR SIR,—The chickens from the Hamburgh-Cochin eggs I purchased from you have done splendidly, and have grown faster and better than any I ever had. I have been most successful in my first attempt at chicken breeeding and farming, and I have now 60 fine birds. It is only doing you justice to say that all my success is entirely owing to your most useful and instructive book, which I can thoroughly recommend. I am, yours truly,
REV. F. F. COLLIN.

1, St. George's Terrace, Cromwell Road, Eastney,
Southsea, Hants.

DEAR SIR,—Three or four months since we purchased one of your poultry books, which we have found very useful, especially when any of our poultry have been ailing. We have also found your powders most advantageous. Yours faithfully, J. WHITEHEAD.

The Schools, Arundel, June, 1885.

DEAR SIR,—Some time since I purchased your excellent little treatise on breeding and feeding poultry, and may say I consider it one of the best investments I ever made. I recommend it to all my friends. Yours truly, J. GREENWOOD.

MR. COOK.

Cross Hill, nr. Lancaster, December, 1883.

DEAR SIR,—I have read your most valuable book on poultry—I may say over and over again. I am sure it is one of the greatest boons to poultry-keepers, and should be purchased by all.

Yours truly, C. J. CLARK.

INDEX.

ADDENDA.

PREFACE.

MY object in writing the first edition of this book was to give, in as few words as possible, such plain and practical information as would enable anyone who had little or no idea of poultry, and only the smallest accommodation, to keep fowls and make them pay well, thus combining pleasure and profit both in towns and country. I am glad to say the information contained in my book has been eagerly sought after; in fact, so much so, that three editions were sold at the end of last year. In this country for many years past new-laid eggs and poultry have been merely luxuries for the rich, many of our working population never obtaining these delicacies; and to those few who have, they have been given in times of sickness by some charitable person. I am, however, glad to say that this kind of thing is fast giving way, and since the first publication of my little work many thousands have indulged not only in eating the eggs and poultry, but have derived a certain amount of enjoyment from their live birds.

There are many thousands of people keep poultry now who formerly thought it an impossibility to keep a few birds in confinement profitably.

I have treated on pure-bred fowls so that a novice may select his or her best fowls for breeding pure stock, and also for crossing purposes, and the best breeds to keep under different circumstances, the best table fowls and egg-producers. I have tried about 50 different crosses, and keep about 48 different pure breds.

The knowledge thus gained has enabled me to give an accurate account of the various breeds, so that the readers may judge for themselves which varieties will suit their varied accommodation.

I have not given any very elaborate description of ornamental poultry houses, &c. My whole object has been to give such practical information as will enable anyone to build the coops, &c., themselves (if time permit), on a cheap scale. I may add that poultry may be likened unto machines for converting waste and worthless things into very good and profitable delicacies, as in most houses there are some scraps from the table, and refuse, such as potatoes, scraps of meat, and cold vegetables, &c., that will do well for poultry, but which in most cases would be thrown away as useless. These things, however, make first-rate food for fowls, when treated as described in the paragraph on feeding; and when poultry are kept in this way, and with good management, I have known them pay over 300 per cent. in a small way. I have received thousands of letters in the past few years, stating how well the writers have done by carrying out the instructions laid down in this book. Ladies and gentlemen who keep their poultry for the purpose of supplying their own household requirements obtain eggs *all through* the year. I know farmers who have made from £10 to £80 in a year. One I know well made £180 clear profit in two years. Many cottagers I have known who have made from £3 to £15 a year by keeping a few fowls.

The chapter on ducks has been very useful to many.

I am willing to give anyone requiring it any help in this way by their enclosing a stamped and addressed envelope.

WILLIAM COOK.

INTRODUCTION.

THE number of eggs annually imported by this country is about eight hundred millions, in addition to thousands of tons of poultry, together worth over three million pounds sterling. As is generally known, the majority of these eggs come over from France, Sweden, and Denmark, where they are produced by the cottagers and small farmers, nearly all of whom keep fowls and make them pay well, although their eggs and poultry have to pass through the hands of four or five different middlemen, each making a profit for himself, before they reach the English consumer. The greater part of the money these people receive from England might just as well go to our own farmers, cottagers, and workmen.

It may be said that in England we could not produce the number of eggs the French do, owing to our variable climate, but I believe the largest number of eggs comes from the north-west of France, where the climate is very similar to our own, and the eggs sent over in the winter are largely composed of those laid in spring and summer and carefully preserved. There are also large numbers of eggs and fowls exported from Ireland, where the climate is much damper than in England. Another point in favour of the home producer is that foreign eggs are generally smaller than

English, and they always fetch less money, as the average value all the year round of each egg, when first imported into this country, is under three farthings, and, therefore, the actual producer cannot receive more than a halfpenny, if so much, when he sells first of all.

The workman who lives in or near a town may say that it is all very well for cottagers, who have commons and lanes for their fowls to range over, where they pick up half their living, to keep poultry, but that he would have to keep his birds in confinement and provide every scrap of food. Against this, however, he must bear in mind that eggs in the country sell for about half the price they would fetch in the town, and therefore the town resident has just as good an opportunity, from a pecuniary point of view, as the country cottager; in fact, I may say far better, for, as a rule, six fowls penned up in a back yard in a town will lay more eggs than ten birds in the country where they have several acres to roam over.

Another reason given by many persons for not keeping fowls is that it is stated in certain books that they must not keep more than so many fowls in one house, or rear a brood of chickens on a piece of ground less than such and such a size, and that they must heat their houses in winter to obtain eggs. These rules, with the exception of artificially heating the houses, are all very well if they can be carried out, but for cottagers, &c., they are impossible, and, as I shall show, they are not necessary, as I have frequently found that workmen and others with very small accommodation for their birds produce more eggs in winter than many gentlemen who keep six times the number. The reason for this is that the cottagers' fowls are well looked after and fed on warm soft food, while the gentleman's are often fed anyhow, and with hard corn only.

From the preceding remarks it will be seen that there is

no reason why the eggs should not be produced in this country instead of paying France and other countries for them, and the object of this work is to show how those with only the smallest and roughest accommodation can do well with fowls and make them pay.

I do not write this book without experience, having kept fowls for many years, which have given a good profit, and I also know of many instances where cottagers with only a very small piece of ground have kept fowls and made them pay well (in many cases having more than paid their rent). In addition to the profit derived from poultry keeping, there is a large amount of pleasure obtained in looking after and watching the birds, and this probably attracts far more people than the idea of making profit.

There are many people who, when they first have the care of poultry, think it a great trouble and nuisance to have anything to do with them ; but these very same persons have frequently said before they had the care of them long what a pleasure they were. I have known people in all stations of life watch and tend poultry for hours ; and what is more interesting to young people in their leisure time than the care of poultry? When a hen becomes broody, with what care and attention they place the eggs under her, and watch and tend her for three weeks ! and then, when the chicks appear, with what joy are they greeted, and how carefully attended, the young owners not denying them anything they fancy will tend to their comfort ! I also think that nothing gives parents more pleasure than seeing their children interested in young quadrupeds or birds ; as, if they are naturally inclined to be cruel, by giving them, say a fowl or other animal to call their own, it not only often cures them of this tendency, but frequently leads to acts of generosity.

In addition to this, who, either rich or poor, has not found it a great boon to have new-laid eggs and poultry in time of sickness? and is there anything more nutritious and nice for a working man after a hard day's toil than one or two new-laid eggs, which, were they not of his own producing, would be quite out of reach, as new-laid eggs are far too expensive a luxury for working men, and if they try ordinary shop eggs they often have the utter disappointment of finding them quite uneatable after breaking the shells.

Those who start poultry-keeping must not be discouraged if they do not get on so well as they could wish for the first year or so; but there is nothing that pays so well in the way of live stock for care and attention. There may be one or two birds die first of all; but losses will come in other things as well as poultry, and if the remaining birds are treated properly they will soon pay for the loss of those that die.

In a few instances I have known poultry clear from 15s. to £1 each bird where only a few have been kept, say from six to thirteen hens, and where from 25 to 40 have been kept they have brought in from £9 to £20 clear profit in a year. I have known many who could not make the fowls pay for the food they ate before my little book was published; in fact, some had given up altogether, thinking it impossible to make them pay, and have re-commenced, gaining not only a handsome profit, but also much of pleasure. It is gratifying to one when a little profit is made out of fowls, but where pleasure and profit are combined it is more so, especially for parents who have to struggle hard through this life to maintain a large family. Fowls are then a great boon to them, being quite a luxury, for they are not only helping themselves, but teaching their children the art of keeping a few fowls profitably; nor does it end here, for there is often a little house or coop to be built, or a small run to be put up. Then the paint or tar brush must come into use for the outside, and the whitewash brush for the inside. Boys usually follow the example of their fathers, and when brought up thus it enables them to be very useful in their after-life, whatever station they may be placed in. What I learned in these little things as a boy has been very useful to me. Since the publication of my little book I have done all I can to encourage poultry-keeping in towns. I have given information twice a week at my London office (Mondays and Saturdays), and have doctored the sick birds which have been brought to me gratis. They have been brought from 20 miles round. In fact, sometimes I have not been able to leave my office till after 10 o'clock at night. Boys and girls bring their precious pets for me to see and relieve them from pain, which I am only too pleased to do. Some bring whole pens of birds to know which are the best to breed from. I have also answered all questions connected with the management of poultry—gratis—from anywhere in the world on receipt of a stamped and addressed envelope. Sometimes these have been more than I could answer in one day (from 20 to 80 in a day). If I can help anyone in poultry-keeping I am only too pleased to do so, as meat is so dear, and corn cheap; and it is always convenient to have new laid eggs, as they are much better for children than meat. When you are not feeling well and cannot eat meat, a new-laid egg is very nutritious, and as you are getting better who could say "No" to a nice roast or boiled fowl; and there is always something sweet about anything that is produced at home.

The convenience of always having them is worth a great deal to many people. I do not know five out of every hundred who have gone by my book these past four years that have not had eggs all the year round. I have had hundreds of letters informing me of this fact.

I have introduced in this edition of my book a chapter on Laying Qualities in Fowls and how to tell the points of a good layer from a bad one. This is, I think, a new subject, as I am not aware it has ever been attempted before. Having made a study of this subject for many years, I am able to pick out the best layers as soon as I enter a poultry yard, and it has enabled me to breed a large stock of good laying fowls of all breeds. This has been a boon to many hundreds of people, as I have given lectures to large audiences on this subject of laying qualities, demonstrating from live birds brought to the lectures the different points good layers possess, as compared with bad ones. I cannot reach the majority of poultry-keepers by lectures, so I have had the heads of some good and some bad-laying hens photographed, and from these illustrations I think my readers will be able to pick out the best layers they may have in their pens, which will enable them to discard the bad layers and only keep profitable birds. I have already brought out two varieties of fowls, viz: the Orpington and the Rose-Comb Orpington, and another variety which will be called the White Rose-Comb Orpington will be out in the autumn of 1889, which I think will find much favour among a certain class of people.

I am pleased to say that the two varieties of Orpingtons already out have been most favourably taken up by breeders throughout the world; and there is not a doubt that the Orpington fowls are the best all round birds that England can boast of at the present time.

I am frequently asked which is the best cramming machine for fowls. Undoubtedly, that manufactured by Mr. John Every, Phœnix Iron Works, Lewes, Sussex, is the best.

"THE WALDENS,"
St. Mary Cray, Kent (Late Tower House, Orpington).

GENERAL REMARKS.

BEFORE proceeding to describe the different branches of poultry-keeping in detail, I think it well to have a short chapter with a few general remarks.

In the first place, it is absolutely necessary to keep only young birds if a large number of eggs are required, as only a limited number of fowls lay so well in their second season, and I have found the best plan in this respect is to get rid of all my birds in the autumn except the very best layers, which may be kept for another season ; however, I do not recommend Brahmas or Cochins being kept unless they are extraordinarily good layers, and shed their feathers early in the autumn, as they rarely if ever do well in their second season, being so liable to make fat instead of eggs. They are also a great nuisance as regards sitting, as they are very frequently broody in the summer. The following treatment, however, will generally cure them, and is by far the best way to treat broody hens when it is requisite to cure them of their desire to sit.

Procure a box about 3 feet wide and 20 inches deep, in which three to six fowls may be kept at one time, and place bars across the front about 2 inches apart, so that the sitting hens cannot get out. The box must have no bottom, but bars from 2 to 3 inches apart should be nailed across, and when the box is stood, say upon four bricks, it will be from 2 to 3 inches off the ground. It will therefore be quite impossible for the hens to sit down in it except on the staves, and this practically causes them to be on the perch day and night. An ordinary coop with bars across the bottom will answer the purpose.

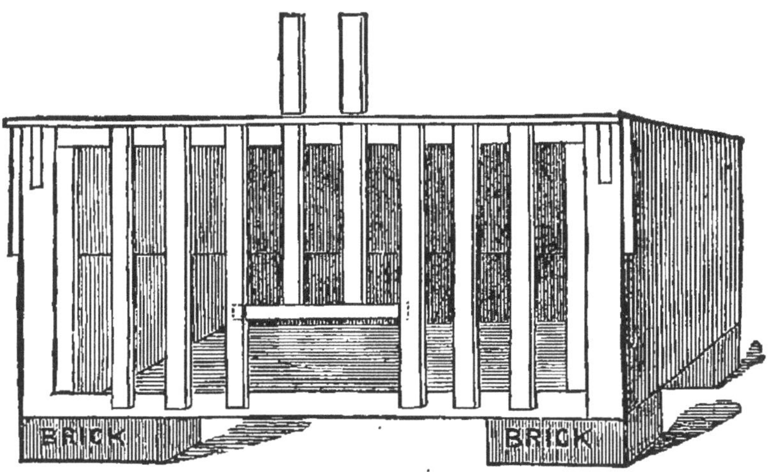

COOP FOR BROODY HENS.

The box or coop should be put in as light a place as possible in the run with the other fowls, and the water for the whole yard should be placed in front, so that the others must come in sight of the sitting hens to drink. They should also be fed all round the box, taking care that the sitting hens get as much as they can eat, as when fed with other fowls they generally eat more ravenously. By these means a broody hen will soon be cured, be in a healthy condition, and quickly come on to lay again. I have had

Cochin and Brahma hens come on to sit, have treated them in this way, let them out in three days, and before the week was up they have commenced laying; in fact, I never found this treatment fail with any fowls.

Some poultry writers tell us to shut the hens up in a dark place and give no food for a day or two, but by so doing the birds are weakened, and the poultry-keeper loses from five to nine eggs each time they come on to sit, which amounts to something considerable in the course of the year.

It is very essential in poultry-keeping that fowls be kept perfectly clean, as they seldom do well when not properly attended to in this respect, although some hardy breeds

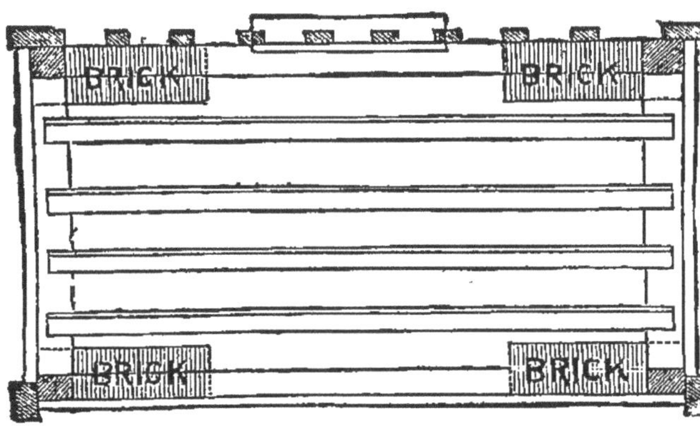

BOTTOM OF COOP.

will stand a good deal of inattention. This subject is one of the most important for those who have only small accommodation, as when fowls are cramped they require great attention in this respect, but where they have plenty of room they will sometimes thrive in a state of filth, although not so well as if properly attended to.

A very important point in poultry-keeping is when to kill or dispose of the hens that are not required for the following season. To be in prime condition for the table, they should be killed just when commencing to shed their feathers, when they will eat tender and juicy, but if not killed just in time they are unfit for at least another six weeks or two months.

A fowl which weighs 6lbs. before moulting, and moults late in the season often loses one-and-a-half pounds by the time it gets its new feathers. It is a great item where many fowls are kept.

Feeding, of course, has a great effect on the profits of the poultry-yard, and fowls are more often mismanaged in this respect than in any other, many people only using hard corn, and of this they give their birds as much as they can possibly eat, and to spare, whereas the proper mode of feeding is to give one meal of warm, soft food in the morning, and only to give the fowls at any time as much as they will eat eagerly.

To obtain eggs in the early part of a cold winter where the situation is cold, damp, or exposed, it is necessary to have young Brahmas, Cochins, Plymouth Rocks or Langshans, or crosses from these breeds, and if these are wanted to commence laying early in the season, they should be hatched in February or early March, as if the birds are properly looked after and fed well, they will generally come on to lay when about five or seven months old.

Pullets may be hatched all the year round, from January to August, but the late chickens must not be crowded with the other birds; if so, they will not thrive.

Other breeds besides Cochins, Brahmas, Plymouth Rocks or Langshans will often lay through the winter, but they cannot be relied upon for certain, especially if the weather be very severe, and the best way to obtain a constant supply of eggs in cold winters is to have young birds of the feather-legged tribes, or crosses with these breeds.

Poultry-keepers are often troubled with rats, that carry away the eggs and young chickens. These nuisances are very often attracted by food being left about, and if this is the case, the first thing to be done is to see that the fowls have only sufficient food for their immediate wants, and do not leave any about. Traps may sometimes be used with good results ; but the rats soon become too knowing, and will not be caught. One remedy I have found effective is to place tar in their runs and down their holes, but sometimes this does not answer. Poison may be used, but there is the risk of the fowls getting hold of it. One of the best remedies is to place small mesh wire netting along the sides of the houses up to the height of a foot, and continue it below the ground about eighteen inches. When this is done, it is quite impossible for the rats to get through, and when once properly done will always be found a certain cure.

In the following remarks, where I describe the different branches of poultry-keeping, it may be thought that I have gone needlessly into small details, and that it is not necessary to follow all the instructions given. This is quite true, as it is not absolutely necessary to do all that is described ; but if the attentions mentioned are given the fowls will pay well for them.

HOUSES & RUNS.

HOUSES.

THE house is a great consideration for poor people, as they do not consider they can afford £2 or £3 for this purpose, and therefore they do not keep fowls on account of the cost. There is, however, no need to go to this expense when starting poultry-keeping, although it is money well spent where it can be spared, and the fowls will soon pay for the trouble and care expended on them.

Where only a few fowls are kept, say half-a-dozen, they may be easily housed in a large box or hogshead bought from the grocer's for a few shillings, as very comfortable homes may be made out of these articles when treated as hereafter described.

If a hogshead is used, it should be laid on the ground longways, and fastened at the sides so that it cannot roll. A few inches of earth or road-scrapings should be put in the bottom and beaten down hard to make a level floor. A small square should be cut out of the farther end, close up to the top, and a piece of glass about 6 by 8 inches put in, so arranged that it may be opened wide when the weather is not too cold. Ventilation must also be provided by boring a few holes in the front and back of the hogshead; these holes should be made as close to the roof as possible, so that the fowls will not feel a draught.

Two perches should be put up crossways, and so made that they may be easily moved; and a nest must, of course, be provided, and so arranged that they may be easily got at,

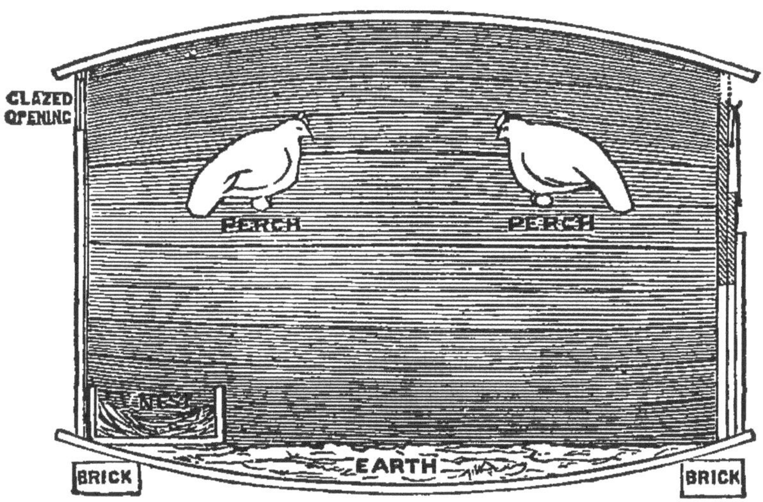

HOGSHEAD HOUSE.

the best place for this purpose being at the end, just under the movable window.

The front should be boarded a little at each side, the door being in the middle, and a hole should be cut in the bottom of the door to allow the fowls to pass in and out. A slide should be made to fit the hole, so that it may be closed in very cold weather.

The top of the hogshead must be covered with a piece of felt or canvas, and well tarred to keep the wet out, and if the cracks are very wide, some brown paper should be pasted inside over them, and this may be torn away in the warm weather. It is well to give the paper a good coating of limewash, to keep insects from sheltering underneath it. A large box may be used in the same way as the hogshead, but the roof must be made slanting, or the box should be tilted up, to allow the water to run off.

If a large box or hogshead cannot be obtained, a few egg-boxes may be bought cheap, and a small house built out of them, if possible, against a fence or in a corner. The wood

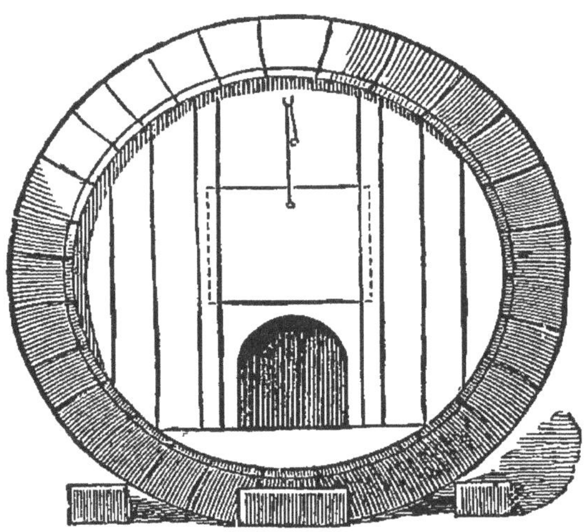

FRONT OF HOGSHEAD HOUSE.

is rather thin, but if covered with brown paper, as in the hogshead, they will do very well, and a nice warm house may be made out of them.

For eight to twelve fowls, a house 5 feet high and 5 feet square will be quite sufficient, and I may mention that I have kept fowls in perfect health and full lay all through the winter in these little houses.

If a larger or more substantial house is required, it may be made with feather-edged boards for the sides, &c., and the roof may be either thatched or made with ordinary half-inch planking, covered with felt and well tarred every year. The feather-edged boards are not so good for the roof, as they do not keep the wet out without being covered with felt, and when felt has to be used, it is better to put it on even boards. Quartering cut down the middle is quite

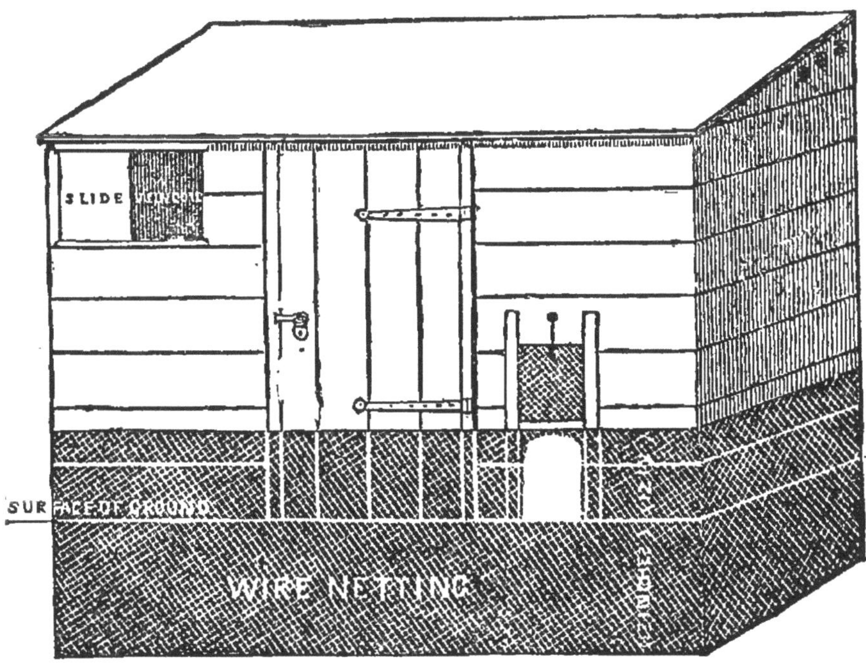

LEAN-TO HOUSE.

Showing Wire Netting above and below ground for keeping out Rats, &c.

strong enough for the framework. The sides must be tarred or painted to preserve the wood.

These houses may be either arranged so that they can be carried from place to place, or they can be made to lean against a wall. When in a fixed position, the bottom should be covered with road-scrapings, or any kind of soil mixed with water and well trodden down, as when the floor is quite hard it may be easily swept and occasionally peeled off with a spade, so there is no stale dirt left on.

The perches should be made to fit in a socket, and must be placed out of the draught. For heavy birds they should be about a foot from the ground, and should be made quite flat, about two inches wide, the edges being bevelled off. For smaller birds they may be placed a little higher, and need not be so large, as small birds like a round perch best. The bark must be stripped off, or it will harbour insects.

The nests may be made in any convenient position, but they are best on the ground in a secluded spot.

Ventilation must *always* be provided in all poultry houses by an opening of some sort at the topmost point of each end of the building. The ventilators must be so made that a draught will pass through over the birds' heads. An opening must be made for the birds to pass in and out, and this should be fitted with a slide to be closed in cold weather. Windows must also be put in where required, and these should be made so that they may be opened or shut according to the state of the weather, as fowls like light.

In building houses it is well to use screws as much as possible, so that they may be easily taken to pieces; and if the sides can be made to fit on in one piece it is all the better, as it is more convenient for moving, and, if required, they may be fixed on with a hinge, so that in wet weather additional shelter may be provided by propping up the side that gives most protection. There are also many houses made complete by well-known manufacturers that can be obtained at a moderate price if desired, as advertised in this book.

People who live in the country will generally have a shed or outhouse that may be used for the poultry; but those in towns will probably have to build their own houses, and if the instructions here given are followed, they will have no difficulty in providing suitable accommodation for their birds at a moderate price. Where two or three small pens are kept for breeding purposes, it is well to make one long house, and divide it inside, leaving a small passage for the attendant to reach each partition.

Small houses may be made with wooden bottoms and fixed on wheels, and these are very useful, especially to farmers, as they can move their poultry from place to place, and in the autumn the young chickens may be turned out on the stubbles in these houses, where in most cases they do remarkably well, as it is entirely fresh ground.

RUNS.

Although Poultry may be easily kept, and will thrive well in small runs if kept clean, the more room they have the better for them; but as many poultry-keepers are cramped for space, I describe the best way to keep them in close confinement.

Half-a-dozen fowls *may* be kept in a run from three to four yards square, but in this case they must be most carefully cleaned out, that is to say, the earth in the run should be constantly changed, and this is best done after wet weather, as the top scum of the yard may then be removed in cakes. When clean, fresh earth should be substituted. The larger the run is, the less attention it will require in this respect, and the only rule I can lay down for changing the earth is, that it should be done in wet weather when the run gets dirty. The owner is best able to judge when it requires attention in this matter. The run should also be dug over once a week, or a part of it, as the loose earth occupies the fowls in scratching. If a part of the run can be covered in, so that it does not cause a draught, it is much better for the fowls, to provide shade in summer and to keep the wet off in the winter; and it is also well to provide shelter from the cold winds. This may be done by boarding up part of the side of the run, or by thatching hurdles with straw, and placing them against the wire outside the runs.

Then under the covered-in part place dry earth or a little loose straw, scattering a few grains of corn under it. This also gives them employment, and circulates their blood.

It is well to put a perch in the covered-in run (length according to the number of birds), as they are very fond of sitting on a perch to clean their plumage. This often prevents them from plucking their feathers, as they do not then stand about in heaps. Where it is not convenient to have a covered-in run, place a perch in the open run.

Where two or three pens of birds are kept, the best way is to keep each lot in an enclosed run, and allow them out separately every day for two or three hours on a larger piece of ground. Each pen will then have the advantage of a good run every day, and after a week or so there will be no trouble in driving them in and out, as they will be quite used to it and know their way.

To give an example, I may say that should one have an acre of ground, and want to utilise it to the best advantage for poultry, divide it across the centre, and place the houses and runs in the warmest part, and have a slide to each pen into the spare half acre, so that each pen of fowls has the advantage of a good run every day. The runs must be made according to the number of birds required to be kept in them, from seven to thirty, but if for breeding purposes not more than fifteen. The runs ought to be swept well in wet weather, or the top crust peels off.

This system is the best way of keeping poultry when pure, or in pens for breeding, and it is also the most economical as regards the ground, for to provide a perpetual grass run for each of these pens by other means would require about three times the quantity of ground. Fowls for general purposes may also be treated in the same manner.

Brahmas and Cochins may be kept in a run with the wire about 3 or 4 feet high, but for the other breeds it should be from 6 feet high, and often this is not high enough for some, in which case some wire netting must be put on the top of the fence or wall, so that it slants inwards over the run, and thus checks the birds and knocks them back when they fly against it. If this is is not sufficient, the run should be covered right in, or one of the fowl's wings must be cut.

One is quite sufficient. The flight feathers should be cut just underneath the first row of small feathers, leaving about two of the long feathers at the end. When done in this way the appearance of the bird is not spoilt.

The more comfortable the run can be made the better the fowls will like it, and the increased expense will be compensated for by the extra number of eggs obtained in the winter.

Plenty of ashes or dust must be kept in a dry spot for the fowls to dust themselves in, and these should be put in the sun if possible. It is also well to have one part of the run higher than the other, to allow the water to drain off.

Where two or three pens of birds are kept in runs joining one another, the first three feet of the side where the pens join should be boarded up, or else very small mesh netting must be used, as otherwise the cocks will be sure to fight and damage themselves.

I manufacture cheap houses and runs. For particulars refer to my advertisement.

WHAT ARE THE BEST FOWLS TO KEEP?

THIS question is one of the most difficult to answer, as different strains of the same breed of fowls vary very much in their egg-producing properties; and I have often known one bird lay well, while another of the same breed was anything but a good layer. A great deal also depends upon the place and circumstances under which the fowls are to be kept.

The following crosses, viz. :—Plymouth Rock-Brahma, Plymouth Rock-Langshan, Plymouth Rock-Cochin, and Plymouth Rock-black-breasted red Game make good winter layers where the situation is cold, damp, and exposed to the north-east winds. They also produce very fine brown eggs, and make excellent sitters, and can be depended upon for that purpose. They are also the best of mothers, and can cover their chickens well from the cold east winds. They are good hens to send on a journey when broody, as the sight of the eggs usually brings them to the nest at once, and they forget they are in a strange place. They are valuable, as they can be depended upon. I may mention that these crosses may be kept either in confined runs or in an open space, and will not disappoint their owners. They are like young turkeys on the table—one will serve a good family. When early chickens are required these crosses are the best to keep, as they come broody early in the season, and can be depended on, as they have so much heat in themselves. They can be set on goose, turkey, or duck eggs. For general purposes I find nothing better than the Houdan cock, mated with P. Rock, Langshan, Brahma, or Cochin hens. When the pullets are hatched from a good laying strain, one is equal to the other. They come so much alike it is hard to distinguish them from each other when side by side. The results for twelve months will not vary ten eggs. Of the four, the Plymouth Rock cross are the best table fowls. They have more breast-meat, and are usually free from feathers on the legs. The laying results are just as good when a Minorca cock is used with the four mentioned breeds, but the cockerels are not quite so good table fowls, as they are not so full in the breast, but they are excellent in flavour, very white and juicy. As a rule the eggs are a little larger than in the Houdan cross. The pullets from all of these crosses will stand confinement well, or do well if they have an open range. They cannot easily be put out of their place. Most of them lay a tinted egg, some quite brown; they are large and saleable anywhere. Those who have tried these crosses have not been disappointed, as they are such good winter layers. Some object to keeping birds that come broody. In this case I recommend a Houdan-Minorca or Houdan-Leghorn cross as the best to keep, as these are excellent layers of white-shelled eggs. They stand confinement well, and if sheltered a little from the cold winds eggs will be found in the nest all the year round. The golden spangled Hamburgh-Cochin are very handsome birds, more so than any other cross. They are extraordinary layers, both winter and summer. The eggs are a fair size; most of them are brown or tinted. They make fair table birds, rather small, but of excellent flavour. They will stand confinement, or search well for their living when they have their liberty. It is rather difficult to get the eggs fertile. They are the choicest cross I know. The Game-Dorking cross are excellent for the table, and very fair winter layers. They come broody very often during the spring and summer. I prefer Houdan-Dorking, if eggs are required as well as good table fowls, as they are much better layers. The Plymouth Rock-Dorking cross will soon stand at the top of the list as table fowls. They are large, of fine flavour, with a good white breast. They make a better price in the market than any other fowl. Early spring chickens fetched 16s. a pair in the London market in 1884, first hand. They put the Game-Dorking out of sight for table birds. The Game-P. Rocks are very good, and I prefer them to the Game-Cochin, as they make so much better table fowls, although not better layers; they make good sitters and mothers, and may be trusted with valuable eggs. They are very strong in the wing to cover their chickens from the cold winds. This cross is very good for gamekeepers. If one has a fancy for pure bred birds, and the place is cold and damp, I recommend Plymouth Rocks as the best, having no feathers on their legs to hold the wet and damp, and they are more active than the Cochins and Brahmas. The Langshans are also good for this purpose, although I give the Rocks the preference where the place is very cold and damp; they do not show the dirt and smoke as many other breeds do, they stand confinement well, and lay a brown egg. The Wyandottes stand confinement fairly well, and are good layers of brown eggs, but they do not breed true to colour. As a non-sitting breed Minorcas are excellent. I prefer them to the Houdan, as they are not quite so subject to colds when in the pure state. They stand confinement well, and will lay all through the winter months if sheltered from the cold winds. This breed is becoming very popular, and will be more so when better known. They lay a fine white egg; the chickens are hardy and grow fast. Leghorns are also excellent fowls as non-sitters; they are remarkably hardy, and will lay more eggs in the cold winter months than the Minorcas. They are the hardiest fowls I know, especially the white variety; the chickens thrive anywhere. The eggs are not so large as the Minorcas', and neither do they make such a good table fowl. In confinement they stand the cold much better than the Minorcas. The Andalusians are excellent layers of large white eggs. They stand confinement well, and if they have shelter they lay during the winter months. The Dorkings are not so good to keep in confinement when in their pure state. I do not recommend the Hamburghs for confinement, as the Leghorns are so much hardier and lay more eggs during the winter months. The black variety is rather the hardiest, the golden and silver-spangled next; the pencilled varieties ought not to be reared in confinement. Game fowls ought not to be kept in confinement if wanted for profit only. Every breed of fowls will lay in the winter, more or less, if bred from a good laying strain and treated properly. It is not so much a certain breed being good layers, as a matter of being bred from good laying strains. I have had two birds of the same breed running together, and treated in the same way, one having laid over 260 and the other only 90 eggs in twelve months.

For tropical climates, the non-sitting tribes, viz., Hamburghs, Houdans, Spanish, Minorcas, Leghorns, &c., and their crosses are best; while for the colder and more changeable countries, the hardy, feather-legged tribes, such as Cochins, Brahmas, Langshans, Plymouth Rocks, &c., and their crosses are best; and for extremely cold climates I recommend the Game and Cochin and Game and Rock crosses.

FEEDING.

ALTHOUGH much good information has been give on the subject of feeding poultry in the last fe years, they are often mismanaged in this respect, th eason being that seven poultry-keepers out of ten conside heir birds are fed properly if some hard corn be give hem two or three times a day. Another great mistake i nade by many people, who think that any quality of foo loes for poultry, and therefore they give their birds an oor stuff they come across, and this is more especially th ase with farmers, who only feed with poor thin corn tha vill do for nothing else. There are also many who neve ive their laying fowls meal, as they consider it would onl e a waste of valuable food ; but this is also a great mistake s fowls fed once a day on meal will produce at least 30 tc o more eggs per bird in the year than others in exactl imilar conditions that are only fed on hard grain. The reason of this is, that the hard corn takes a certain time to get soaked in the crop and ground in the gizzard, while soft meal passes into the system immediately, and gives the fowl nourishment at once, thereby enabling it to consume (or turn into flesh and eggs) more food than if fed only on hard corn. It will, therefore, be seen by the above remarks that it pays best to give soft meal once a day, and this is best given in the morning, and may consist of nearly any kind of meal—such as barley-meal, oat-meal, buckwheat-meal, &c., mixed with fine and coarse pollard, middlings, or "sharps." The quantity of pollard used depends greatly upon the other meal, but it will generally be found that one part of barley-meal with one part of fine, and one of coarse pollard make a very good mixture; but the best way is always to have sufficient coarse pollard or "sharp," so that the meal mixes easily, that is, without sticking about in soft, doughy lumps. Pea-meal may be used occasionally with pollard for a change, and sweepings from a mill also make very good food, as they contain a large quantity of flour. The full description of my Poultry Foods will be found in the end of this book—advertisement pages. The meal should always be mixed with hot water, or hot skim milk is better if it can be had, and given warm, especially in the winter months. Care should be taken not to mix it too damp, as it is not at all good for the fowls when it is sticky and clings to their beaks. Any scraps of fat or grease can be mixed with the meal, and in the winter, if there are not many scraps, it is desirable to buy some liver, lights, paunches, or tripe (the sheep's paunches can be bought for 2d., and the tripe for 1s. each, the latter weighing from 9 to 18 lbs. each), and give to the fowls the last thing before they go to roost, as they will then eat ravenously of the meat. If, however, it is given with or before their corn they will eat the meat and refuse their other food. The lights, &c., must, of course, be boiled, and the water in which they are boiled should be used to mix the meal. It is more convenient to use granulated meat in the soft food, as that does not require boiling. It is best to pour boiling water over it, and then mix it with the meal while it is hot. Any vegetable refuse, such as small potatoes and cabbage, or pieces of fat meat may also be used, as when these are mixed up with good meal, they make a first-rate food. Turnips, mangold wurtzel, in fact nearly all vegetables, may be used in the same way, especially in the winter months, when green food is scarce. In the autumn and winter the fowls should have their morning meal as hot as they can eat it, and it is well to give them warm water to drink, first thing in the morning, when the weather is cold, as after drinking cold water they will often stand moping about with one foot up, whereas the warm water seems to revive the whole system on a cold morning. Also, it is very beneficial after the birds have had their warm breakfast to drive them back into the house for three or four hours. This causes them to be very active when they are turned out. After they have been driven into the house for a few mornings it will become customary to run into the house after having had their breakfast. Of course they must be fastened in.

If the simple rules I have given in this little manual are followed, eggs will be found all the year round. Biscuit-meal is one of the best meals that can be used, given alone, or occasionally other meals mixed with it. When this meal is not used, a little oyster shell, mixed with the general meals, helps them very much, as it not only furnishes material for making the shell, but assists in digesting the food, and is far superior to old mortar. If the fowls do not have lime in some form or other it weakens the laying birds very much, and often causes them to lay shell-less eggs.

When this occurs they are apt to break before the fowls can pass them, and when this is the case the fowls often die or are ruptured for life; but more often they are found dead on the nest or underneath the perch in the morning.

Bone-meal strengthens the egg-organs more than anything I have used. I do not have five soft eggs in three weeks from 400 laying hens. It is well to use a little salt for flavouring the soft food.

The following table will show the different proportions of flesh-forming, &c., food contained in wheat, barley, and other grain, &c., used for feeding poultry. It was, I believe, originally published in the *Poultry Diary*, but the copy given is taken from L. Wright's *Book of Poultry*:—

There is in every 100 parts, by weight, of	Flesh-forming material like gluten, &c.	Warmth-giving and fattening material, viz.:—		Bone-making materials or mineral substances.	Husk or Fibre.	Water.
		Fat or Oil.	Starch.			
Beans and Peas ...	25	2	48	2	8	15
Oatmeal	18	6	63	2	2	9
Middlings, Thirds, or Fine Sharps	18	6	53	5	4	14
Oats	15	6	47	2	20	10
Wheat	12	3	70	2	1	12
Buckwheat ...	12	6	58	1½	11	11½
Barley	11	2	60	2	14	11
Indian Corn ...	11	8	65	1	5	10
Hempseed ...	10	21	45	2	14	8
Rice	7	a trace.	80	a trace.	...	13
Potatoes	6½	...	41	2	...	50½
Milk	4½	3	5	¾	...	85¾

In the preceding remarks, I have mentioned what are the best things to feed poultry on; but perhaps the most important part is when and how to feed, and what quantity to give; and although some writers mention certain definite allowances for each fowl, I think the exact quantity must be left to the feeder's discretion, as fowls' appetites vary so much, two birds at some times often eating as much as six at others. The golden rule, however, is never to give one morsel more than the birds will run after quickly, if thrown some distance from them, and on no account whatever should food be left lying about or in troughs, as not only does the sight turn the fowls against it, but it also attracts sparrows, mice, rats, &c., and the latter are not content with the food alone, but often kill the young chickens as well. If there is a dry piece of grass or gravel, the fowls should be fed on it; but in the winter and wet weather both meal and grain should be given in troughs, unless a very clean dry place can be had, as otherwise the dirt sticks to the food, and makes it very injurious to the fowls. Another advantage in feeding with troughs is, that they may be taken away directly the birds have had sufficient, if they have not finished their food.

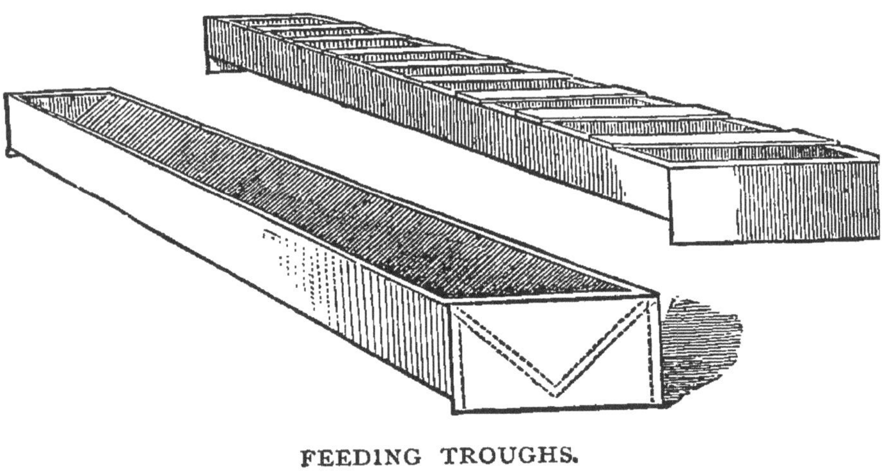

FEEDING TROUGHS.

Except in winter the fowls should be let out of their house for half-an-hour or so before giving them their breakfast, as this gives them a better appetite for their food.

In the winter months, and more especially in October,

when the mornings are chilly and many of the old birds are moulting, poultry require very generous treatment, and at this period they are often better for a little in the way of "stimulants," such as hemp-seed, &c. My Powders, advertised in the end of this book, will be found very beneficial for health and egg-production all through the spring, autumn and winter months, as they strengthen every organ of the body, enabling fowls to produce a larger number of eggs, and do not leave them weak, as many other laying-powders do. They impart vigour to the birds, cause their combs to be redder, plumage more glossy, and make a marked difference in them before the Powders have been used ten days. They have been used these last few years with great benefit for rearing chickens, pheasants, turkeys, and early ducklings by hundreds of breeders. (Refer to testimonials on the use of these Powders.)

These little attentions take time and money, but the fowls pay well for them, as, when they are thoroughly well looked after and fed on warm, stimulating food, they will often lay while they are moulting.

Perhaps, however, the most important, and very often the most neglected, thing that poultry in confinement require is a supply of grit, for without it they are unable to digest or grind their food. A miller cannot grind his corn without stones, and it is the same with poultry, and if they fail in getting a supply of small sharp stones (which the greater part of the grit should be composed of) they suffer in health, as these things are to poultry what teeth are to human beings—they digesting or grinding their food with small stones or grit, while we masticate ours with our teeth.

When I have had poultry suffer in health and die, I have opened them and often found an absence of these necessaries, and very often when fowls mope about and do not care to eat their food, it is simply for want of these small stones, and very often, when in this state, they do not care to pick up the small stones, &c., in which case some should be mixed with the meal and forced down their throats, when, as a rule, they will soon be all right.

The round shingle which is sent from the seaside, and used by hundreds as grit, is simply useless, as it, being round, cannot perform the necessary work. Very sharp small stones are required, in fact the edges cannot be *too* sharp. The friction of the water constantly flowing over the shingle causes it to become in time as smooth as glass. Egg-shells help to form the new shell; but they should be broken very small before being given to the fowls, otherwise it may teach them to eat their eggs. Sand and small gravel, such as may be obtained at the bottom of steep country roads after a storm of rain, or ordinary road scrapings, are also much liked by poultry, and if none of the above can be obtained flint or pebble stones should be broken up small and given them, as grit they must have in some shape or other.

Too much maize is not good for fowls, as it brings on liver disease sooner than anything I know. It makes too much internal fat, and also makes blood too fast. Fowls that are fed liberally on it are lined with yellow fat, especially in the abdomen. I have taken it out when it has been half an inch thick; the egg organs become so weak they often lay shell-less eggs. Even this is not the worst part of it, as fowls that have liver disease are susceptible of many other diseases, especially roup. It is not always the liver that actually kills them. It is very often that other diseases follow through their being in a weak state. When roup has been incurable, I have found on examination that the liver was diseased—it is called scrofula—having white spots on it Sometimes they are only as large as the head of a pin. It no other disease sets in, the spots become very large, also the liver. I have weighed it when it has turned the scale at 9 ozs. In-breeding also brings on liver disease. There are more fowls die of this disease than all the others put together. I have known farmers use maize for years together, and it has affected the progeny so that they could scarcely rear a chicken. They died off when from four to six days, and from four to six weeks old. It is used so largely as it is such a cheap food. A little maize for a change does not hurt the fowls, especially in the cold weather. I use more wheat than any other grain, as that does not make so much internal fat as most other grains do. Next to wheat I use French buckwheat, dari, and a little barley. Good oats are a splendid grain for a change, but they ought not to weigh less than 40 to 42 lbs. to the bushel. If 44 lbs. so much the better. Hempseed is also an excellent grain for the breeding-season, especially for the male birds. If this seed is given, there will not be many unfertile eggs. It helps them very much. It is also very good in the autumn through their moult, as it is stimulating. It is used largely for bringing young chickens into good condition for the show pen. It is well to change the grain, as the birds like variations.

From October to March it is well to soften the corn by boiling from 15 to 30 minutes, and standing the pot on one side till it soaks up the water used for boiling, giving it to the fowls when hot. Care should be taken not to boil the grain too much, or to use too much water, as it causes it to burst and become very sticky, in which state it is not at all liked by the fowls.

They ought not to have as much boiled corn as they can eat, but should have a little hard corn to finish up with. When meat is given to the fowls, care should be taken in cutting it into moderate pieces, just so that they can swallow it. If left in large pieces, one hen gets hold of a large piece and runs away with it, and while she is trying to peck it to pieces, the others eat all theirs, and then have a good run to the large piece, in which case the hen which ran away with it usually has not any, and worse than this, the hen that swallows the large piece often gets into trouble, as it sometimes causes a stoppage between the crop and gizzard. When fowls are deprived of a grass run and fed liberally, and at the same time are rather short of green food, their blood gets very hot, especially in the spring months. It is well to use a little flour of sulphur (sometimes called brimstone). There are two sorts, the dark and the yellow; the latter is the best; one heaped-up teaspoonful for ten fowls is the quantity to be used. Sulphur, unfortunately, causes the eggs to have a strong taste. This is partly counteracted by using the same quantity of common salt as sulphur. It is not well to use this medicine too early in the spring, as it opens the pores of the skin too much if it is given in cold weather, or when the cold wind is blowing. One heaped-up teaspoonful of mustard to ten fowls, given once or twice a week, will help them very much, especially if they are breeding stock; the same quantity of sulphur, mustard and salt to be given.

Fish is also a very good thing to give fowls where convenient. Unless it is oily fish, and given very liberally, it does not taste in the eggs. English people do not cultivate herbs as they ought to for the use of their poultry. There are two herbs most valuable in the poultry yard, and yet they are trodden under foot and thrown to the rubbish heap, or rooted up altogether as the most wretched things that grow. These herbs are stinging nettles and dandelions. The stinging nettle is one of the most cooling for the blood that can be found among all herbs. At the same time fowls do not catch cold after having them (as they are liable to do with sulphur). The nettles should be got when young; they can be cut short and boiled, and then mixed with the soft food, and the water they are boiled in will also do to mix with their food. If time will not permit boiling them, they can be put in a vessel of some kind, and boiling water poured over them. Cover them over, so that the steam cannot evaporate. The nettles and the tea can be mixed with the meal; also add a little salt. When given in this way they are both food and medicine. It is rather difficult to gather them, unless a glove is put on to handle them. They can be cut with a knife or scissors, not pulled; then they grow again very quickly. Nettles are invaluable for fowls. Dandelions are an excellent herb for the liver. They will often put the poultry right when everything else fails. The leaves can be pulled from the roots and cut in small pieces, and given just in their raw state. If the roots of these two herbs are set in the autumn or winter (not later than February) they will grow anywhere if they are put underneath the soil. The nettles can be found by the side of hedges, and dandelions by the roadside, or on any waste piece of ground. They have a yellow flower which grows upon a round stem. Watercress is an excellent green food for poultry, but rather too dear to buy. Where there are many poultry kept, and spare ground at command, cow-cabbages are the most economical to grow, as they grow very large, and if grown properly, one is sufficient for fifty fowls in one day; the fowls are particularly fond of them. A mangold wurtzel for a change is very good. It is well to cut them in half; then there is nothing left but the skin. Those who live in towns, and have but little space, cannot grow either cabbage or lettuce, but can grow rape, mustard, or maize. These can be grown in boxes with a little earth and manure, and must be well watered. The seed springs very quickly, and in the hot weather is ready in a few days.

By having seven boxes, and sowing every day, there is a daily supply of green food.

The maize springs twice or three times without sowing again. It can either be cut, or the box placed in the run for the fowls to peck it off. The size of boxes must vary according to number of fowls kept; not more than two or three inches of soil is necessary in the boxes. If the space is very limited, the boxes can be placed on the top of the fowl-house, but in the sun as much as possible.

This green food can only be grown in the summer months.

HOW TO BREED, AND WHAT TO BREED FROM.

ONE of the most important points towards successful poultry keeping is to breed only from the best birds, and never on any account to set an egg from an inferior or sickly bird. If fowls for laying are required, the poultry should be watched, and the eggs of the best laying hen set, when the chickens will generally all be good layers. This can be done where only a few birds are kept. If, on the other hand, they are required for table, the eggs of the finest and plumpest birds only should be used.

Whatever sort of poultry is kept, whether pure breeds or the commonest mongrels, if they are watched, and the eggs from the best ones only set, the stock may soon be easily improved, as there is almost sure to be one good layer in the very worst half-dozen. It is always best to have a pure bred cock, as most pure breeds have some distinctive quality that it is well to introduce in mongrel birds. If, however, a mongrel or half-bred cock is an extra fine bird, or comes from an extraordinary laying hen, it may often pay to breed from him, although I do not recommend this course as a rule. It must always be borne in mind that while a bad hen only causes a portion of a brood to be inferior, an indifferent cock spoils the whole hatch.

The number of hens to be allowed with each rooster, to obtain fertile eggs, differs according to the nature of the bird, but as a rule, a Cochin will take from four to six hens, and a Brahma from six to nine, while six is enough for most other breeds; but with some, such as Game, Hamburghs, Houdans, Leghorns, Minorcas and Rocks, nine or ten hens may often be allowed. It all depends whether the birds are highly bred or not. A heavy Cochin or Brahma, if he will breed, will not manage half as many hens as a smaller one. I have known as many as thirty hens running with one cock, and early in the season all the eggs were fertile, but not for long.

Too much attention cannot be given to the subject of introducing fresh blood into a poultry yard, as the chickens never make such fine birds, and are seldom so strong and healthy when the parents are related.

Where it is desired to keep, say a dozen hens and only one cock, the best way to obtain fertile eggs is to shut off with the cock, for a few hours every morning, just the hens from which it is desired to breed, as the eggs of, say half-a-dozen hens, may then be depended upon for hatching.

INCUBATION.

Artificial incubation is very much in vogue at the present time, not only where large numbers of chickens are required, but also where a very limited number are kept, especially by ladies who have time to attend to them properly. Cottagers frequently make their own. Some of them answer very well, hatching 12 chickens out of 15 eggs. The high price of incubators prevents the working classes investing in them. I feel sure a much cheaper one could be produced than those already in the market. I have tried several makers' machines, and many have come under my notice, but I find no maker turns out all good machines; that is, some of them fail to do their work, and yet to all appearance it is no fault of the makers. Nevertheless, it remains a fact. I have known those which have no self-regulation work equally as well as those which have. I am much more in favour of incubators now than I used to be, as they are very much improved. They are easily worked, and save a great deal of trouble running after hens. Another advantage is, the eggs can be put in every few days while they are fresh (by those who breed from their own poultry). If fresh eggs are put in the drawer with others previously put in, a piece of flannel or cotton-wool should be put between them, as the cold eggs are apt to chill the others, especially if they have only been in a few days. If they are near hatching it does not hurt them. I am often asked which is the best in the market. This I cannot always answer, as in some cases I have known them all fail, and on the other hand, at other times nearly every egg has hatched a live chicken. A really good incubator is a great boon to poultry-keepers. The machines which have obtained the best results under my notice are Hearson's, Ellis & Tyler's, Christy's, and Tomlinson's. There may be others good, but I have not met with them. Those mentioned are easily worked. A pamphlet would be forwarded from either place if applied for—Christy, Ellis & Tyler, and Hearson, London; and Tomlinson, Birmingham. There are some people who think if chickens are hatched in an incubator they do not grow so large nor do so well. This is only superstition. They do equally as well if taken care of. They are not so liable to vermin as when hatched under hens, as the hen breeds them during the period of sitting. Care must be taken in dusting her. I think there are a larger proportion of cripples hatched with an incubator than under hens, but there are no chickens killed by the incubator as there are by the hen trampling on them. Incubators are a great convenience, save time, can be worked any time in the year, and there are many who enjoy attending to them. A few common eggs should always be put in first to see if the incubator works right. This frequently saves disappointment, as it takes a few days to get them into working order. When non-sitting breeds are kept they are indeed very useful.

SITTING AND HATCHING.

Opinions vary regarding the proper way to set hens, for while some persons prefer a nest on the ground in a damp situation, others always set their birds in as dry a place as possible. I have found the best way is to imitate nature as much as possible. for, as a rule, hens that choose their own nests usually bring off large broods.

If a hen that is sitting in a stolen nest is watched, it will be observed that she chooses a dry, secluded spot for her nest, and though the ground may be dry when she selects her nest, the heat from her body draws a certain moisture from the ground to the eggs, which, of course, is a very gradual moisture ; she also leaves her nest early in the morning to search for her food, and as the grass is quite wet with the dew, the bird's breast also gets wet, and in this state she returns to her eggs, and consequently damps them.

It will therefore be seen that it is best to make the nest on the ground, and to cover it in from the others. Where possible, a separate house should be used for sitting, and the hens left quite to themselves; but this may be done without, and a nest made in the usual house and covered over with an old piece of bagging, &c., so arranged that it may easily be moved every morning.

The best way to make the nest is by scooping out a little earth from the floor, and then beating the soil quite firm in the shape of a nest. Where the earth cannot be removed, a few shovelfuls should be obtained, and moulded into the same shape in an ordinary nest box, a turf being placed on the top and well beaten into shape. It is easier to make a nest with loose earth than a turf, and it is well to sprinkle a little lime in the nest and beat it in with the hand. If the soil is damp it forms a crust and holds well together.

The nest should be made quite round, so that all the eggs are covered if the fowl moves her position; it should be hollowed somewhat in the centre, in order that the eggs come together and do not roll out of reach when the fowl steps into the nest. Plenty of room must be given, as, when a bird is cramped in sitting, many eggs get broken. The nest should be made of soft, fine hay, the inside being lined with feathers just at the bottom of the nest in cold weather. Hay is much better than straw, as it sticks closer together, and therefore holds the warmth better, and the hen may consequently be allowed more eggs. Straw being hollow, it conducts the cold air to the eggs, especially in frosty weather.

When it is required to set fowls in a strange nest, it is best to put them on their new nest at night unless very tame. They should not be forced or hurried, but ought to be placed in front of the nest they are to occupy, with a few common eggs in it, when they will generally take to it at once, and if not disturbed again too soon, they will stick to it and sit well. Some hens, however, *won't* sit in a strange nest, and the only thing that can be done with them is to patiently allow them to have their own way, or else not to set them at all. Hens that have travelled a journey, or have been removed, should be put in a coop and fed well with hard corn and water, and then be placed on their nest in the evening, and covered in so that they are partly in the dark, and should not be taken off the next day, but the day after. This enables them to be well settled down before being disturbed. For the first few days they should be fed in a coop or other small place; if not, they become too wild, and will not go back to their nest. They should be handled very gently. It is well to place the feeding-coop before the nest, so that the hen may see her nest; she will then walk straight on.

I cannot give the number of eggs that should be allowed a hen, as both the hens and eggs differ so much in size, and a great deal also depends on the state of the weather; but, for fair-sized hens, about thirteen ordinary eggs will be sufficient in the early spring, but a larger number may be given if the hen be set in warmer weather. I have set twenty-four eggs under one hen, and hatched out twenty-two chickens; but this is far too many as a rule, and if any doubt is felt as to the number to give a hen, it is best to be on the safe side and give one too few; for if a hen has too many eggs she may let a different one get cold every time she turns them, and thus spoil the whole batch.

When the nest is made without soil or turf, the outer skin of the egg becomes very dry during the last week of incubation, and the chickens usually hatch out very badly, and often one-half do not crack their shell. To prevent this occurring, it is best to moisten the eggs slightly during the last few days. In moderate weather cold water will do to wet the eggs with, but in cold weather it is best to use warm. I find it is best to dip them in warm water and let them remain in for one or two seconds. The last three or five days of incubation is sufficient.

Should the hen break any of the eggs, they should be removed immediately, and if any portion of the broken egg is on the others, it should be wiped or washed off in warm water at once, as when it dries it stops the pores of the shell, thus preventing the air passing through to the chick.

The hen should be lifted off the nest every morning, and about the third morning she will rise up when her attendant goes to her. Care must be taken in lifting the hen, and this is best done by placing a hand under each wing to make sure there are no eggs lodged there, and then take hold of the legs with the fingers and lift steadily, letting the wings rest on the wrists. In cold weather the hen should not be allowed to stay off the nest more than fifteen minutes, but in warm weather she may be out from forty to sixty minutes. The nest should be closed to prevent the other hens going in it, and in very cold weather it is well to cover up the eggs with a piece of flannel or wadding to prevent their being chilled.

A supply of dust or ashes must be kept in a dry place for the hen to clean herself with, and food and water must, of course, be placed so that she may help herself. As sitting hens go so long between each meal, it is best to feed them on some sort of hard corn, as this lasts them longer than soft food.

Sometimes a hen when sitting will lose her appetite. When this is the case she ought to have a little hemp seed, soaked bread, and pieces of meat. She must be tempted with these, as, if she does not eat she cannot sit her time, and the whole sitting of eggs will consequently be spoiled.

It is well to examine the eggs about the eighth day to see if they have chicks in. This may easily be done by turning them slowly round in front of a small lamp or candle in a dark room. If there is a chicken in the egg there will be a dark spot in the middle, while those that appear quite clear are unfertile. The brown-shelled eggs are rather more difficult to tell, but if there is any doubt they should be left under the hen a few days more and then tried.

The unfertile eggs should always be removed, as it gives the others a better opportunity; and where a large number of chickens are hatched, it is well to set three or more hens on the same day, and if many eggs are unfertile, those with chickens in may be given to two hens, and the other hen turned off or supplied with some fresh eggs, as it does them no harm to sit for a month. This may be done all through the season, and by these means trouble is saved and each hen will have a good brood instead of wasting time with only a few chickens.

The eggs that are set should always be marked in ink, with the date they are placed under the hen, so that they may be easily known. The unfertile eggs that are taken away may be boiled hard and chopped up for the chickens, as they are quite sweet and as good as many of the French eggs we use

When the hen is hatching, I always find it best to remove the chickens every two or three hours, and it is, therefore, well to accustom her to the hand being put under her, or she will be restless and spiteful when the chickens are removed, and perhaps crush some of them or the hatching eggs.

As the chickens are removed, they should be placed in a box in wadding before the fire until they are all hatched, when the hen should be let out for a good run and feed; for, as a rule, they do not come off the nest for two days before hatching. The chickens should then be placed in the coop, when the hen will walk in and brood them quietly. If the hen is very wild and restless, it is best to leave her quite to herself when hatching, or she will flutter about and trample her chicks to death.

When the eggs are fresh—and by rights none but fresh eggs should be set—they will often hatch in nineteen-and-a-half or twenty days, but if at the close of twenty-one days the eggs are not chipped, they should be examined, which may be done by tapping the egg and holding it close to the ear, when if the chicken is alive its beak will tap against the shell, or it will chirrup. A small hole should then be made with a penknife, to give the chicken a start, at the large end. If the chicken is alive, the skin next the shell is white; if dead, it is a dark colour. After the hole is made, the egg should be turned gently round, to ascertain where the chicken's beak lies. Then break a small hole where the beak is. If the blood follows, put it under the hen at once; if no blood appears the chicken can be taken out at once. There are thousands of chickens die in the shell for the want of a little help. It is when the beak lies in a slanting position against the shell, and, as the egg is oval, when the chick endeavours to free itself its beak slides. After making the hole in the shell, the egg should be placed under the hen for twelve hours longer, and at the end of this time the chick will have drawn the blood up into its body, and be quite prepared to leave the shell, if not already out of it.

CHICKEN REARING.

There are many different systems pursued in rearing chickens, and I have tried most of them and found them answer more or less; but I think that the following lines will describe the best and simplest method.

When all the chickens are hatched they should be placed in a coop with the hen where they can get as much liberty as possible. If not cooped on or near grass they must be provided with a supply of green food chopped up small, and the more they have the better they will thrive.

There are many kinds of coops used, but the best is made with match-boarding, the size being according to the fowl; 2 feet wide, 2½ feet long, is a fair size, but large hens should have a coop 3 feet long and 2 feet 3 inches high in front and 1 foot 6 inches at the back, thus giving it the appearance of a lean-to roof. A 6-inch board should be nailed along the top of the front part of the coop, and the

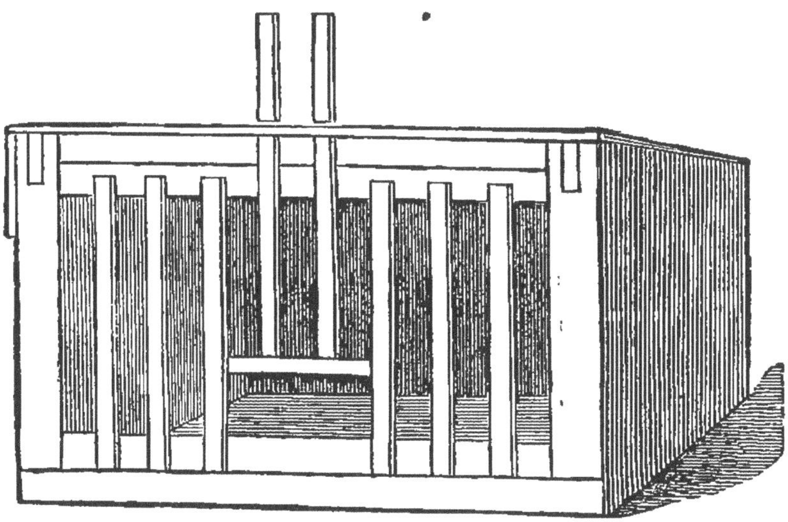

CHICKEN COOP.

pins or bars should run from this to the ground, not cross-ways; they should be about 2½ or 3 inches apart, so as to give the chicks plenty of room. A little door may be made in the middle, about a foot wide, worked with hinges; or a better way is to arrange for one or two of the bars to fit in a socket, so that they may be withdrawn at any time and answer for the door. It is well to board up part of the front of the coop, so as to prevent the rain beating in. This kind of coop will be very light, and may be easily carried about, and will last for years if well tarred or painted and kept out of the wet when not in use.

There are many elaborate coops, much more expensive than these, for those who wish to buy them, and there are also some less expensive that may be made out of an old soap-box or tea-chest, after the cracks have been stopped with stiff brown paper glued on and afterwards well lime-washed. As the roof will be flat, an extra piece of wood must be nailed on the top, to allow the water to run off. I have used coops made in this manner for many years, and

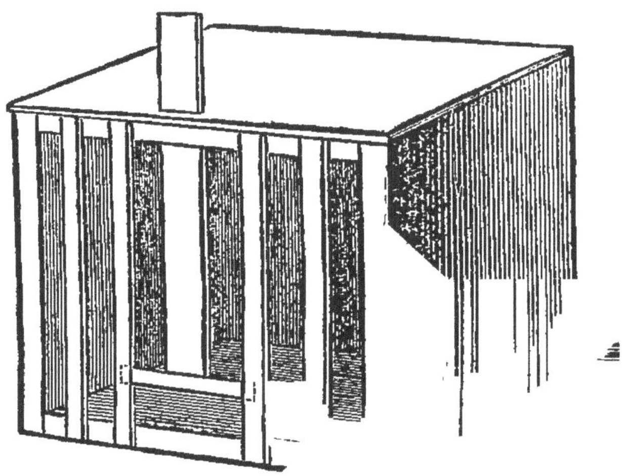

CHICKEN COOP MADE OUT OF A TEA CHEST.

found them answer well, as they may be made very snug and warm.

It is a disputed point as to whether coops should have bottoms to them or not, for while some people hold that the boards keep the chickens dry, and prevent the hen drawing up the moisture to them by the heat of her body, I say that the boards produce cramp, unless they have a fair thickness of some loose stuff on them.

Chickens are much more liable to have cramp, especially

in the winter and early spring, when they are allowed to run on hard or solid floors such as boards, bricks, or concrete. It is for want of circulation of the blood in the legs and feet, or, in other words, the blood becomes chilled while it is passing through the chickens' legs and feet. If the cramp is not checked the toes refuse to do their proper work, and become doubled under their feet. When they get to this stage they soon begin to show a roughness in their plumage, denoting the cramp is in the body. In very bad cases they become quite unable to move. There is often more than half the early broods die with cramp. This is very discouraging after all the trouble of hatching them out, and early chickens are so very valuable, whether crosses or pure bred. When chickens first show symptoms of cramp it is well to catch them at once and rub their legs with a little turpentine. In bad cases it is well to use a little spirits of arnica. This will soak in very quickly. A little vaseline should then be rubbed on the legs and feet after the turpentine or arnica has been used. The vaseline supples them and makes their legs and feet more pliable. It is well to wrap their legs up with a little cotton wool. This keeps them warm, and the blood soon circulates freely again. For binding up the toes refer to paragraph on "Cramp." Sometimes chickens are hatched with their toes turned under. When this is the case the splints, as described in "Cramp," must be put on in the same way. If chickens are kept under glass after they are a fortnight old they are very subject to cramp and many other diseases. It is not good for them to be kept entirely under glass, and therefore they should have their full liberty if possible, however cold the weather. If there is a shed or cover of any sort that they can go under when they like, so much the better. When the weather is very cold or wet the front of the coop should be covered with an old sack or bagging in the night;

but in moderate weather they do just as well without any covering.

As chickens do not drink for the first day or two, they require something both moist and nourishing; hard-boiled eggs chopped up fine and mixed with groats or coarse oatmeal is the best food for the first day or two. The hen should always be fed with plenty of corn before feeding the chickens, or she will eat all the food intended for them. When the hen is a long time hatching, the elder chicks often require feeding before the others are out. All of them may not eat the first day they are hatched, but if they do not eat the second day they should be carefully fed once or twice with a few small pieces of egg and groats, and after this they will look out for themselves. A supply of clean water must always be kept with the chickens in a shallow pan, and they may be taught to drink by putting a few pieces of groats or egg in the water. When the chicks are two or three days old they should be fed outside, the coop on a board or sack, and it is a very good plan to sprinkle a little silver sand or fine grit on the sack, as it clings to the food and serves as grit, with which they must be kept supplied.

After the chickens are two or three days old the egg may be discontinued, and the food consist of biscuit meal soaked with hot water; not made too wet; if so it is liable to give them diarrhœa, and dry groats, which is better than oatmeal for them. A little soaked bread may be given now and then, and if a little finely-chopped meat can be spared, it will help them on wonderfully. For the first week or so they should have food to run to all day, as, when there is a large brood, some will be running about for food all day, and they cannot be fed too often when young. After this they should be fed every hour until a fortnight old, commencing with the rising of the sun and ending with its setting. No food must be left lying about, or it will make them dainty. When a fortnight old, every two hours will be sufficient until they are about a month old, when they will do if fed every three or four hours. A mixture of meal is very good to use for the chickens, such as buckwheat meal, barley and maize meal, locust meal and sharps when they are growing large.

Sometimes there will be one or two chickens that do not care to eat, and when this is the case, a pill should be made with the advertised powders and some fine grit, and put down the chickens' throats, and this will generally bring them round again.

Chickens thrive best if fed on groats, but as this is rather expensive, it is well to give them biscuit-meal when they are a week or so old, and this may be varied occasionally by using a little other meal, such as buckwheat meal, ground maize, oats, &c. The meal should always be given to them warm.

Bone meal is excellent for young chickens, as it prevents leg-weakness, and they grow so much finer, especially the male birds. It is a cheap meal, as they do do not require much of it. It can be used with any other meal—proportion, about one pound of bone meal to four or five of any other. More can be used if necessary.

Rice is very good for a change, and should be boiled; it may be obtained very cheap with the husk on. Potatoes, &c., are also very good for them, and as they are generally very fond of these things it is well to give them plenty, for they will often eat them when they do not care for meal. It is best to feed the chickens on grain for the evening meal, and this should consist of groats for the first two or three weeks, and afterwards any kind of grain except maize, which must be kept out of their way until they are about six weeks old, as it is too much for them to digest. It will be found of great advantage to the chicks if the hard corn is boiled occasionally as described.

For the first week or two the hen should be kept in the coop; but after this period she may be let out with the chickens to roam at will. Cottagers, however, should always keep the hen in the coop, and let the little ones run where they like, when they will not fly to be an annoyance in a neighbour's garden. The same remarks apply to others than cottagers, and it is always well to place the coop in the midst of the kitchen garden, when the chicks will eat up worms, insects, &c., and thus prevent damage to crops; but they must, of course, be removed as soon as they begin to scratch, and younger ones put in their place.

Gardeners may complain of the chickens being allowed in the garden; but if they are only allowed in while they are small, they will cause no harm, but will do a deal of good by eating up the small insects, &c.

The hen should be allowed with the chickens until they are about six weeks old, when they will be able to take care of themselves unless the weather is very severe.

When possible, the chickens should be allowed to roost out in a coop or in an open shed, until a short time before commencing to lay, when they should be put in the house with the others.

If chickens are fed in the manner I have described they will not require much fattening before they are killed, as they will be in first-rate condition for table. It is much the best plan to keep fowls in this way, for they may then be picked up and killed just as required, choosing the largest first, and leaving the others till they are in a better condition, unless required for market, and they must be well-fattened or they will not fetch a good price.

There is not sufficient attention given to the chickens as regards dusting themselves. When they droop their wings and their feathers look rough they ought to be caught and examined at once, especially round the head and under the wings, to see whether there is any vermin on them, as when this is the case they cannot thrive. Lime will destroy them, but it is apt to get into the chickens' eyes and blind them. I have found my Insect Powder, advertised in this book, the best, as it does not injure the fowls in the least.

There are six things to be observed in chicken rearing :— 1. A constant supply of fresh water. 2. Feed so that there is not a kernel of corn or grain of soft food left; if so, it soon becomes sour, and not only turns the fowls against it, but harbours the rats. 3. A good supply of green food. 4. Always see that they have a good supply of sharp grit to digest their food, if not, they cannot thrive for long. 5. The dust-bath is very essential. 6, and lastly, see that they have plenty of ventilation in the sleeping house and are not too thick on the ground. If these six rules are carried out, success is sure to follow, more or less. Any green food will do for chickens, if cut fine so that there are no large pieces; if so, they swallow them, and it causes a stoppage, usually between the crop and gizzard, usually at the mouth of the latter, if the green food is of a tough nature, such as withered grass or dead cabbage leaves. When there are hairs or pieces of soft wood adhering to the soft food the chickens are apt to swallow them. Anything of this sort blocks the passage to the gizzard entirely up. I have had many sent to me for examination, and these simple things have been the cause of death.

PURE BRED FOWLS.

I HAVE only given the outlines of the pure breeds, just so that an amateur may distinguish one breed from another. To describe all the points of all pure breeds, mating birds for exhibition, &c., would be impossible, as space in this small hand-work could not be allowed. I have just stated what is the best breed to keep under different circumstances. Plymouth Rock is the most fashionable breed now, and the public choice is not a bad one. It matters not what breed is kept, as they do not always thrive so well one year as another. They vary very much in their laying qualities ; it is not so much the breed but the strain. No pure-bred pullet ought to lay before she is six months old. Before this age I always endeavour to keep them back if I see them reddening up too early, as nature must have time to do her work. If they get on too fast they should not have any flesh food, or anything to stimulate, and change them from one run to the other.

This will put them back. On the other hand, if they do not comeon till very late they require a stimulant, for at times nature requires assistance.

PLYMOUTH ROCKS.

This breed has made its way into our country most rapidly. It can be found among all classes, from the highest to the lowest. It can be found not only in parks and paddocks, but in the back yards of cottagers in almost every town and village. If a bird is the colour of the Rock it is picked up at once. The past three years I have given them a good test. I have tried 31 different breeds, and out of that number the Plymouth Rock has proved one of the best all-round birds. I will point out a few of their good qualities, and also what some people call their bad ones. Firstly, they are very hardy, inasmuch as they will stand confinement, and the cold and damp does not affect them. They are good winter layers, but come broody when the warm weather sets in; but they are very easily checked if treated as described in paragraph on broody coop. If they are required for sitting they make splendid sitters and good mothers. As they have only four toes on each foot and are very strong in the wing, they cover the eggs and chickens well. They also lay a brown egg. In this they vary a little, some having a very brown shell, and others a pale brown. Sometimes purchasers are a little disappointed, as the eggs vary in colour. This makes no difference to the quality of the breed; but, at the same time, most people like to get them as brown as possible. They are not large eggs for the size of the birds; some lay much larger than others. Taking them all round they are about the size of the Brahma. I have had some larger, but this is about the average. They are eggs which will sell in either town or country. When set, the eggs of Plymouth Rocks hatch out

PLYMOUTH ROCK COCK.

well; better than the Cochin or Brahma. The chickens do not appear to grow so fast the first two months as many other breeds do, especially the cockerels (as they do not feather so quickly as the pullets). After that age they fill out very fast. A great many of the cockerels come very light in colour, and are useless for breeding pure birds. Those that are rejected do very well for crossing with any other breed. There is one disadvantage in breeding Plymouth Rocks (if it may be called so)—many of the pullets come black, and their legs are usually very dark. The only way they can be detected from a clean-legged Langshan is, that they have yellow feet, especially the underneath part and between the toes. These usually make the largest pullets and are good layers. Unfortunately there are no black cockerels among them; if so, a black breed could be established. There are some breeders who mate a very light cock with yellow legs and beak with black hens, to obtain dark-coloured cockerels with yellow legs and beaks and good, evenly-marked plumage all through. It is not well to breed from a dark-coloured cockerel when the pullets or hens are dark; if so, many of the pullets will come black. This breed requires great care in mating up; if not, the results are unsatisfactory.

It is not those who keep the best birds always breed the best fowls. The mating of them is the secret—that is, when required for the show pen, or to realise a good price. There are a few little things to avoid, and others to cultivate. If fowls for the above purpose are required, first see that the cock has red face and ear-lobes; the latter should be free from streaks of white, comb evenly serrated and standing erect yellow legs and beak (if possible), the former being the most important. The breast and shoulders should be broad, and the bird should have good carriage. The more evenly the cocks are marked the better. White feathers will appear in the tail, but this is one thing to avoid; but it is difficult to get them without a little white in the tail. It is not a matter of light or dark shade, but of even marking. The hen's comb should stand erect, and be firmly set to the head and evenly serrated. The plumage should be of two distinct colours; each feather should be marked with a very light slate, almost white, and a very dark slate. In those birds which are of a dark shade, the dark marking looks almost black, especially in the hens. When one feather is examined separately, it should be marked to the quill, one bar of light and then of dark. The last bar or spot of white should just show, and the tip of the feather should be edged with the dark shade. When they are evenly marked it gives the birds the appearance of being beautifully spotted all over. The more evenly the hens are marked in this way the better. The light markings must not run into the dark. The hackles (the neck feathers) are marked finely, but should be the same shade. The cock's breast should be the same colour as the hen's body, and the hackles and saddle are of a much finer marking. When the birds are of a fine colour, the markings should be of a bright grey, showing distinctly the light and dark shades. Care should be taken in mating Plymouth Rocks. If not, there are many of the cockerels come very light, and *vice versa*, and the pullets black. If the hens are of a dark shade, a light cock, with yellow legs and beak, should be mated. This is the colour that usually produces the best-marked pullets, but the cockerels are very light. It is very difficult to produce good pullets and cockerels from the same pen, unless there are a good number of stock birds to pick from. If good cockerels are required, a medium-coloured cock may be mated with dark hens. If mated in this way, a few black pullets must be expected. If the hens are of a light shade, a dark cock may be mated with them,

PLYMOUTH ROCK HEN.

Great care should be taken in mating this breed. A light-coloured cock, with bright yellow legs and beak, will produce the best marked pullets, and a dark-shade cock the best coloured cockerels. When chickens of this breed are brought up under trees or shade, their plumage keeps a much brighter colour, as the summer tans them very much. In the summer months Plymouth Rock hens usually lose the yellow cast from their legs—in fact, some become quite white, especially if allowed to sit. Their legs become yellow again when they change their feathers, but not such a deep colour as when pullets. I do not mind a Rock hen having pale legs if I know the blood is right. This is not always a point to go by, as there are many half-bred Rocks which have much brighter legs than the pure ones. This is one reason why the purchasers of this breed ought to be careful from where they procure their stock.

If Plymouth Rocks are only required for table and eggs these points may be lost sight of, and birds with short legs and an intelligent-looking head sought after. I like to introduce fresh blood every year, when eggs only are required, as it always pays in the end. The chickens are much stronger, pullets lay earlier, and the cockerels fledge much faster. I knew a Plymouth Rock pullet in 1884 lay when under four months old. This, of course, is unusual. They usually commence laying when about seven months old. This is the average, but some commence at six months. It depends upon how they are attended to when young, and whether they are bred from a good laying strain. I have known them lay 60 eggs before they were eight months old. This is an exception, and not a rule. I had one hen which laid over ten months out of twelve. The pullets bred from this hen laid when five months old. The cockerels were very short in the legs and broad in the breast. I have bred from four of the cockerels this year. This breed will, I am sure, still spread, as they possess such good qualities. They are heavy, broad in the breast, stand confinement well, do not show the dirt, lay a brown egg, are very hardy, with no feathers on the leg, and stand the cold weather well. I prefer them to the Cochin this year. I bred from 125 of them to 35 of the Cochins. They are much more active, and better table fowls. Where table birds are required, this breed ought to be kept, especially if cross-breds are kept. They improve them very much. They can easily be bred with white legs and skins, if these are preferred. The plumage of this breed fades very much when exposed to light, and especially if not sheltered from the sun. Some shades fade more than others. The dark markings, which some people call black, fade and turn brown, especially in the cocks. It can be noticed more particularly on the top of the back. It is well to avoid this as much as possible. Sometimes, when they are a rusty colour before they moult, their new plumage will come quite a distinct colour, fit for exhibition. They are good birds for a town, as they do not show the dirt. The chickens can be distinguished from other breeds. When all hatched out together, they are very dark on back. This part may be called black, and light colour underneath. The mark of distinction is at the back of the head; it is a small grey spot. The legs and beak are usuaally very yellow. They do not show the markings on their plumage until their feathers grow. I put the Plymouth Rock down as one of the best all-round breeds, as I have thoroughly proved them to be. One vigorous cock may run with nine hens, and almost every egg will be fertile.

MINORCAS.

This breed has been the best known in the West of England, especially in Cornwall; they abound there like

W. COOK'S MINORCA COCKEREL.

PRIZE BIRD.

cross-bred fowls do in many other parts of the country. I visited Cornwall a few years since, and was surprised to see so many there; but I thought, as most other visitors have done, that they were a good bird for that warm climate—as they are non-sitters—but not for colder climates nor for confined runs; but to my great surprise I find it is not so. They are excellent for confined places, and they can now be found in almost every town in England and in many country places, even on farms. I have tried many experiments with them these last three years, both in cold and sheltered places and on different soils; I have reared them and not put them in a house or shed from the time they were hatched until they laid; I have tried them against my Houdans, and they surpassed them for laying purposes altogether. As a rule they have laid from a month to six weeks earlier than the Houdan, all hatched at the same time and brought up together. This is the only way to test which really are the best fowls, so that they all have the same treatment. The eggs of the Minorcas are very fine; they lay one of the largest eggs of any breed; some strains of Houdan lay as large, but they are very scarce; also the Creve Cœur, Spanish, and La Fleche lay large in some instances. I find all breeds that are accustomed to lay large eggs differ very much; the reason often is, that they lay at an earlier age. A pullet that commences to lay at from four to five months old will not lay such a large egg as one that does not commence until she is six or eight months. Although they lay white eggs they are very saleable both in town and country. This breed is not the most popular of the day, but one of them; even now I do not think they stand so high on the list as they ought to do. They are without exception one of the best non-sitting breeds to keep if large eggs are required, as there are so many thousands who want eggs and do not care whether they are good table fowls or not. The Minorca is not considered a good table fowl by the public as a rule, and yet there is no fowl eats so much like a turkey, that is in flavour and colour of flesh, as this breed does (and who is it that is not fond of turkeys ?). They have remarkably white flesh, nothing can be whiter as a table fowl; they may not be quite so juicy as a Dorking, but the flavour is quite equal. If care is taken they may be bred to a large fowl, and are what I should call a medium-sized fowl at present. I weighed a pullet this year that turned the scale at 6¼lbs. at seven months old; that was the largest I ever saw at the age. They have small bones, and comparatively short legs, so there really is no offal about them. Where they have not been bred for size, the ordinary weight is from 4½ to 5lbs. at six or seven months old. The cockerels are much larger, and they would not disappoint any nobleman at the dinner table. They ought to be kept more among all classes of breeders. I am breeding many of them now, as they are not only good in their pure state, but make excellent layers when crossed with any other breed. The eggs from the Minorca hatch out well; cockerels fledge fairly, and pullets fledge very quickly, and are very strong and healthy, easy to rear. They are a very active fowl, and scratch well for a living when they have their liberty, and yet when penned up they are quite contented. The plumage of them is very nice; they are a black fowl, and have a splendid gloss on their plumage, especially the cocks. They have very large single combs. The hens' fall over on one side, and when bred for the show pen are very long, and should be evenly serrated; fine combs, the cocks' standing erect, and evenly serrated. are preferred, not a rough comb. Their faces should be red when they are in full lay, and free from streaks of white. When required for exhibition they ought to carry their tails well out, that is to say, not too upright; if so, they are called squirrel-tailed. This is also a fault in the show pen—they

BLACK MINORCA PULLET.

should have dark legs, not blue, like those of the Spanish; four toes on each foot, well spread out from each other; white ear-lobes, free from red spots. The cocks should answer to this description in face, ear-lobes, and legs, but the combs should stand very erect; the straighter they are the better; and the ear lobes much larger than those of the hens, and should be free from wrinkles as much as possible, and as soft as a kid glove. This breed, like all other breeds that have white ear-lobes and large combs, should be shut up 14 days before they are sent to a show; the place should be so that it can be darkened. Some have shutters to the windows of the house; this is not always convenient. The coop or pen that the fowl or fowls are put in should be large enough for them to turn round in without ruffling their tails. They ought to be supplied with grit; the best way is to mix it in their soft food, then there is no doubt about them having it. They should be supplied with dust or moss peat—the latter is much better—so that they are kept quite clean, and water by them. A large thin sack or bag can be covered over the front of the pen, or anything of this description, so that the fowls are shaded from the light; this not only whitens the ear-lobes, but the combs grow very much and usually become very red. They should have green food every day, also a little meat is beneficial to them: it helps the combs, especially the cocks'.

Sometimes a cockerel will be perfect in every point but his comb, and it will hang over on one side, as it is very fine, and has not strength in itself to stand up; of course, he will not do for the show pen. Such birds are usually killed, because the owner thinks they are no good. This is a great mistake on the part of many breeders. It is quite a common occurrence to hear breeders say they are the finest birds of the whole number that have been bred by them, and yet no good because the comb is over. These cockerels make the best pullet-breeders. They produce birds with very fine combs, just those that win in the show pen. They look quite different from pullets that have been bred from a cock that has a good erect-set comb, as many of the pullets bred from the last-mentioned cockerel have heavy, thick combs —what are sometimes called fleshy combs. They are too strong to fall over on one side of the face, so that makes a great part of the comb double over the wrong side of the face, or, rather, come both sides of it. This is a fault in exhibition fowls. If Minorcas are not required for exhibition, the comb is no detriment to the cockerels when it hangs over a little on one side, or a streak of white in the face. These little defects are nothing when the fowls are only required for laying and table purposes. The chickens of this breed when hatched are white underneath and black on the upper part. When the feathers begin to grow the black covers the white. Sometimes white feathers remain in them for three months, but they usually shed them before that time. I have not treated upon the white Minorcas, as their points are much the same, only white plumage instead of black. They ought not to have a coloured feather of any kind. The comb, wattles, face, and ear-lobes should be just the same and the legs white. I like black much the best. An active Minorca cock can run with from seven to ten hens of the same breed.

LEGHORNS.

Much has been said in favour of this breed the last two years, both as layers and hardy birds. They cannot be spoken too highly of, although they are small. There is not much of them if required for table; their skin is also rather yellow, and another drawback is they lay white eggs; nevertheless their good qualities counteract their failings. In the

WHITE LEGHORN COCKEREL.

first place they are very hardy and stand confinement well; they even thrive in the back yards of towns, and lay all the winter through if properly housed and fed. They are easily reared as chickens, they fledge fast, and mature early. They commence to lay at from four to six months old, although the former age is too early. If they lay under five months old they usually commence to shed their feathers like old hens, but they get over it quickly, and soon come on to lay again. Leghorn chickens may be hatched out from January to August. They do not grow quite so large when hatched in June or July as if they had been earlier. They often lay at Christmas, most of them being in full lay in the month of January.

They are a beautifully-shaped bird, and often take the eye in preference to the larger breeds, as they are very active, and when allowed their liberty they range a long way from home, but do not lay away, as many other breeds do, if they have good accommodation in their roosting-house.

There are four varieties of this breed, brown, white, black, and cuckoo. I prefer the two former, as when bred from they come more true to colour, and there are more of them kept, so that it is easy to obtain fresh blood. This is very necessary with this breed; if not, they deteriorate very much and become very small. In former years I found the brown the best layers, but the last two years my white have left the brown a long way behind in the laying qualities; in fact, I have found them stand my cold place better than any other pure breed. This year my white Leghorns lay a larger egg than the brown, and the hens weigh three-quarters of a pound heavier, some of them over a pound more than the brown. The latter look rather the best in a confined run, as they do not show the dirt. They stand confinement equal to the white. All varieties will do this if necessary.

The black often throw white feathers in the tail, and their

ear-lobes are a bad colour (yellow) unless bred from first-class stock. They are excellent layers.

The cuckoo frequently come a bad colour, especially if they are exposed to the sun. They often throw a great many brown feathers, especially the cocks. All four varieties should have yellow legs, white ear-lobes and single combs. The cock's should stand very erect and be evenly serrated, The hen's should fall over on one side. The white variety should have no coloured feathers if required for show.

The cocks of the brown are very handsome, much the colour of a black-breasted red Game cock. The hen's hackle feathers should be well marked, slight brown edged with black. These are the hens to breed from if good-bred fowls are required.

The egg-table of the Leghorn varies very much, like most other breeds. I know a cottager who keeps fifteen white Leghorns. The average is close on 250 each per bird in a year; another I know whose birds do not average higher than 120 eggs per bird. There are single specimens which will lay 300 per year, but these are very rare at present. Another pen of white Leghorns, fifteen in number, laid over 650 eggs from the 1st of November, 1884, to the 28th of February, 1885. I mated some of my cockerels with these hens, and supply the eggs at 6s. 6d. per sitting of thirteen eggs. When I meet with a good-laying pen of birds I always endeavour to keep them up, or even a single fowl, if a good layer. I encourage them to breed from her or buy her myself.

Leghorns are very fertile fowls and the eggs hatch out well. One cock may run with from eight to ten hens (six in a confined run), and twelve hens are not too many if they have an open run (grass field). They are non-sitters. I prefer them to Hamburghs, because the chickens are much hardier and the eggs are also larger. They give good value for their food. This breed ought to be more encouraged in our country. The eggs are about as large as those of the Dorking.

I can recommend Leghorns as the best breed to keep if only eggs are required for home consumption, either in confinement or in an open range. The white variety is my favourite. This variety keeps more free from disease than any birds I ever kept.

DORKINGS.

There are four varieties of this breed, viz., the coloured, silver-grey, cuckoo, and white.

All four varieties resemble each other in having deep, square bodies with broad breasts and short white legs, with five claws on each foot. The comb should be single and evenly serrated in the coloured and silver-grey, while the white and cuckoo should have double or rose combs.

The coloured or dark Dorkings are very large birds, the cocks weighing about 10 lbs. and the hens about 7 or 8 lbs. The cock's breast and tail should be black, the hackle and saddle feathers being striped grey and black ; the upper and lower part of the wing is greyish white, while the middle bar should be black.

The feathers on the top part of the hen's back should be very dark, each feather showing a light brown stripe in the centre. The breast is of a reddish-brown shade, each feather being just tipped with black at the end. The tail should be black and the hackle feathers striped grey and black.

The silver-grey resemble the coloured in shape, but are not quite so large. The cock's plumage is also much the same as that of the coloured, but the hackles, &c., are lighter or more of a silvery colour. The hen's back should be of a delicate pale grey, the breast being of a light brown colour—

rather paler than that of a robin—and the hackles striped white and black, appearing very bright. Cuckoo Dorkings are smaller than the coloured, but are very handsome, each feather being a greyish-white tipped with slate at the end. They are rather the best layers of the four varieties, and are often called speckled Dorkings. These resemble the Plymouth Rocks in colour.

White Dorkings are about the same size as the cuckoo variety, but rather longer in the leg, and they are also rather delicate unless they have a good open range.

As is generally known, Dorkings carry a large quantity of white meat, and as they are the best birds for table purposes they command the highest prices in the London markets.

They are not good layers in confinement, and most people find them delicate to bring up, although I have never found any difficulty in rearing them; but the chickens do better if they have a good open space with short grass to range over.

No fowls require the introduction of fresh blood more than Dorkings, and unless a change of blood is frequently brought in it will be found that the eggs and chickens get smaller every year.

CREVE CŒURS.

The nature of this breed is much the same as that of Houdans, but the colour is different, Creves being quite black, and they are also larger birds, and lay about the same sized eggs as Houdans, but they do not lay such a large number.

The cocks should weigh about 8 lbs., and have a large comb divided in the middle like two horns; the wattles are long and the top-knot ought to be large, as also the whiskers and bib. The hens are non-sitters and good summer layers; they have top-knots, &c., the same as the cock, but the

BLACK HAMBURGH COCK.

combs and wattles are much smaller. The legs are blue, with four claws on each.

Creve Cœurs are not much known in this country, and where they are known are generally preferred for cooking purposes, as they make fine table birds.

HAMBURGHS.

There are five varieties of this breed, viz., silver-pencilled, golden-pencilled, silver-spangled, golden-spangled, and black.

With the exception of black, which only differs in being rather larger, all the varieties of Hamburgh resemble each other in having small white ear-lobes, rose combs ending in a point behind, and small but somewhat plump bodies with blue legs and four claws on each foot. They are also non-sitters.

In the silver-pencilled the hens are evenly pencilled nearly all over the body, the only part not marked being the hackle feathers, which are almost white. The cocks are nearly pure white, the exception being the tail, which is black slightly edged with white, the feathers on the lower part of the body between the end of the wings and the thighs, which are evenly pencilled, and some of the wing-feathers, which are slightly touched with black.

The golden-pencilled are marked in exactly the same way, but with rich brown colouring on the feathers in place of white.

In the silver-spangled variety the hen should be spangled on the breast, back, saddle, and thighs, the tail and long wing feathers being white with black spots on the ends; the neck hackles should be striped black and white. The cock's breast is spangled and the hackles and tail white, each tail feather being tipped at the end with black; back and wings grey and white with a few dark feathers, the wing being marked with three distinct bars of black.

The golden-spangled are marked nearly in the same way, but the feathers are coloured rich brown instead of white, the cock's tail being pure black. They are often known as "Moonies," or pheasant birds, especially in the Midland counties.

GOLD-SPANGLED HAMBURGH COCK.

The black have pure black feathers, which look almost green in the sun. They appear to have a slight touch of the Spanish build, from which breed they no doubt obtain the extra size.

Hamburghs are well known on account of their laying qualities. They lay medium-sized white eggs, which do not sell well for market. Although smali they make fair table fowls, as they are plump and the flesh is white and tender.

They do best with a large range, but if shut up securely and kept clean they will thrive well in confinement.

These fowls are largely kept in our country, and still retain their reputation as layers. I have tried them against the Leghorn the last three years, but I must give the Leghorn the preference for several reasons. Firstly, they are much hardier when exposed to the cold and wet; secondly, they lay better in the winter months, laying larger eggs, which make a better price than the Hamburghs; thirdly, the chickens are much hardier, and can be reared considerably easier, being much less subject to colds in the winter months, that is, they do not feel the changes in the weather so much. Hamburgh chickens ought not to be brought up with other breeds; if they are they do not thrive so well. They also ought to be kept from the damp grass early in the morning, and if reared in confinement should be kept very clean.

SCOTCH GREY.

This breed is very little known in England, although they are good useful fowls. In Scotland they are very popular, and are thought very much of. The colour is much the same as the Plymouth Rocks, but the markings are finer, and the dark markings of the feathers are of a lighter shade than the Rocks, and the lighter marking not so light. In well-bred Scotch Greys the markings are very even of two shades of grey, one light and the other dark, so that if one single feather is examined, it will be found that the bars of light and dark shades run right down to the stem of the feather. The markings are so distinct that many of our English breeders have crossed them with the Plymouth Rocks to get the even markings. It may be noticed, by those who attend Poultry

Shows, that there are two distinct varieties of Plymouth Rocks, one with large bone, especially in the legs, which are long reachy birds with very large frame, the others are more the shape of the Dorking, short legs, with very compact bodies, and the markings are very fine or small.

The Scotch Greys are very hardy, with fairly short white legs, broad in the breast, skin very white, and may be classed as a good table fowl. The chickens grow fast and are very hardy. A few of the cockerels are a little delicate, but this is where they have been bred-in too much. If bred from a good laying strain the pullets will commence laying when from six to seven months old, and make good layers of fair-sized white eggs. They stand confinement fairly well, but do better where they have a good range; they are good sitters and mothers, and can be crossed with any other variety. If the owners of Scotch Greys wish to increase the number of eggs, and do not mind white shells, the best breeds to use for crossing are Houdan, Minorca, or Leghorn cocks. When crossed with either of these breeds they make excellent winter layers, and will produce from thirty to fifty eggs each more than in their pure state in twelve months, and also commence laying earlier. When a Leghorn cock is used many of the pullets commence when five months old. When the Houdan cock is crossed the best table fowls are produced. When the Minorca cock is mated the eggs are a little larger than from the other crosses. When a white Leghorn cock is used most of the pullets come white. If the Houdan, most of them come black, with small top-knots. If the Minorca, sixteen out of twenty come black. The laying results from these crosses are marvellous. If table fowls for market are required, I recommend the Dorking cock to be crossed, as when this cross reaches the London markets, they are bought up at once, as their legs and skins are so very white. If brown eggs are required, I recommend a

Langshan or Brahma cock to be used. The two latter are the best, if the situation is very cold or damp, as they will lay when the snow is on the ground ; in fact, if the two latter crosses are hatched out in February, March, or April, they will lay more eggs in October, November, December, January, and February, than they will in March, April, May, June, and July. If the birds are required for pheasant-rearing, I prefer the black-breasted red Game cock to be mated with the Scotch Greys, as the pullets from this cross are hardy, good winter layers, and are excellent sitters and mothers. If these crosses were tried in the North of Scotland their egg-list would be doubled in the winter. I have had pullets of the Scotch Grey cross commence to lay at five months old. If this breed were only better known in England they would be kept largely, being a favourite fowl in Scotland.

LA FLECHE.

These birds should be pure black in colour, and of a fairly good size. The comb is very peculiar, dividing into two distinct and upright pieces a short distance from each other, giving the bird the appearance of having two horns. The legs are slaty-blue and rather long, with four claws on each foot.

Although the hens are non-sitters, and moderate layers of large white eggs, I should not advise any one to keep this variety, as there are many others more profitable.

This breed is very subject to roup where the situation is cold or damp. I do not keep a bird of this breed on my place.

POLISH.

The three best known varieties of this breed are the golden-sdangled, silver-spangled, and white-crested black. All three varieties resemble each other in having a large crest, and the silver-spangled and golden-spangled also have feathers under the beak, commonly called a "bib." They are moderate-sized birds, and should have short, blue legs, with four claws on each foot. In the golden-spangled the cock's crest should be a bright brown, some of the feathers being tipped with black and white. The hackles and middle of the wing are also brown, the tail being black, edged with brown, and the breast spangled. The hen should be spangled all over, with the exception of the tail and lower part of the wing, which should be brown tipped with black. The silver-spangled are marked in exactly the same way as the golden-spangled, but the feathers are white and black instead of brown and black.

In the white-crested black the cock and hen should be black all over the body, the crest being pure white.

Polish are non-sitters and fair layers of moderate-sized white eggs. They thrive best on a sandbank, or in a dry wood, but, although they make very fair birds for table, I do not recommend them, as they are not one of the most profitable breeds to keep.

Their crests get very dirty and irritate their eyes. They often lose the sight if great care is not bestowed upon them.

GAME.

All varieties of this breed resemble each other in having a sharp strong head and neck, long vigorous legs with four claws on each foot, and broad firm breast, and the general appearance of the bird should be firm and hard, caused by the feathers being very strong and lying close to the body. The comb is single, and of a moderate size, standing erect in both sexes. The cock's comb and wattles are often cut off or "dubbed" when the bird is about four to five

INDIAN GAME COCK.

FRENCH HOUDAN COCK.

months old, as they are then less liable to injure themselves should they get fighting.

There are so many different varieties of Game that to describe all would take too much space, but the most common variety is the black-breasted red, the cock of which should have a black breast and tail, and the lower part of the body should also be black; the hackle and saddle feathers are of a rich brown-red colour, the upper part of the wing is of a deep red with black edging, the centre part being black and the end a reddish brown, something the same colour as the hackles. The hen's back and wings should be brown, and the under part of the body rather lighter. The hackles are striped black and brown. I find this variety are the best layers.

Game are fairly good fowls to keep when they have a good range, as they search well for their own living and are very hardy. The hens are poor layers in confinement unless they are bred from a good laying strain, but lay fairly well if they have a good range, and they are also good sitters and mothers, as they will defend their brood against anything but they are spiteful to chickens not their own.

They make much better table fowls than one would expect, as they are very plump and fit to kill at a moment's notice; but I should not recommend this breed to anyone desirous of keeping fowls for profit unless they have a wood or a grass field for them to run over, in which case they will, practically, take care of themselves.

HOUDANS.

This breed is the most general of the French varieties known in this country, and holds about the same position in France as Dorkings do here. They are much the same shape as the Dorkings, and are first-rate table fowls, having small bones, short legs, and plenty of very white and rich meat on the breast. They are, however, much better layers than Dorkings, as they produce a large number of fine white eggs in the year, and are also much hardier and stand confinement fairly well.

The hens are non-sitters, and should have black feathers tipped with white, the markings being as regular as possible. The cocks weigh from 6 to 8½lbs., and are the same colour as the hens on the breast, but darker on the back, with greenish-black feathers in the tail. Both sexes have large top-knots, with feathers round the ears and under the beak, known respectively as the "whiskers" and "bib." The cock has a large comb opening in the middle, and often known as a leaf-comb; the hen's is the same shape, but much smaller. The legs are short and of a blue colour, with a few white spots, and five claws on each foot.

As will be seen by the above description, Houdans are very fine fowls to keep for crossing purposes, when a supply is wanted of eggs, and also of chickens for the table.

COCHINS.

All varieties of this breed should have four claws on each foot, and the legs should be of a yellow colour, short, and feathered down to the toes, with a great deal of fluffy feathers on the thigh. Comb single, rather short, and standing erect. Breast appearing very broad, and the genera attitude of the fowls rather leaning forward. The cocks ought to weigh from 7 lbs. to 11 lbs. and the hen from 7 lbs. to 6 lbs.

The most common colours known are buff, white, and partridge, but black and cuckoo Cochins are frequently met with. I prefer the buff and partridge varieties.

Buff differ in colour a great deal, some being of a pale

lemon colour, and others much darker, while the cock's feathers are very glossy, being of a rich brown-red colour on the wings and back.

The white and also the black variety, to be pure, should be free from any feathers other than those of their respective colours.

PARTRIDGE COCHIN HEN.

Partridge hens are mottled, something like a partridge but rather darker; the feathers on the body are pencilled, and those on the neck are black and brown, tinged delicately round the edges with light brown. The cock should have black feathers on the breast and under part of the body, and red on the wing and back.

Cuckoo Cochins are of a pale slate colour, usually known as "speckled;" they are not so heavily feathered as the other varieties, and no doubt derive their colour and existence from cuckoo Dorkings and Dominique. Cochins are often disliked on account of their being such bad table fowls and so often wanting to sit; but, in spite of these failings, they are very good fowls to keep for anyone with only a small space, and that cold and damp, as they stand confinement well and are very hardy. I have known disease go through every breed in the poultry-yard with the exception of Cochins, and even Brahmas will take diseases that will not touch Cochins. As chickens, they are hardy, and may be hatched all through the winter, although they fledge very slowly. In breeding, care should be taken to select a young cock, hatched about May, as then they are more active and do not grow so large, and by breeding in this way, as many chickens may be hatched from two broods as would be obtained from four without taking this precaution.

The best varieties to keep in confinement are buff and partridge, but of the two I advise partridge, as they lay a month earlier than the buff, often laying when six or seven months old, while the buff are often eight months old before commencing. They are first-rate layers, and will lay well in winter, as their feathers being long and strong, they can stand any weather. They lay a good-sized egg, very rich in flavour, the white being thicker and more glutinous than any other fowls', and the colour of the shell being quite brown they sell well, and command a good price in any market.

These birds are also very valuable for crossing, and may be crossed with any other fowls; but I recommend non-sitters, as they are so often broody, and many farmers who have crossed Cochins with Dorkings, to obtain good table birds, have been tormented with broody hens. Care should also be taken in selecting birds to cross with Cochins to

SILVER WYANDOTTE COCK.

choose those with short legs and plenty of breast-meat, or otherwise the half-bred birds will be very lanky.

Cochins require careful feeding, as, when fed entirely on corn, they will only lay a few eggs, and then become broody, and, although they make good sitters and mothers, they are a nuisance when so often broody ; they are also very liable to feed internally, which, of course, stops their laying, and often causes death by apoplexy.

WYANDOTTES.

This is one of the most recent breeds from America, and is not very popular yet. It is comparatively but little known in our country. Some praise the Wyandottes, while others are disgusted with them. I have found them excellent layers; there are not many pure breeds to surpass them (if they can be called a pure breed) ; they may, indeed, be classed amongst our best layers. The eggs are brown and rather small—some would call them a medium size—and the fowls themselves are fairly hardy, will stand confinement well, and make fair table birds, as they are short and compact, and very full in the breast. Occasionally a few of the cockerels have yellow skins, which is not in their favour as table birds. The hens make good sitters, and mothers will often lay in the coop before the chickens are three weeks old. If not required for sitting they are easily checked, two days in the broody coop often being sufficient. They will often commence to lay before the seven days are up. Those who first brought this breed out ought to have kept them about three years longer, and then they would, no doubt, have been better, as they do not breed true. Doubtless the English breeders will improve this for them, as they have done with many other breeds. A few years' careful breeding will bring them round to a more set colour, as when first hatched they look like an ordinary mixture, some being black, others brown, a few a mixture of black and white, and others almost grey. Some turn out black when matured, some a greyish black and white, speckled, or between a spangled and pencilled; the latter are the correct colour. In the hen the breast, back, and wings are more of a spangle, while the under feathers are slightly laced, and at the top of the thighs, the hackles are nicely laced, the middle of the feathers being white, edged all round with black. I call it a laced neck, much the same as that of a silver Sebright Bantam. The centre bars of the wing are white, slightly edged with black. Both the cock and hen should have rose combs, rather small, with a peak protruding over the back of the head; face and ear-lobes are red. The beaks should be strong and of a pale yellow; legs, bright yellow, free from feathers, with four claws on each foot well spread out from each other; tails should be black. The cock is much the colour of a dark Brahma cock; the saddle and hackles white evenly striped with black. The back and wings are of a silvery white, slightly edged with black. Many of the cocks come with black breasts, but they should be laced on the breasts very evenly (some use the word "mottled" breast). I do not hesitate in saying they are really a cross between the silver-spangled Hamburgh and dark Brahma. I have reasons for stating this, as many of the chickens from this cross come marked exactly the same as the Wyandotte. The first cross between these two breeds comes truer to colour than the Wyandottes do. The second cross—that is, when the silver-spangled Hamburgh and dark Brahma are crossed and their offspring are bred from—do not breed true to colour. (This is the case with most crosses: the first cross usually comes very uniform, but when bred from again they come all different colours.) This cross usually throws a few feathers on the legs, but if the Brahma hen that is selected for breeding is fairly bare of feathers, many of the offspring do not have a trace of them on their legs. I believe the Wyandottes will be very popular in a few years, as they are good layers. When this breed is mated to produce exhibition birds, or for good marking in the pullets, a cock with a good mottled breast should be used, and a mixture of white in his fluff feathers. When this colour is selected, well-marked pullets may be expected. It is rather difficult to get a nice-shaped comb with a good peak at the back in the cocks, but it is an important point.

BLACK SPANISH.

These birds should have perfectly black plumage and blue legs, with four claws on each foot; the face should be large and quite white, comb very large, and standing erect in the cocks, but falling over in the hens.

The general build of the birds is rather slim, and therefore they do not make good table fowls, but are very profitable layers when they have a suitable place, but not, as a rule, when confined, unless well sheltered from the cold north-east winds. Generally they do well when shut up in some of the back gardens of towns, as in these places they are warmer than in the country, and well sheltered from the cold winds, and when properly treated I have known them to pay about 300 per cent.; the chickens, owing to slow fledging, are difficult to rear, unless a warm situation be provided and care taken; when crossed they are much hardier, and once fledged they are healthy and strong. Some people say that Spanish chickens are strong and healthy, but my experience differs from this. When I have reared many breeds together, and the others have got on well, the Spanish have drooped their wings and died. As a rule it is not a good plan to bring different breeds up together, as some require more care than others; but when a number of different breeds are

SILVER WYANDOTTE PULLET.

brought up together on the same treatment, I think it plainly shows which are the hardiest and which are the weakest.

LANGSHANS.

Though this breed have been so much ridiculed, they are becoming favourites, and will more so when they get better known. They are, indeed, a good all-round fowl for table, hardy to bring up, splendid layers of a brown egg, which is saleable everywhere, good birds to breed from, excellent sitters and mothers, stand confinement well, do not show the dirt, and are good foragers if they have their liberty. They have a beautiful green-black gloss on their plumage. A black fowl is much easier to breed from than any other colour. There is in the Langshan what is wanted, viz., laying and table qualities combined and also a handsome fowl. If breeders would only keep to the best layers and make this a special point of compass, it would be a grand thing. The Rocks at the present time are the most fashionable breed, though Langshans are much easier to breed. The beautiful brilliant gloss upon their plumage is quite different from a black Cochin, though they are mixed up a great deal.

The Langshan has much more tail than the Cochin, and has black legs slightly feathered down to the outside toe, not the middle one, which should be quite free from feathers. The thick fluff (vulture hocked) is a fault with them, especially the cocks. These are rather long in the leg, and should be broad in the chest, and should carry themselves very erect. Their combs should be evenly serrated and erect, the hens the same, but sometimes the latter's incline to one side (this is not a serious fault), and should also have very red ear-lobes. They often have a few white feathers on their feet; this ought to be bred out, although they are often passed thus in the show-pen. They should have four toes on each foot. Sometimes the male bird throws a few red feathers on the neck and saddle.

If the cock is a very active bird he can run with from seven to nine hens in a confined run, or in a large range (grass field), ten or twelve hens, and, as a rule, eleven eggs out of thirteen will be fertile.

If breeding for exhibition, run less hens, when for this purpose they are much heavier, and it is not well to run more than five or six hens. The pullets fledge moderately well, the cockerels rather backward, but all are very hardy. If they are required for table they ought to be killed when from three to four months old, or from six to seven months old. At the latter age they are like young turkeys.

I am so pleased with them and the Rocks that I shall use both breeds for crossing purposes in preference to the Brahma or Cochin, as they both make better table birds when crossed, and the laying qualities are equal. I breed very largely from Langshans and Rocks, both pure and crosses. The Langshan chickens when hatched are black on the back and a whitish-yellow the underneath part. The first feathers sometimes come tipped with white, but these pass away in the first moult.

BRAHMAS.

There are two varieties of this breed—viz., the light and dark. Both are of large size, and should have a broad substantial appearance. The cocks weigh from 8½ to 10 lbs. and the hens from 7 to 9 lbs. The legs are yellow, rather short, and well feathered down to the tip of the middle claw. The comb should be small and set close to the head, and is what is called a pea or triple comb, having the appearance of being cut down or rounded-off, like three small peas, the centre one being the largest.

In light Brahmas the plumage of the cocks and hens should be of a white colour all over, with the exception of the hackle feathers, which are striped grey and black, and the tail feathers, which are black slightly edged with white. The hen should have a white body and black and white hackles.

In dark Brahmas, the cock's breast, tail, leg feathers, and under part of the body, should be pure black. The upper part of the wing is of a greyish-white, the centre being black, and lower part white, tipped at the end with black. The hackle, back, and saddle feathers are of a greyish white and black. The hen's hackle feathers should be black and white, the tail being black, and the remainder of the body a slaty colour, each feather on the breast, upper part of the wing, and back, being marked with a darker slate, giving the bird the appearance of being beautifully pencilled.

Brahmas are very good fowls to keep for confinement, as they are very hardy, and do well in a small space. They are good layers of brown eggs in the winter months ; but in spring and summer they are often broody, and, as they make good sitters and mothers, it is often well for people who keep non-sitting varieties and wish to hatch a few chickens to keep a few Brahmas, as they may then be sure of a broody hen sooner or later.

If this breed is especially bred for laying only, they are excellent layers. I have known them lay from 130 to 170 eggs each in twelve months, while the show Brahmas have not averaged 40 each. A good laying strain of this breed will come up to the Rocks and also the Langshans ; they will lay from 30 to 40 eggs without missing a day. I have known several specimens not to come broody the whole of the year. They do not make as good table birds as the Rocks and Langshans when they are pure, but are equal for crossing purposes. The Brahmas breed so much better than the Cochins ; eleven eggs out of thirteen are usually fertile, where not more than six out of the same number of Cochins would produce chickens. This is a consideration. It is more difficult to get good layers from the dark variety than the light. I have been years in procuring a good laying strain of dark Brahmas, and did not succeed until 1884. They have laid all through the past winter, and some months have produced more eggs than the Rocks and Langshans. Notwithstanding this, I prefer the above breeds. If Brahmas are bred for laying only, they do not disappoint their keepers; if they average 110 per bird that is what may be called very good; it depends much upon the treatment they receive. When they become broody and are not required for sitting purposes, they ought to be shut up at once in the coop mentioned; then they lay again in a few days. The Brahma is a good fowl to cross with other breeds. Looking over my egg-book, I find that some of my dark Brahmas have laid 170 eggs each from the 1st of October to the middle of September.

REDCAPS.

This breed is a very old one, though but little known in many parts of the country. They are best known in Yorkshire, Derbyshire, and Staffordshire. In Yorkshire the farmers call them mooney fowls, and in Staffordshire pheasant fowls. I have known better layers from the latter place than either of the others. I have tried all three. I have found them a good breed as layers of a fair-sized white egg. One pullet has been known to lay 70 eggs in seventy days. The strains differ very much. They do rather better in an open range than in confinement, although they do fairly well anywhere when once matured. They are rather delicate to rear in confined back gardens, and where they are attempted to be brought up with large numbers of other chickens they usually succumb to an early death. If only a brood or two are required, and a little care is bestowed upon them the first three or four weeks, they will grow and feather well, both cockerels and pullets, and make fair table birds, white skin and blue legs, with four toes on each foot, free from feathers on legs and feet. In plumage they are much the colour of the golden-spangled Hamburgh. They are a reddish-brown with a tip of black, a kind of half moon. The Hamburghs are more of a spangle and also much brighter in colour, and have smaller combs. Redcaps should have red ear-lobes and very large rose combs. When the chickens are hatched out they are of a light buff colour underneath, and they have two stripes on the back, light and dark brown. They occasionally come rather buff, and only show a dark stripe at the back of the head, and others are almost black. They are very pretty as chickens. The cockerels can be told from the pullets when hatched, or at least in a week or two, as they have such a large comb. The cockerels are ready for the table when about four months old if fed and attended to well.

ANDALUSIAN.

This breed is a favourite with some fanciers, and also those who only require eggs. The colour of their plumage is different from any other variety, being slate colour. When the hens are properly marked they are very handsome. The ground colour is rather a light slate, each feather edged with a very dark shade. They look as though they are pencilled. The neck hackles are very much darker than the body, white ear-lobes, red face, single combs lying over on one side, dark legs rather a blue-slate, four toes on each foot. The cock has face and ear-lobes similar to the hen, comb single and should stand erect and be evenly serrated and well set to the head. Their back should be dark, almost black, and the breast more the colour of the hen. Andalusians do not breed true to colour; some come black and others white, and a few a very light slate with no dark marking. Those who do not understand the breed, when buying a sitting of eggs, must not be surprised if three or four different coloured chickens are produced. They are excellent layers of large white eggs. If the birds are sheltered from the cold winds they will lay in the winter, and spring and summer months in abundance. The chicks do fairly well, the pullets thriving best and also feathering better than the cockerels. They usually commence to lay at from five to six-and-a-half months old. One cock can run with seven or eight hens.

BLACK ROSE-COMB BANTAMS.

BANTAMS.

THESE small birds are often looked upon as useless by many, and even those who keep the larger breeds. The day of small things should not be despised, as small beginnings often produce large endings. There are many large breeders of the present day who only commenced with a pair of Bantams, and trace their success and love of poultry to their parents keeping these pets. I think it so nice to allow a boy or girl to keep a few fowls ; and Bantams can be kept where the larger breeds cannot. Young people must have something to do in their spare time ; and if parents do not find it for them, they will for themselves, and not always in the best direction. It would be well for parents to study their children a little more in this respect. It gives the young people a love for their home, whether the pets are fowls, pigeons, or rabbits. I have kept all three, and the former not only gave me as much pleasure in looking after them, but also paid for their food, and a little over. I always had an eye to pleasure and profit combined. Bantams usually give young people a great deal of pleasure. There are many people keep them all their lives, and make a study of them. If one cockerel and pullet are purchased, they will soon breed a pen of birds. A dog-kennel, or large box, will serve as a roosting house. A 4-feet square house is large enough for about twenty The game Bantams are kept more than any variety, especially the black-breasted reds.

The Duckwing and Pile are favourites with many. The colour of them should be much the same as the Game fowls of these varieties. If persons are desirious of keeping good specimens, it is well for them to go to a good show, or to where the best Bantams can be found. Mr. Entwistle is one of the cleverest gentlemen in the Bantam fancy that I know. He breeds some of the best birds in England. Any fancier wishing to obtain good Bantams cannot do better than apply to him. They will have their money's worth, and will be well suited. He is not only one of the best breeders, but also one of the best judges of all varieties. I believe he keeps almost every variety. It is well to prepare Bantams for the show pen, especially the black rose comb. This variety requires great care. Refer to the chapter on "Preparation for the Show Pen."

BLACK ROSE-COMB.

This breed is rapidly spreading through our country, and is becoming one of the favourites in the Bantam fancy. They are my favourites, as they are not only a very pretty little bird, but such good layers and very hardy. Being black they do not show the dirt when kept in the back yards of towns. There are many of our leading fanciers who first started by keeping a pair of these birds. I always like to encourage young people in keeping these pets. This breed should have nothing but black feathers, with a splendid gloss on their plumage, especially the male birds. Both sexes should have a neat rose comb, red face free from spots or streaks of white, and small white ear-lobes free from wrinkles and red spots, black legs, four toes on each foot. The cock should be very full in the breast. The smaller they are the better if they are compact and well-shaped. Where so many make a mistake in breeding Bantams, they hatch them out too early in the season. If they are not required for the show pen until November, May or early June is the best time to hatch them out. If for the summer shows, they may be hatched out early. The smallest Bantams I ever bred were hatched in the month of September. I have found this variety the best layers of any Bantams, and also of the largest egg according to the size of the bird. They can be kept in a very small pen if required. One male bird may run with about four or six hens. In all cases where they have not a grass run they ought to be supplied with green food. Nothing is better than watercresses if they can be procured reasonably. The chickens hatch out strong. When first hatched they are black on the back and a light colour underneath. Occasionally they throw white feathers in their wings, but usually shed them in their chicken moult.

CROSS-BRED FOWLS.

BEFORE proceeding to give some description of cross-bred fowls, I wish to make it quite plain what they really are, for I often hear mongrels called cross-breds. What is called a first cross is a bird obtained when two pure-bred fowls of different varieties are bred together, say a Dorking and Game, and if their offspring are crossed again, the chickens may be called a second cross. If first-cross hens are bred from, with a pure cock, the progeny are called a second cross. Say a hen crossed between a Rock and Langshan, if mated with a Dorking cock her offspring have three breeds in them, half Dorking, a quarter Langshan, and a quarter Plymouth Rock, and if these are bred from again their progeny may properly be called mongrels.

The question is often asked, why we do not breed from cross-bred cockerels? The principal reasons are—1st, the chickens obtained eat a great deal more; and 2nd, they do not lay so early by six weeks or two months, and altogether do not show such good qualities as the first crosses; but, of course, there are exceptions. I have proved that first crosses are best by running a cock with pure and cross-bred hens all shut up together; have saved eggs from each hen, hatched the chickens, at the same time brought them up together and treated all alike, and the first cross have laid before they were six months old, while the chickens obtained from the cross-bred hens, but with the same cock, did not lay until they were seven or eight months old; and although they laid as well as the others when they did commence, there was the loss of two months, which is a great consideration, especially in winter, when the price of eggs is so good.

There are many opinions as to the advisability of breeding and keeping cross-bred fowls, for while one eminent author will write, "Cross your fowls as much as possible; you cannot have too many breeds mixed," another will say, "Pure-bred fowls are best, as, while some of them average 170 to 200 eggs per bird in the year, cross-breds will only lay 80 to 120 in the same time." My experience is that first-cross bred fowls are much the best for general purposes, and I recommend them, as a rule, in preference to the pure-bred ones. If a pure hen will lay from 120 to 130 eggs in a year, and she is mated with a pure cock of another breed, and he has been bred from a hen which laid about the same number in the time, the offspring will produce from 150 to 190 eggs in a year, for, in a cross, there are the qualities of two pure-bred fowls together; for instance, in half-bred Hamburghs and Cochins, there is part of the hardiness and size of the Cochin, and part of the plumpness, non-sitting, and wonderful laying qualities of the Hamburghs; and, besides this, cross-breds are generally larger and hardier, on account of fresh blood being introduced. I do not wish to run down pure fowls in any way, for without them, of course, no cross could be produced; but I do most decidedly prefer a half-bred for purposes of laying, &c., and have, therefore, written fully on some of the principal crosses I have tried.

There are, of course, many I have not mentioned, but I have written on those I consider best. For instance, if it is more convenient, a Leghorn or Minorca cock may be used instead of Hamburgh or Spanish, or Creve Cœur in place of Houdan, or Brahma in place of Cochin, &c.

The La Fleche may be crossed with any of the breeds I have mentioned, but they do best with Dorking or Hamburgh. Malays are also another good breed, and, if crossed with the Brahma, produce excellent layers and sitters well suited for confinement.

If anyone has a curiosity for crossing, and still wishes to retain their pure-bred fowls, they may easily do so by letting two pure hens run with a cock of the same breed and four more of a different kind. I may mention that a Houdan cock, with two Houdan, two Spanish, and two Cochin hens, answer very well, and that it is always best when crossing non-sitters to have a Cochin or Brahma, to be sure of a broody hen for sitting in the spring.

The number of eggs I have given as being produced by certain crosses may seem very large, but it must be understood that it is only birds bred from the *very best* laying strains that will produce these numbers; and great attention must, of course, be paid to their feeding and management. Amateurs must, therefore, not be discouraged if their birds do not produce any such numbers for the first year or two. Those, however, who give attention to the birds, and follow my instructions, will find an increase in the number of eggs they obtain every year.

I have known fowls lay from 100 to 275 eggs in a year. It is according to the laying strains, and how they are treated. The owner must have practical knowledge, and this is obtained by closely watching the habits of the fowls. It is usually those who are fondest of their fowls that succeed the best in the end. A book may be a great help and guide, but this will not do all that is required in the poultry yard.

HOUDAN-COCHIN.

For many years Dorkings have been crossed with Cochins with very good results, with the exception of being inferior layers in the summer, as they become broody so often. I have found it best to cross Cochins with the French Houdan, as this breed possesses most of the good qualities of Dorkings, such as small bones, short legs, plenty of very white and rich meat, especially on the breast, and are plump when cooked. The best way of crossing is to run a Houdan cock with from six to eight Cochin hens, and if the cock is an active bird nearly all the eggs will be fertile. The chickens from this cross will hatch out well and fledge quickly, especially the pullets, but occasionally there may be a cockerel rather naked, but not for long; they are very hardy, and will do well in cold or *wet* weather, while, as a rule, chickens cannot stand wet weather; but I have reared these chickens from a week old, and have not lost more than one chick in three years, although they had never been inside the hen-house, or had a shed to protect them from wet and cold at night, until a short time before laying. They make good table birds, often being ready to kill when three months old, and are then plump and of good flavour, the skin on the body being very white. Most of the pullets are black, but a few have brown bodies and are spangled on the breast; generally they have white legs, but there are a few with dark, and some a bronze colour like those of

Game fowls. The hens lay fine eggs, generally brown, that will command a good price in any market. They do well in confinement or with a large run, are very healthy, and I have never had them suffer from anything except cramp, which was caused by their laying so much in cold weather; but have known this cross suffering from cramp, and yet not miss laying more than a day or so. I have had from two to five eggs dropped in one night from fifteen hens. Altogether these are capital fowls to keep, and may be classed as one of the best for confinement.

I first tried this cross in the year 1874 and hatched six pullets on the 4th March, one of which laid at the age of four months and three weeks; this, of course, is not the rule, but the others all laid before they were six months old, which is about the average age for these birds to commence laying, although, if well fed, they will lay a fortnight before this time. I kept these six hens for two years, and during the whole of that period I do not think I was more than a day without one or two eggs, as there were never more than three resting at the same time. One hen laid 263 eggs in eleven months and one day. In the winter months of both years they averaged 26 eggs per week, some weeks as many as 33 or 34, others 22 to 25. In December, January, and February they averaged 27 eggs per week, but after this not so many, as they wanted to sit. The first year some laid while moulting, which is very unusual for any fowls to do. In the whole year the six hens laid about 1,360 eggs, and brought up four broods of chickens, each hen laying when the chicks were about three weeks old; and if I allow a loss of say 20 eggs to each bird while sitting, &c., this would bring the number of eggs produced in a year to 1,440, or an average to each bird of 240 eggs, most of which were laid from September to February. The birds were sold when two and a-half years old, and the average weight was then

6½lbs. I may mention that these birds were kept in a run about 7 yards square

The preceding remarks refer to the buff Cochin and Houdan cross, but I advise partridge Cochins being used for crossing, as they are the best for the table and commence laying earlier ; they are also shorter in the leg, with broader breasts. I may add that the chickens are usually black, whichever variety of Cochin may be used, and that I recommend half-bred Houdan and partridge Cochins as one of the best fowls to keep for all general purposes. If mongrel-bred fowls are kept, and the owner does not wish to part with them, it is well to use a Houdan cock with them. The pullets obtained from this cross make very good winter layers, and some are good sitters. The cockerels are first-class table birds, and should be killed when about three or four months old. The chickens are very healthy, grow fast, and can be hatched out early if required. The Houdan cock being used as mentioned, brings the offspring of a uniform shape and colour, and destroys the mongrel appearance altogether. The Houdan-Brahma cross are about the same in every respect if bred from a good laying strain. They do not vary five eggs in twelve months from the Houdan-Cochin. They cannot be distinguished one from the other, especially the pullets. They are equal both in laying and table qualities.

HOUDAN-MINORCA.

The birds to produce this cross can be mated either way. I prefer the Houdan cock, as the eggs are more fertile when crossed this way. Houdan hens having a crest and beard, are often a little timid, as they cannot see behind them, neither side face. Owing to this, rather a large proportion of the eggs are unfertile. If the Minorca cock is used, six

Houdan hens are sufficient; if the Houdan cock with Minorca hens, eight or ten, and in many cases twelve hens are not too many if they have a good range. The eggs are very fertile from this cross. The chickens when hatched are dark or black on back, and yellowish-white underneath. The heads are usually black and white, and show a small top-knot and beard; they are fairly strong, fledge well, and grow fast. Most of the pullets come black, and make good sized fowls; they have blue legs. The cockerels usually have coloured feathers in their hackles and saddles, a kind of straw colour. They require to be removed from the pullets at an early age—about three months—as they become rather troublesome. They make very fair table fowls; certainly not large, but the meat is of a superior flavour and very white; not a popular fowl for the market, unless hatched early and sold as spring chickens, then they make a good price, as they are very plump and have not much bone. This cross is noted for the size of the eggs, as they lay one of the finest of any cross. The Minorca-La Fleche lay about the same size, but not so many in number. They are eggs that always command a good price in the market, notwithstanding they are white. A few of these mixed with smaller ones is often the means of obtaining a longer price for the small ones. Where fowls are kept for the purpose of selling eggs, I recommend some birds of this cross to be kept. In the number of eggs they differ very much according to the strain, from 105 to 220; I put the average down at 150 eggs per bird per annum. I have had them lay 240 in a year, but these are exceptions and not rules. They will stand confinement well, and lay all through the winter months, especially if they can be sheltered from the cold wind. They are very active and want employment. They are fowls that will suit all classes of people, in town or country. They are non-sitters, but occasionally there is one that will want to sit, but they cannot be depended upon. As non-sitters I recommend Houdan-Leghorns and Houdan-Minorcas, especially where only eggs are required. Both are good foragers, hardy, and easy to rear, and good layers.

HOUDAN-PLYMOUTH ROCK.

I have tried this cross against the Houdan-Cochin and Houdan-Brahma as layers, and the result is about an equal number of eggs of about the same colour, but for table fowls the Houdan-Plymouth Rock is far superior. They are clean-legged, with very fine breasts of a good flavour, and may be classed with the best table fowls in the market. Many of the legs come white, a few a dark bronze colour. They hatch out well, grow fast, fledge quickly, are remarkably hardy, and will stand confinement or do well in an open range. They stand the cold east winds well. The pullets lay when from six to seven months old; some are in full lay at six months. Where fowls are required for laying and table purposes, I know of no better class to keep, as they are a good saleable fowl. They can be hatched all the year round if required. They make splendid spring chickens, especially if short-legged fowls are used for breeding. It is the best to use the Houdan cock with from seven to nine Rock hens. If the Houdan cock is a large and active bird, from ten to twelve hens are not too many. If closed in a back yard with no extra run, six hens are sufficient. When the chickens are first hatched they are of a yellowish-white underneath and round the head, and dark on the back. Occasionally there is a grey spot at the back of the head as on the pure Rock. If a Rock male bird is used, many of the chickens will grow up the colour of a Rock. The other way they are dark and sometimes black. The pullets are a splendid shape and very handsome. They have the little crest on the head, and many of them a small beard. About five out of every twelve become broody. They make good sitters and mothers, as they are very strong in the wing.

Many of the eggs are tinted; a few are quite brown. I strongly recommend this cross; the owners will not be disappointed with them.

HOUDAN-LEGHORN.

For a non-sitting cross this cannot be surpassed in number of eggs and hardiness of fowl. Houdan-Minorca lay a larger egg, but not so many in number. They can be brought up in small backyards, and will grow fast and feather well, giving but little trouble. They are remarkably active as chickens; when first hatched they are black on back and yellowish-white underneath, and usually show a small top-knot. The cockerels ought to be killed off early, as they become very troublesome when they are from twelve to fifteen weeks old. If kept longer they ought to be separated from the pullets. They do not make large table fowls, but are very plump, have small bones, and the flesh is very white and juicy. I do not recommend them as a market table fowl, unless it is for early spring chickens, when they are not required so large. They stand the cold weather, very well, and are ready for the table earlier than the large breeds. Some of the pullets commence to lay very early, sometimes at four months old. This is rather too early, as if they commence when from five to six months old it is better for them, and the eggs are larger. These are white, of a medium size, a little larger than a Dorking's. Most of the pullets come black, and if brown Leghorn hens are used, some have brown hackles; if white hens are mated one occasionally comes white. They are very compact fowls, and will work well for their living when they have an opportunity. They fly if they have their liberty, but if brought up in a wire pen they are very contented. Where eggs are required all the year round I strongly recommend this cross, as they will not disappoint their keepers. If bred from a good laying strain they often lay 200 eggs each in a year, when kept in confined runs. They, of course, vary very much according to how they are managed. The average is about 170 eggs each per annum. Some specimens have laid over 260 eggs in twelve months. The eggs from Leghorn hens with Houdan cocks running with them hatch remarkably well, very seldom less than nine chickens, out of thirteen eggs, and in many cases twelve. Leghorn hens are very good to breed from. It is much the best to run a Houdan cock with these hens ; from seven to ten of the latter to one male bird, but if he is very vigorous, twelve hens may safely run with him For those who only require eggs, and especially if only for home consumption, a more profitable cross cannot be kept, if they can be sheltered from the cold east winds a little, and something given them to scratch to keep them employed. The egg production is marvellous, and if six hens in their second year and six pullets can be kept, the owner would never be without eggs in the cold, dark days of winter. This cross can be hatched very late in the season when it is necessary. July and August hatched chickens will often lay by Christmas. This cross ought to be named the "Amateur's Friend," considering their good qualities, as they hatch out well, are very hardy as chickens, can be reared in small back yards, grow fast, fledge well, lay early and constantly, and cannot well be put in the wrong place. If they are allowed their liberty they travel a long distance, but seldom lay away from home. This is one of the crosses I recommend to those about to start poultry-keeping, and to any who cannot spare much time in looking after their birds. If a breeding-pen have the advantage of a grass run, the eggs are more fertile, and a larger number of hens can be allowed with the male birds.

HOUDAN-SPANISH.

This cross is so much like the Houdan-Minorca, when the birds are grown up, that they cannot be distinguished. The laying qualities and size of eggs are much the same. The chickens are not quite so strong when hatched, and do not fledge so fast, especially the cockerels. The chickens hatch much stronger from the Houdan hens than from the Spanish. Not more than six Houdan hens should be allowed to run with the Spanish cock; but if the Spanish hens are used, the same number may be allowed to run with the Houdan cock as in the Houdan-Minorca cross. It may happen some have Spanish hens and not Minorcas; in this case use them; the result of eggs from the pullets will be about the same, and the chickens same colour.

HOUDAN-ANDALUSIAN.

This cross produce the same results as regards the laying qualities, and size and shape of fowl, but some differ in colour, as many of the chickens are of a slate colour when hatched, the pullets more particularly; they are blue or slate colour when grown, and are called a smoke colour by some. It is a matter of fancy of colour with some people. The quality of this cross is the same as Houdan-Spanish and Houdan-Minorca.

HOUDAN-HAMBURGH.

This cross is a very good one, as the birds can be reared in small runs. They are hardy and good layers, and as a non-sitting cross are very short in the leg. They are compact fowls, rather small, and not good for market purposes. The majority have black bodies and occasionally straw-coloured hackles, with a small crest. I have had birds of this cross lay over 200 eggs each per year. A Hamburgh cock can run with five Houdan hens, or a small Houdan cock with nine Hamburgh hens. They can be crossed either way, it making no difference in the laying qualities. I prefer the Houdan-Leghorn cross, as they are much the best.

HOUDAN-DORKING.

The best way of crossing is to run a Houdan cock with ten Dorking hens, and twelve out of thirteen eggs will be fertile; in selecting the Houdan cock for breeding, choose one with but little black on the legs. The chickens may be bred all the year round, as they hatch out well, are very hardy, and fledge quickly, not one being naked in a whole brood; they pay well for good attention the first fortnight, but after that they grow very fast, and make first-class table birds, being quite equal to the Game and Dorking cross in this respect. The cockerels may be killed at any time after they are eleven weeks old, but are better if shut up for twelve days before killing, although I have killed them at eleven to twelve weeks old, and they have been fine and plump.

The hens are mostly black, very large, short in the leg, and full of breast-meat. A few will have dark legs. They are good layers all the year round of very large white eggs. As a rule, they commence to lay at six months old, but I have hatched them in the beginning of March, and had two laying at the age of five months; about half will become broody, and these make good sitters and mothers.

Taking all their qualities into consideration, I do not

think there is a better cross for the farmer or gentleman with plenty of room, or a cottager that has a good sale for his young chickens and eggs and a large space for the birds to range about, and I can also recommend them to any one requiring good table birds and large eggs.

I may add that from 10 to 25 per cent. more is realised from these birds than from pure Dorkings. If any one keeping pure Dorkings would like to try this cross, he can do so by allowing a Houdan cock to run with the Dorkings.

HOUDAN-LANGSHAN.

This cross is so very similar to the Houdan-Cochin and Houdan-Brahma in every respect, that I do not think I need treat fully upon them. The laying qualities of each are the same. There is a slight difference in the Langshan cross having a little more meat on the breast. They may be preferred as a table bird, but in this quality there is only a trifling superiority. I can strongly recommend them as hardy fowls which will stand confinement well. The qualities of this cross can be seen in the description of the Houdan-Cochin, they being so much alike. The pullets of each cross cannot be distinguished. I have no preference for either of the three above-mentioned crosses.

HOUDAN-WYANDOTTE.

As Wyandotte hens are very expensive, it is best to allow the Wyandotte cock to run with Houdan hens, as the cross can then be obtained much cheaper. Seven hens may be allowed to run with the male bird. When crossed in this way, the chickens usually come dark brown, especially round the head. If the Houdan cock is used they come black on the back and white underneath, much the same as other

Houdan crosses. They are excellent layers of fair-sized eggs, but most of them tinted. They hatch out well, grow fast, and fledge quickly. They are not such good table birds as the Houdan-Rocks, neither is the egg quite so large. In other respects they are about the same, but a little shorter in the leg. The pullets are very compact fowls. A few of them come broody, but as a rule cannot be depended on. I am very fond of the Houdan-Wyandotte cross.

HOUDAN-GAME.

This cross may be produced by running a cock of either breeds.. The best results are obtained when the Houdan male bird is used, as a rule. From ten to twelve hens may be allowed to run with either male bird, providing the fowls have a good range. The chickens hatch out well, are remarkably hardy, fledge and grow very quickly They have a great deal of breast meat, and can be killed any time after they are about twelve weeks old. They do not often require fattening, but can be killed straight from the yard unless required for market. The pullets make good winter-layers of fair-sized white eggs, especially if they have their liberty, and have a wood to range in. The eggs can usually be depended on all through the winter months. If the Game cock is used, many of the chickens come brown when first hatched; if the other way, they are black and white.

MINORCA-PLYMOUTH ROCK.

This cross may be classed as one of the best to keep for laying purposes, both in confinement and with an open range. They cannot well be put out of their place. They are very compact, and can be produced either way, but care should be taken if the Minorca hens are used to select them large, and the Rock cock rather small if possible. A Minorca cock may run with from seven to ten Rock hens, or a Rock cock with the same number of Minorca hens; the results are good either way. This cross resembles the Minorca-Brahma, Minorca-Cochin, and Minorca-Langshan, especially those that come black. They cannot be distinguished one from the other, except that the Minorca-Rock cross are free from leg-feathering, or ought to be. If bred from good laying strains the result will be much the same. If the Minorca cock is used most of the pullets come black, and the cockerels a mixed colour as in most other crosses. If the Rock cock is used part of them come that colour. All have single combs and four toes on each foot. As chickens they are very hardy; pullets fledge fairly well. A few of the cockerels may be a little backward. They may be hatched early or late in the season, and usually do well. Frequently a few of the pullets commence to lay when very young—under five months old. The average age to commence laying is from six to seven months. Most of them lay a tinted egg, and are good summer and winter layers. About half come broody; if allowed to sit they make good sitters and mothers, and are very docile, and will not often peck each other's chickens. The pullets can usually be told from the cockerels, as they feather much quicker. The cockerels are usually a long time getting their tail feathers. The latter are usually ready for table when from 13 to 16 weeks old. They make fair table birds; eat very moist, flesh white and juicy. Their legs are coloured, some being black, bronze, or yellow. I recommend this cross for laying, and fowls for home consumption. They are a good general cross.

MINORCA-BRAHMA.

This cross is an improvement on the Spanish Brahma, although they are much the same class of fowl, but have better qualities. They are shorter in the leg, fledge better as chickens, and grow faster. Cockerels make better table fowls. I prefer this cross to many others. They cannot often be distinguished from pure Langshans, as they usually have a single comb (about seven out of every ten pullets have an erect comb, and the majority have a few feathers on the leg). When the Minorca cock is used he should have from six to nine Brahma hens mated with him. The eggs hatch well ; the chickens are strong and very hardy. I recommend this cross for confinement, as they can be reared in a small space, and when once matured, cannot be put in their wrong place. Most of the pullets come black, with straw-coloured hackles, when the Minorca cock is used. When the Brahma cock with Minorca hens, they take after the Brahma in colour, whichever variety is used. When crossed in this way, the Minorca hens should be as large as possible, if not, the result will be a failure. A short-legged cock should be selected, and if a bird of this description is used, he may run with from six to nine hens, and eleven out of every thirteen eggs will prove fertile.

The pullets from this cross produce remarkably fine eggs, saleable anywhere. One hen has been known to lay 270 eggs in twelve months, but this is an exception. The pullets at the age of 12 months, after their first season of laying, weigh from 5½ to 7 lbs. each, and are at that time excellent for the table. The average number of eggs per annum is from 150 to 180.

MINORCA-HAMBURGH.

As Hamburghs and Minorcas are excellent layers in their pure state, the result is very good when they are crossed, as the half-bred chickens hatch and feather well, grow fast, are very good layers, and altogether more hardy than Hamburghs in their pure state, as the chickens hatch out stronger.

I prefer a Minorca cock with Hamburgh hens. As a rule in crossing the smallest bird should usually be on the male side, but this cross is rather an exception, as the Minorca egg is very large, and the Hamburghs are a small breed; the young chickens do not fill the egg out sufficiently before hatching, consequently many are not able to liberate themselves from the egg without assistance. I like the golden-spangled Hamburghs best for crossing, though, as there is no difference in quality, but only in colour, any variety may be used.

The chickens from this cross mostly have blue or black legs, which is a disadvantage for the market, but the flesh is very white and good.

The pullets are non-sitters, have short legs, and are very compact; they generally have black bodies and sometimes rose combs, and when the golden Hamburghs are used in crossing they are very handsome, often with part of the body spangled or pencilled. They are extraordinary layers if they have a large range. With this they will lay from 230 to 250 eggs per bird in the year, but if shut up in a small run they will only average about 200 each, and often very much under this number, unless they are sheltered from the cold winds, as they are not suited so well for confinement as many other breeds. The eggs are about the size of Cochins, only pure white, and the average weight of the fowls is from 4½ to 5 lbs.

As the fowls are not readily saleable for table purposes, they are best kept when the owner requires them for his own household consumption.

MINORCA - LANGSHAN.

For a black cross-bred fowl I know nothing that will breed truer to colour than the Minorca-Langshan, or Langshan-Minorca, whichever way they are crossed. Nineteen out of every twenty come black, with a beautiful gloss on their plumage. All have single combs and black legs, with four toes on each foot. There may be one occasionally with five toes on each foot, but this is very seldom. They are an excellent-shaped fowl, and take the eye of those who are partial to black fowls. They are splendid layers in confined runs or with an open space; they cannot well be put out of their place. A Minorca cock may run with from seven to nine Langshan hens, or a small Langshan cock with about the same number of Minorca hens. The latter must be large and strong, if not the results will be unsatisfactory. Great care must be taken when mated in the latter way. It does not make any difference in colour and qualities of offspring which way they are crossed. They hatch out well, and make strong chickens, pullets fledging fairly well, cockerels being a little naked for a time. They lay good-sized tinted eggs, some being brown. They average from 150 to 170, and many will lay 200 in the year, usually commencing to lay when from 5½ to 7 months of age. About half of them become broody. They make food mothers, but are rather timid when sitting; they want handling gently. They make good table fowls, skin and flesh exceedingly white, of good flavour, and juicy. I do not know of a fowl a better flavour, but of course their black legs go against them in the market. The cockerels should be killed early, from 13 to 16 weeks old, if not they must be kept from the hens and pullets. The best laying hens of this cross may be kept until two or three years old. They do not get so fat internally as many other crosses do. This cross may be classed with some of the best layers, both winter and summer. They are excellent for confined runs, as they do not show the dirt. A few of them are slightly feathered on the legs. When first hatched the chickens of this cross are black on the back and yellowish-white underneath. I strongly recommend this cross when large eggs are required all the year round. In shape and attitude they resemble the Minorca-Brahma and Minorca-Plymouth Rock.

BROWN LEGHORN-BRAHMA.

A Leghorn cock may run with from six to eight Brahma hens. If he is a large and vigorous bird of his kind, ten hens are not too many for him. It is well not to use large Brahma hens if it can be avoided, as, if they are large, not more than six hens must run with one cock. In this matter the owners must judge for themselves, as the Leghorn is a small, and the Brahma a large fowl. This cross hatch out well, and are very hardy; they grow fast, the pullets fledge well, and a few of the cockerels are rather naked for a time. Most of them have yellow legs, and a few yellow skins, especially the cockerels. This is, of course, against them as table fowls, though their flesh is of good flavour. They grow very fast and the pullets mature at an early age; some of them commence to lay at five months, and are in full lay at six and a half months. They are remarkably hardy, and can be reared in confinement. They are excellent layers of good-sized eggs; most of them are brown. About six out of twelve want to sit. They make good sitters and mothers, and lay early after having brought up a brood. Many of the pullets come brown, much the same colour as black-breasted red Game hens. When the light Brahma hens are used, a few of them come buff or pale cream. They are very compact and have short legs.

BROWN LEGHORN-DORKING.

The best way to obtain this cross is to run a Leghorn cock with from seven to ten Dorking hens. It does not make much difference what variety of Dorking is used, as they make just about the same sized fowls, and are also the same in laying qualities, which are very good. If the brown Leghorn cock is used, the pullets come much the same colour as black-breasted red Game hens. They are very plump, and splendid-shaped birds; a few of them have yellow legs, although the majority have white. They make very plump table birds, the flesh being very white and juicy, and of excellent flavour; they are not large, but are saleable. The cockerels can be killed at an early age, any time from twelve weeks to six months. If not allowed to run with the hens and pullets, they can be picked up at any time and killed. I do not recommend this as a general cross, although they are very hardy, and stand confinement fairly well, and, if they have their liberty, scratch well, and, in some cases, six pullets of this cross will lay more eggs than twelve pure Dorkings. If it is desired to breed from this cross again, a clean-legged Langshan cock is the best to use, or a Rock cock with white legs. The progeny then produce brown eggs. If the Rock has yellow legs, eighteen chickens out of every twenty will have bright orange legs and beaks, and the cockerels yellow skins.

LEGHORN-PLYMOUTH ROCK.

The Leghorn cock can run with from seven to nine Plymouth Rock hens if he is a strong bird, and 11 eggs out of 13 will be fertile. Any variety of the Leghorn may be used. If the brown is used many of the pullets come that colour, and a few the colour of the Rock. If the white, there are a variety of colours, some quite white, some a mixture of white and drab, and a few the colour of the Rock. They make excellent layers of a fair-sized tinted egg, saleable in market. I recommend this cross to be kept where the birds are exposed to the cold east winds, or where there is a cold or wet soil. They are very active, and so hardy they cannot be put in the wrong place. They do as well in confined runs as in a grass field. For number of eggs and hardiness of fowl, there are but few to surpass this cross. There are some pullets that will lay over 100 eggs before they are 12 months' old, and in a few cases 120. Where birds are wanted for laying only, this is one of the best crosses that can be kept, and will become one of the most prominent of the day for egg-production. There are many specimens that lay 260 eggs in 12 months. These are, of course, bred from the best laying strains, and are well looked after. The average number of eggs per annum is from 170 to 200. They can be hatched all the year round if required. They are so hardy they fledge like partridges, many being fully fledged at three weeks old. There are a few of the cockerels a little backward in fledging. I cannot recommend them as table fowls for the market, as their legs are a bright yellow, and many of the skins the same colour, which many people object to. The flesh is white and juicy, they are of fair size, mature very quickly, and may be killed at three months old. If kept any longer, they must be separated from the hens and pullets; if not, they become very troublesome. The pullets are more of an uniform colour when the Rock cock is used, as many of them are marked like the Rock. The legs and beak are a much brighter yellow. A large Rock cock should never be allowed to run with Leghorn hens; if so, many of the latter will be injured dangerously. Late-hatched Rock cockerels should be used for this purpose. The birds are much shorter in the leg, and the eggs wlll prove more fertile. If the Rock cock is an active bird, not less than nine hens should run with him, rather over than under that number. It does not affect the size or colour of the eggs which way the birds are crossed. About five out of 12 of the pullets want to sit.

LEGHORN - MINORCA.

This cross can be obtained by using either male bird, and the results will be much the same. One cock may run with from seven to ten hens. The chickens hatch out rather stronger when the Minorca cock is used, but the result in pullets when six months old is much the same; the colour is also the same whichever way they are crossed. They make both excellent summer and winter layers of large white eggs. Chickens are very hardy, grow fast, fledge well, and may be hatched all the year round if required. They do not make good table fowls (not saleable in market), though their flesh is very white and juicy. The legs come various colours, yellow, black or bronze; all have single combs. The drawback to this cross is, they do not come an uniform shape and colour. Some are like poor-bred Minorcas, and others like poor-bred Leghorns. They ought not to be kept where either of the pure breeds (Minorcas and Leghorns) are, if so, some of the chickens are difficult to distinguish from the pure, and they may get mixed up in a mistake. I do not recommend this cross to be kept unless the owner has the stock birds all ready in hand, and the old stock birds are Minorcas, and the egg-list not what it ought to be; this will be improved, and if the old birds are Leghorns, size will be obtained both in eggs and fowls.

LEGHORN-COCHIN.

The best way of crossing is to put a Leghorn cock with six Cochin hens, the chickens from which hatch out well, stand cold, and are altogether hardy. They can be reared in confinement, and grow fast, the pullets fledging quickly. They make pretty birds. I prefer the brown Leghorn for crossing, as the progeny are more uniform in colour. The pullets lay at the age of six months.

The cockerels are fair table birds, but the pullets are much better, as they have short legs and broad breasts, but many have yellow skins. They stand confinement well, keep free from disease, and lay good-sized tinted eggs, generally all through the winter, but more in summer. About five out of twelve become broody in the year, and if these are allowed to sit, they make good sitters and mothers, as they have small feet with only four claws.

The hens are about the same size as Houdans, but with single combs, and shaped like cuckoo Dorkings, mostly with yellow or brown legs, but with careful breeding many will have white legs.

I prefer the Leghorn and Plymouth Rock cross, as they are better table fowls, but lay about the same number of eggs, viz., from 130 to 200 in the year.

LEGHORN-HAMBURGH.

These may be crossed by running a cock of either breed with not more than six hens. The chickens hatch out well, are very healthy, fledge early, grow fast, and require but little care.

The cockerels should be kept by themselves or killed early, but they do not sell well in the market for table purposes, as they are rather small and have coloured legs.

The pullets grow to a moderate size, and make compact birds with short legs; they lay sooner than most other crosses, sometimes commencing when only four months old, produce from 240 to 270 eggs per bird in the year, and as a rule lay more eggs by the time they are twelve months old than any other cross I have tried.

The eggs are white and rather small, and although not rich, are of fair flavour. They make very poor table birds, of no good for the market, being so small, although of good flavour.

DORKING-BRAHMA.

This cross is the most general farmers now have, and if the parents are carefully chosen, the half-bred chickens are very good in many respects. The best way of crossing is to have a Dorking cock, with from six to nine Brahma hens; either variety of Dorkings may be used for crossing, but the cuckoos are best if the chickens are wanted for laying, and the coloured or silver-grey if they are wanted for table and laying.

The chickens from this cross are healthy and strong, may be hatched early, grow very large, and make good table birds. The cockerels should be killed off when they are from three to four months old, as, after this, they will not be so fit to kill until they are seven or eight months old, and the cost of their keep, while they are growing to this age, will be more than the additional value of the fowl. The pullets commence laying from eight to nine months old, and lay better than the pure Dorking, but are often broody; and if any are allowed to sit, care should be taken to select those with small feet, as, when the hens have five large claws on each foot, they break the eggs and kill the chickens when hatching out; if those with large feet are used for sitting, the young chickens that are hatched first should be removed while the others are hatching and placed in wadding in a box or basket by the fire to prevent their being trampled to death.

If desired, Cochins may also be crossed with the Dorking; the chickens from this cross will resemble the Brahma-Dorkings in many ways, but the cockerels grow a little longer in the leg, and, as a rule, the pullets lay rather better.

If the owners of such cross-breeds, as mentioned above, wish to do away with broody hens, and, at the same time, desire to have an increase in the number of eggs laid, and retain delicacy of the flesh, I advise their running hens with a Minorca or Houdan cock, using the Houdan, if possible, as the colour of the legs is more suited for table.

By breeding in this way there will not be half so many broody hens, and those that are broody will more easily be cured and commence to lay much sooner; the chickens will be quite as hardy, grow shorter on the leg, feather earlier, have more breast-meat, and only about two out of twenty will have blue or dark legs. The cockerels will be ready for table two weeks sooner, and the pullets will lay six weeks to two months earlier, laying, as a rule, when they are from five to six-and-a-half months old. These birds are excellent for any one with plenty of room, as they scratch and look well after their living; and about 10 to 20 per cent. more would be realised by again crossing in this way than by breeding the first cross of Brahma-Dorkings or Cochin-Dorkings.

In selecting the birds for breeding the above, care should be taken to choose the hens that lay best, and a Houdan cock with as light-coloured legs as possible.

GAME-HAMBURGH.

The best way of crossing is—run a Game cock with seven or eight Hamburgh hens. The chickens are very hardy, may be allowed to run loose, and if they have a wood to roam in, they will pick up a great deal of their own food and roost out at night. They are very pretty, and when young can fly like pheasants ; the pullets commence to lay when from five to six months old, and are mostly good layers of small eggs. They make better table birds than one would suppose, and will do very well if they have a large range ; but, otherwise, they should not be kept.

GAME-PLYMOUTH ROCK.

This cross can be produced either way. A vigorous Game cock can run with from nine to twelve Plymouth Rock hens. I prefer the black-breasted red cock for crossing. The chickens can be hatched all the year round, if required, and are very hardy and strong. They keep very free from cramp, fledge quickly and grow fast. They make heavy table fowls, having a deep breast, meat white, but unfortunately many of them have yellow skins and legs, and occasionally a few have bronze legs, which is rather against them for the market. They can be killed very young, as early as 11 weeks old ; from this age to six months they are always ready to kill when well attended to. The cockerels are rather long in the leg, but in this respect the pullets are very moderate ; they have a splendidly-shaped body. Many of them come the colour of the Game hens, but when a Rock male bird is used, 18 out of 20 come that colour. A Rock cock may run with from eight to twelve Game hens, if they have a good range. This cross make good autumn and winter layers of fair-sized, tinted eggs. They are good sitters, and may be trusted with valuable eggs; not one in a hundred will fail. They are excellent mothers to their own chickens, but if other chickens, of different sizes and ages, are allowed to run with them, they will kill them, as they are so very spiteful. They will defend their chickens from rats, stoats, hawks, cats or dogs in the daytime, if they have their liberty. Nothing comes amiss to them. They are an excellent cross to keep where young pheasants are reared, as they can be depended on as sitters, and are very gentle mothers to their own little ones. They become broody early, so that they will usually hatch out chickens or ducks in January, or early in February, and bring up their brood if required, and then sit again early enough for pheasants' eggs. They are a most valuable fowl for gamekeepers, or to those who have a large range for their poultry, and wish to have eggs in the autumn and winter months, early sitters, and good table fowls for home consumption. This is one of the best crosses to keep for these purposes.

GAME-DORKING.

These birds may be crossed either by running a Game cock with ten Dorking hens, or a Dorking cock with seven Game hens. The chickens will hatch out well, are remarkably hardy, and feather well, often being fully-fledged at three weeks old. They make *very good* table birds, being ready to kill at ten weeks old: but they may be kept much longer, if required. as the breast meat does not waste away on the young cockerels after they are four months old, as in most other breeds, but, on the contrary, increases. If well fed they do not require fattening, but may be killed at a moment's notice, and will be found in splendid condition, the flesh being white and well-flavoured.

The pullets make fine birds, and lay a medium-sized egg, but very rich in flavour; they average about 130 to 150 eggs in the year, being fair layers in autumn and winter, but poor in summer. Both parents being sitters they are often broody. They make good mothers where only a few chickens are reared; but, if many of different sizes are brought up together, they often kill them if they go in the wrong coops.

I do not recommend these birds to anyone with only a small yard, as they require a good open run, but they are very well for a gentleman with plenty of room.

PLYMOUTH ROCK-BRAHMA.

Where brown eggs are required this is one of the best crosses to keep. They can be produced either way, by running an active male bird with from seven to nine hens of either breed. I prefer using the Rock cock, as the pullets come a more uniform shape and colour; eighteen pullets out of twenty will take the colour of the Rock. The chickens hatch out well, are remarkably hardy, and stand the cold weather. They make splendid, large birds, and if early hatched the pullets will often weigh 9lbs. each at ten months old. The chickens do not grow very fast the first two months, not feathering very quickly; but after that period their growth is very rapid. They commence to lay when from six to seven-and-a-half months old. They are excellent autumn and winter layers of brown eggs, some very deep in colour, which makes them very saleable, and especially as they are laid in the winter. They will often lay over 100 eggs from the middle of October to the middle of March, if not allowed to sit. They make splendid sitters and mothers, and can be sent on a journey, as removing them to a fresh nest does not put them about in the least. If not required for these purposes, they should be shut up at once in the broody coop; if not, they become very troublesome. The cockerels come various colours, and are rather long in the leg. They do not make the best of table fowls, as many of them come with yellow skins. Notwithstanding this, their flesh is excellent, being both white and juicy. They should be killed at the age of four or seven months, as between these ages they lose much of their breast meat; but if kept until seven months old, they are like young turkeys, and will weigh from 9lbs. to 12lbs. each, if well fattened. For a cold, damp, exposed place, this is an excellent cross to keep, as they will lay when the snow is on the ground, and stand confinement well. They should not be overfed with hard grain, especially maize; if so, they get too fat internally, unless they have boiled rice at the same time; this counteracts the maize.

PLYMOUTH ROCK-DORKING.

This cross may be obtained either way. If active, a Rock cock may run with from eight to eleven Dorking hens, that is if he is mated early in the season. This makes a vast difference, as Dorkings are not very early layers in the winter months, but at the same time are very partial to the male birds, so that many of the eggs are fertilised before the hens commence to lay. It is much the safest way to use the Rock cock if early chickens are required, as the cold winds do not affect the male birds of this breed as in the Dorkings. There is not sufficient attention paid to male birds in breeding, especially early in the season, and yet this is chiefly where the success or failure commences. Cocks for breeding in all cases should be strong, healthy, vigorous, and not brought up in glasshouses or heated fowl-houses, as when such birds are mated with hens many early-hatched chickens are almost out of the question. The Rock hens lay much better in the winter than the Dorkings, so that it is easy to obtain eggs from the Rocks. If it is very early in the season a Dorking cock should not have more than five hens, or six at the most, less if anything. When the weather is warm he may have from seven to ten, and most of the eggs will be fertile. Too much care cannot be bestowed on mating fowls for breeding purposes. The chickens hatch out remarkably strong from this cross, and can be hatched all the year round if required; the pullets fledge very quickly, also most of the cockerels, but about two or three in twenty are a little naked. The cockerels grow to a very large size, and if well fattened will run from eight to ten pounds each at the age of six or seven-and-a-half months old. This cross not only producesa large table fowl, but is excellent in quality. I know no other cross to equal it, taking everything into consideration. As chickens they are remarkably hardy, grow fast even in cold weather; the legs are usually white if mated right. Not two in twenty will come of a yellow cast; flesh remarkably juicy and of excellent flavour, and if fed properly will command a higher price in the market than any other table fowl. This cross ought to be bred more for market and also home consumption. This will be when it becomes more known and there is an increasing demand for good table fowls in all the leading markets, especially in London. A Rock cock that is selected for mating with Dorking hens should have white or very pale yellow legs, and white skin if possible, broad in the breast, and have a good carriage; plumage is nothing. When the Rock cock is used, seventeen out of twenty will be marked much the same as Rock hens. When the Dorking cock is used they come more of a mixture, and the skins and legs are usually rather whiter in colour. The pullets are of excellent shape, and make good autumn and winter layers, most of them laying a good-sized tinted egg, saleable anywhere. This cross will stand confinement fairly well, but should not be kept a second year for laying as a rule, unless very good layers, as a few specimens have been. When kept in close confinement they frequently become very fat internally. They do well in a moderate run for the first year, but after the pullets have laid one year, that is when they are from eighteen to twenty months old, just before they commence their first adult moult, they will weigh from six to nine pounds each, and are in good condition for the table. They make excellent sitters and mothers, and come very broody in the season. March-hatched pullets will sometimes sit in December. They have a great deal of heat in their bodies, and can be set on Goose or Turkey eggs if required. They are very quiet, and can usually be removed to a fresh nest, and can cover a large number of eggs. If it is cold, frosty weather not less than thirteen should be put under them; I do not put less than eighteen. I would recommend less rather than more to those who may not understand making the nest; it is best to be on the safe side. I give this cross the preference for good table fowls as one of the best to keep.

SPANISH-GAME.

I do not recommend this cross, as the chickens grow very moderately, come long in the leg, and are altogether awkward table fowls. The hens have black bodies spangled round the neck; they commence to lay when about seven months old, but often later than this, and make fair layers of moderate-sized eggs ; a few will want to sit, but they do not make good mothers.

SPANISH-BRAHMA.

These may be crossed by running a Spanish cock with six or eight Brahma hens. The chickens do not hatch out so well as many other crosses ; they also require great care the first month, as they fledge very slowly, and on this account they are best hatched in the middle of March or April.

Mostly they have black or bronze legs, and as the cockerels are also very lanky, they do not make good table birds. The hens are very fine, generally being black with a few straw-coloured feathers on the neck ; about half become broody, and if these are allowed to sit they make good sitters and mothers. They commence laying when six or seven months old, and are excellent layers both in summer and winter of large eggs, generally slightly tinted, and if bred from a good laying strain they will often lay the whole twelve months. They produce from 190 to 230 eggs the first year, and from 150 to 190 the second ; but the moulting goes very hard with them, on account of the Spanish blood. They stand confinement well if in a dry and warm run, and thrive in the back yards of towns, as there they are generally sheltered. They also do well if they have a good wide range.

There are defects in this cross, but, having given them a good trial, I value them much, as they are first-rate layers.

SPANISH-COCHIN.

The drawback to this cross is that both Cochins and Spanish fledge badly, but in spite of this the half-bred birds are very good to keep in confinement.

The bes. way of crossing is to run a Spanish cock with six partridge or buff Cochin hens ; these birds will produce some very fine pullets, most of them having black feathers on the body and brown hackle feathers with fine stand-up combs, and weighing from 6 to 7½ lbs. each when full grown. They are one of the best cross-breeds to keep, being excellent layers of large, tinted eggs, and taking the year round these birds, owing to their laying so well in winter, will produce a greater weight of eggs than any other cross-bred fowls except the Houdan-Spanish ; they lay more eggs in moderate confinement than with an extensive range, and keep very free from disease. About five out of every twelve want to sit in the year ; these make good mothers, and can bring up from fifteen to eighteen chickens in one brood. The cockerels do not make the best of table birds and the chickens feather badly, but this latter defect may be remedied with care.

This cross and those of Brahma and Spanish, Hamburgh and Cochin, Houdan and Cochin, and Hamburgh and Dorking may be kept for laying after they are two years old. These may be kept for three years, and will lay well if kept warm when moulting, and fed on warm, stimulating food.

The Minorca is much the best fowl to use in the place of Spanish (if it is convenient). The pullets cannot be distinguished, unless it is that the Minorca cross are a little shorter in the legs. The colour of plumage is exactly the same. When the Minorca is used the pullets usually lay six weeks earlier.

SPANISH-LEGHORN.

The chickens from this cross are tolerably hardy, grow moderately, and make good layers of a moderate-sized white egg. They are ready for table when about three-and-a-half months old, but do not make very good birds for this purpose. The pullets, however, are the best, as they are more compact than the cockerels, and resemble Minorcas very much in shape and carriage.

Either male bird can be used. The Leghorn cock may run with from eight to ten Spanish hens, and the Spanish with seven or eight Leghorn hens.

SPANISH-DORKING.

This cross produces some very fine birds that have been considered the best farmers possess. People might well think so when it was thought that 80 or 90 eggs in the year from each bird was a good number, while this cross produced from 140 to 150, and I know of one instance in which a cottager's daughter kept a single hen of this description that laid 360 eggs in two years.

Either way of crossing will do, but the best way is to run a Spanish cock with seven Dorking hens, the chickens from which will hatch out well, but want care the first three weeks, after which they grow fast and require little trouble and attention. The cockerels are ready to kill when from three to four months old, and make good table birds, as the flesh is white and good, and many have white legs. The pullets are good-sized birds, and, as a rule, about half want to sit, They commence to lay when about eight months old, and are good layers in spring and summer, and fair winter layers. I do not, however, recommend them for confinement.

The Minorca cock is much the best to use with Dorking hens, as the birds produced are better layers and finer table fowls. The chickens are much hardier and grow faster. The pullets are shorter in the leg, and lay from three weeks to a month earlier. This, of course, is a consideration. The Minorca-Dorkings are good birds for a farmer, and where there is a grass field, one Minorca cock may run with from ten to twelve Dorking hens when the birds have a good range.

LANGSHAN-BRAHMA.

The best way of crossing is to run a Langshan cock with six Brahma hens, taking care to select the hens with short legs, or the half-bred birds will be very lanky. The chickens are very hardy, and if required may be hatched all through the winter. The cockerels fledge badly, but the pullets get their feathers fairly well. They make fair table birds, as they are large, have plenty of breast-meat, and the flesh is of good flavour. The cockerels should be killed when about three-and-a-half or four months old, when they are plump, but if kept after this age, they grow long in the leg. Most of the pullets have single combs and very red faces; generally they are quite black, with black or bronze legs, and often pass as pure Langshans; but sometimes a few have coloured feathers on the breast or neck. If fed on good stimulating food, they commence laying when from six to seven months old, and lay very fine brown eggs, generally producing from 130 to 180 in the year.

This cross resembles the Brahma and partridge Cochin cross in many respects, and make excellent winter layers, and I can recommend them to any one with only a small place, as they stand cold and damp well.

This cross are often exhibited in the show pen as pure Langshans. I saw one not long since with a second prize card attached to the pen.

LANGSHAN-PLYMOUTH ROCK.

This cross can be procured either way by running a male bird of either breed with seven or nine hens. I prefer the

Langshan cock to run with Rock hens. When crossed in this way, most of the pullets come black, and make splendidly-shaped fowls. The greater part have black legs, and a few are slightly feathered down the leg, but some are clear. The chickens hatch out well, but feather rather slowly, especially the cockerels. They do not appear to grow very fast the first two months, but after that time they fill out very fast and make good-bodied birds. Although large they are very active, and if they have their liberty will search well for their living, but if in confinement, they make themselves very happy and will do well. This cross is very similar to the Plymouth Rock-Brahma in many respects, laying about the same number of eggs, and much the same colour, a little smaller, if anything. They commence to lay when from six to seven-and-a-half months old, and are excellent winter layers, good sitters and mothers, and can be depended on for this purpose. They are quite equal to the Rock-Brahma for hardiness. They will stand cold and damp, and when the east wind blows and the snow is on the ground, eggs are usually to be found in the nest-box. I strongly recommend this cross to be kept where it is cold, damp, or exposed. They can be hatched out all the year round if required. The skin of most of them is very white, the meat being of excellent flavour. They are very full in the breast, and may be classed as an excellent table fowl. When well fattened they sell well in the market, in spite of their dark legs. This cross is a valuable one, as they possess so many good qualities—good winter layers of brown eggs, hardy, will stand confinement, and are a large table fowl. Those that have pure Langshans or Rocks should be careful, as a few of them come much the same as the pure fowls, especially when the Rock cock is used for crossing. This cross is frequently sold as pure fowls.

COCHIN-BRAHMA.

For close confinement, Cochins cannot be crossed with anything better than with a Brahma cock, and this cross produces very good winter layers ; in fact, they lay more eggs in winter than in summer, as, after January or February, they are frequently broody, when, unless wanted for sitting, they should be treated as described in paragraph on broody coop. The chickens are very hardy, can be hatched all through the winter, and with proper treatment will even thrive when snow is on the ground, Cochins and Brahmas being the hardiest birds introduced into this country. They stand close confinement well, and can therefore be kept healthy in a very small space, say from three to six birds on a piece of ground three or four yards square, with a fence about 3 feet high, as they are heavy birds and cannot fly as high as this ; they are very tame, can be driven about easily, and scratch but little in a garden, if occasionally allowed to run over it. The cockerels should be killed when about three or four months old, as after this they get very long in the leg and cost a great deal more for keep. The pullets begin to lay when about seven or eight months old. Some I have had laying when only six months old, and the cottager with six square yards of ground can produce more eggs from six of those birds than the farmer with nine pure Dorking hens, although his birds have fields to range over, plenty of pure air, and pick up a large quantity of insects. In breeding, care should be taken to select the eggs of birds that are good layers, short in the leg, and full in the breast ; the plumage is not of much importance, as the birds are wanted for laying purposes only.

A Cochin cock should only run with four hens of his own breed and six of other breeds, as they are very inactive birds as a rule.

One reason why I recommend this cross is they do not fly, and cannot in this way annoy the neighbours. They should be hatched early in the spring; in fact, they cannot be hatched too early.

COCHIN-DORKING.

This cross makes very large and handsome birds, especially when the buff cock is used. Most of the pullets come with buff bodies and black and brown hackles, which give the birds a very nice appearance. They are good autumn and winter layers, most of the eggs being brown, of good size, and saleable in market. The chickens are very hardy, grow fast, and will stand confinement moderately well. The cockerels are not the best of table fowls, and ought to be fattened rather young, (from 11 to 15 weeks old), if not, they have long legs, and are rather deficient in breast-meat. The pullets lay when from six to eight months. They make splendid sitters and good mothers. They are very troublesome in the spring and summer, as they come broody so often if not set.

HAMBURGH-PLYMOUTH ROCK.

This cross produces very compact and neat-looking birds, and excellent layers of a moderate-sized tinted egg, some quite brown, usually commencing to lay at about five-and-a-half months old; about four out of twelve want to sit. The pullets grow fast and fledge well; the majority have rose combs, legs dark, some bronze, almost the colour of Game fowls' legs; they are very compact fowls for the table, not large, with white skin. I do not recommend them for market purposes. The cockerels should be killed when from 14 to 16 weeks old. The best way of crossing is to run a Hamburgh cock with seven Rock hens. Any variety of Hamburgh can be used for this purpose, either black, golden, or silver-spangled. The pencilled are too small. I prefer the black variety, as then most of the pullets come that colour. If the silver-spangled is used, many come much the colour of the Wyandotte, and also about the size and shape of them. If the golden-spangled is used they come a variety of colours. A few are marked like the golden-spangled hens, some black, and some with black bodies, and black and brown hackles. This cross stand confinement, and lay well. I have not kept a strict account of the number of eggs they produce in the year; some lay over 200 eggs in the 12 months when bred from good laying parents. They are very strong in the wing if allowed to fly when young, but if not, they are very contented.

HAMBURGH-DORKING.

The best way of crossing is to run a Hamburgh cock with five Dorking hens, and the eggs will nearly all prove fertile; but, if crossed the other way, not more than four eggs in a sitting would be good. Either variety of Hamburghs may be used for crossing, but I prefer the golden-spangled and black. The chickens hatch out fairly well, fledge quickly, grow fast, and make very plump birds, as they have short legs and small bones, at the same time carrying a great deal of very white breast-meat.

This cross can be hatched late in the season if required, and are good layers when they are old hens from three to four years old, and look better than many other breeds. They do not get so fat internally as some; they may be killed when from twelve to thirteen weeks old, and are often very handsome, as many are pencilled or spangled, with rose combs; generally they have white legs, but a few will be found with black. The pullets lay, as a rule, when about six months old, and make very good layers when they have a large run; about six out of twelve will become broody, and these will make good sitters and mothers.

HAMBURGH-COCHIN.

Some persons think, the Hamburghs being small birds and the Cochins large, they cannot well be crossed; but this is a mistake, as I have been very successful with this cross in every respect.

The best way of crossing is a Hamburgh cock with four hens, either partridge or buff Cochin; any variety of Hamburgh may be used for crossing, only, as a matter of fancy, I prefer the golden-spangled and black. Not more than three or four Cochin hens should be allowed to run with a cock, unless he is a very large bird of his kind, as the hens are so large. A Cochin cock should not be mated with Hamburgh hens, if so, the results will be unsatisfactory. The chickens will grow fast, feather well, and give little trouble; they make very good table birds, being compact, with short legs, and the flesh is also very white and juicy; most of them have white legs, but a few black, and a few yellow legs will be found amongst them. The plumage is very handsome when a golden-spangled Hamburgh is used for crossing, some of the cock birds having the prettiest plumage I have ever seen, with rose comb, black tail, brown-red body, and the breast full spangled, the tip of each feather being black or dark-green in the sun; generally, the pullets are the same colour as the cock on the body, and striped on the neck; but some are spangled all over like golden-spangled Hamburghs, and about five out of six of both cocks and hens have rose combs; and, altogether, they are splendid-looking fowls. They fly very much, if not checked when young; if hatched early, they weigh from five to six pounds when a year old; their eggs are generally slightly-coloured, rather small the first year, but larger the second.

They are enormous layers, but I cannot say exactly how many eggs each bird would average in the year, but should think from 240 to 250.

They have been tried in all parts of the country the last two years, and in most cases have given great satisfaction, both in town and country, in small and large runs. They are so handsome they do not look like cross-bred fowls.

I will give one or two instances to show they are first-rate layers, and really good fowls to keep.

In March, one year, I hatched fifteen pullets from a golden-spangled cock and buff Cochin hens, and, as they feathered and grew so fast, I decided to set some more eggs in June and July, as I wanted some chickens for the table. The young cocks were ready for killing before three months old; of course they were not large, but plump and well grown. The pullets that were hatched in March began to lay in August, and those hatched in June and July laid in the following January. I give below the number of eggs from these early and late-hatched pullets up to the end of May, most of them being sold or killed after that date. Fifteen pullets hatched in March laid in September, 265; October, 222; November, 278; December, 213; total, 978, being an average of 65 eggs per bird in four months. The above fifteen, and fifteen pullets hatched in June and July, laid in January, 506; February, 764; March, 696; April, 624; May, 589; total, 3,179, an average of 106 eggs per bird in five months. I may mention that I have had seven eggs dropped from the roost in one night from these thirty birds, mostly with perfect shells.

These eggs were produced without any artificial heat in the fowl-house in winter, and without flesh food, the birds being fed as described in the paragraph on feeding.

I let a cottager have a few eggs of this cross, from which he hatched three pullets, and from these three he had fourteen eggs per week during the winter ; they were reared and kept in a run $3\frac{1}{2}$ yards square, where fowls had been kept for eight years, with four other cross-bred hens, and, as they were always healthy, this shows they will do well if kept in confinement. A farmer had six of these at the same time, and he said he never had fowls to lay so well.

These fowls do well in confinement or with a large run, but they lay rather more eggs when shut up in a medium space, and let out for a good run once a day. These birds were kept in a run about 10 yards square—in fact, it is not easy to put them in a wrong place, as they will thrive where some others would not live ; they are very active, and will search well for their food when they have their liberty, but are very contented when shut up, if the run is made secure.

From five to seven out of every twelve become broody in the year, and if these are allowed to sit, they make excellent mothers, and often commence laying in the coop before the chickens are three weeks old, taking good care of their young family at the same time.

GAME-COCHIN.

These make a very good cross, especially for sitting purposes, and are therefore very useful when hens are required for sitting on prize eggs, or when wanted by a gamekeeper for hatching out pheasant or partridge eggs. They have only four claws on each foot, and therefore are not so likely to break eggs when sitting as many other fowls; they also have the advantage of long feathers, and this enables them to cover chicks or young birds very effectively.

The best way of crossing is to run a good Game cock with nine Cochin hens, and twelve out of thirteen eggs will prove good. As chickens, they hatch out well, are very hardy, and give no trouble in rearing. The cockerels are very long in the leg, but with broad breasts, and the flesh is of good flavour; but, unfortunately, they have yellow legs and skin. The pullets are very fine and well shaped, and commence laying when six or seven months old; they lay small eggs, but very rich, as they contain very large yolks; they are inferior summer layers, but lay well in winter.

As the feathers of Game fowls stick close to the skin, like a bird's, and Cochins' feathers being long and thick, when the two are crossed the half-bred birds have the thickest plumage of any fowls, and are, therefore, very hardy, and will even keep laying, if roosting in the trees, when snow is on the ground.

ANDALUSIAN-COCHIN.

As Andalusians are non-sitters, they may be crossed with Cochins if fowls are wanted for confinement. The chickens from this cross are hardy and good layers; but I cannot recommend them for general purposes.

They are best hatched in April or May, as they do not feather well; commence to lay when about seven months old, but are not handsome birds, having rather long legs. The colour is one that some people are very fond of; they usually come slate, with a mixture of brown. It is a very unusual colour. I know of no other fowls that produce the colour in the pullets as this cross does.

CREVE CŒUR-COCHIN.

Some may prefer to cross Cochins with Creve Cœurs in preference to Houdans, and if this cross is tried the result will generally be fairly satisfactory.

The chickens very much resemble the Houdan-Cochins, except that the latter have five claws; the qualities also are much the same, but the Creve Cœur cross lay more eggs in summer than in winter, while the Houdan cross lay best in winter.

WHITE DORKING-WHITE COCHIN.

There are some poultry keepers who are very partial to white fowls, and will not have any others on their place. They are usually those who have a good range for their poultry, such as a meadow or large orchard. White Dorkings are a favourite fowl with many people, only there is a great drawback to them in the winter months, namely, a small number of eggs. There are two breeds that can be used for crossing with the white Dorking so that a coloured feather cannot be found on them, viz., white Leghorn and white Cochin. If brown eggs are preferred, the latter will be the best to use for crossing. They can be mated either way. A Cochin cock may run with five or six Dorking hens, and a Dorking cock with seven or nine Cochin hens. It makes but little difference which way they are crossed, as the colour and shape of the fowl are just the same. When the Dorking cock is used most of the offspring have white legs and skins; but when crossed the other way many of the cockerels have yellow legs, and a few yellow skins. They make good table fowls; the flesh is very white and juicy, and of excellent flavour. A few of the cockerels are a little long in the leg, but the pullets are a good shape, and grow to a very large size. They will weigh from 6½ to 9lbs each, at eighteen months old. The largest should be killed off after they have laid one season, as those that grow so large are usually the worst layers. When boiled, they eat very tender at this age. The cockerels should be killed when from three to four months old, or left to run on until they are six months. They can be allowed to run with the pullets until this age. As chickens, they hatch out well, are very hardy and stand the cold weather well. The egg-table is rather low, from 90 to 130 each in the year. They make excellent sitters and mothers, and can cover from 15 to 17 eggs in the cold weather safely.

WHITE DORKING-LIGHT BRAHMA.

Sometimes, when the owners of light Brahma fowls are satisfied with the laying results, and still a little disappointed in the cockerels for table purposes, there not being such a deep cut of meat on the breast as they would like, they often ask the question, "Can I still retain my white, clean-looking fowls, and have as many eggs, and a little better table fowl?" I answer, "Yes; the white Dorking is just the fowl you require." When the white Dorking cock is used with the light Brahma hens, the results are very satisfactory. The hens lay quite as well, and sometimes a little better; about 20 eggs more in the year. The chickens grow faster, fledge quicker, lay about three weeks earlier, and the cockerels are much better table fowls. They will stand confinement moderately well, if required, but are better for a grass run. A Dorking cock may run with seven to nine Brahma hens. The chicks may be hatched out all the winter, if required. Eighteen out of every twenty will have white legs; flesh excellent, fit for any market or a nobleman's table.

WHITE LEGHORN-WHITE DORKING.

This cross makes very neat, compact fowls, which are admired by all who see them, including the owner. The best way of crossing is to run a white Leghorn cock with from seven to ten Dorking hens. If crossed the other way, the Dorking cock should be late hatched, so that he is small; if not, many of the hens get very much injured, and many eggs are unfertile. If the Leghorn cock is used, eleven out of thirteen eggs produce a chicken, and often twelve or thirteen chickens. They are very strong when hatched, fledge very quickly, grow fast, and are but little trouble, and can be hatched all the year round if required. They are not large table fowls, but very plump, full in the breast-meat, very white, and of good flavour. A few of them have yellow legs, and occasionally a cockerel may have a yellow skin; but this is very rare. For early spring chickens they are excellent, as they truss up so well, and can be killed from eleven weeks old if required, or may run on to six months; in fact, they may be killed any time when from eleven weeks to six months old if kept from the hens and pullets, and are always ready for table. The pullets lay from five-and-a-half to six-and-a-half months old fair-sized white eggs, as a rule quite as large as the pure Dorking, and some larger. Where a pure Dorking will produce from 85 to 110 eggs annually, a cross will lay from 130 to 160, and often more. There are a few specimens that will lay over 200 in the year. Except in very severe weather, this cross will lay all through the winter months. Many of the pullets have double combs, a few single, some with four claws on each foot, others with five. About six out of every twelve will want to sit, and, if required for this purpose, will make fair sitters; they are rather timid unless used very gently. They are good mothers, but leave their chickens rather early. They will sometimes lay before the chickens are twenty-one days old. For pure white fowls and good layers these are evidently the best. They never disappoint their owners if bred from a good-laying strain. If the Dorking hens are rather indifferent layers, and a Leghorn cock from a good laying strain is mated with them, many of the pullets prove to be very good layers. This cross is more adapted to those who have a good range; the white fowls on the green grass look splendid. There is both beauty and quality in this cross. It is always well to select a good large stand-up cock or cockerel in the Leghorns, as they are rather small in themselves. The white Leghorn and white Cochin make good layers of tinted eggs, are hardy, stand confinement well, but are not good table fowls, as they have yellow legs and skins. They are very neat-looking birds.

SURREY AND SUSSEX FOWLS.

THE Surrey fowl takes the lead in the London market because the Surrey people were more successful in fattening poultry years ago; no fowls could equal the Surrey fowls for fulness of breast, whiteness in colour, and at the same time an excellent flavour, so much so the consumers of fat poultry usually ask for Surrey fowls, and when the salesman in the London markets is selling poultry, all the best fowls take the name of Surrey fowls, no matter where they came from. Surrey takes the lead. I have heard for this last few years from the people who have visited Surrey what a number of birds were bred there, and also went myself to several towns and villages in that county, but was not quite satisfied with what I saw. I heard of these notable breeders, but could very seldom find a place where the poultry were fattened for the market, and always returned home a little disappointed. This summer of 1885 I was determined to find out more about these notable fowls. I drove through Surrey, Sussex and Kent twice, taking a different route each time, driving in all about 244 miles, calling at farm-houses and cottages, and having a little chat with many of the inhabitants. I think I may say I returned a wiser man. In some cases I was able to obtain a little information and in others to impart a little, especially in the way of breeding, as there is plenty of scope for this. In many places their breeds want reviving. In a few cases I had introduced fresh blood, which they needed badly; where I had done this, many pressing invitations had been given me to call upon them, as they said they could then show me the difference in their birds. Where they had introduced fresh blood there certainly was a marked difference in the chickens. The laying qualities are what they most need in those localities, which I will refer to later on.

Though the fowls are called Surrey fowls, the greater part of them are bred in Sussex and Kent, and I believe there are more than double the number of fowls fattened in Sussex than in Surrey. There is one firm there which, I believe, fattens more birds than any other firm in England—the name of Oliver. There are two brothers. They have as many as 4,080 birds fattening at once (besides ducks and geese), and do not breed a single chicken. They employ men to go with horses and carts to buy the chickens up from the farmers and cottagers. Some go as far as three days' journey buying The chickens are from eight to twelve weeks old when they are purchased, that is in the spring and summer; in the autumn and winter they are older—from four to six months old. I have known them hatched in May, and weigh 10lbs. by Christmas. Of course they are fattened by those who thoroughly understand their business. These large fatteners will kill from 300 to 500 in a day, according as the market runs. When the London season is principally over they send them to sea-side places, Brighton, Eastbourne, Hastings, &c., so they really command a good price all the year round.

The firm I referred to use fifty sacks of ground oats in a week, besides other foods, although the ground oats is the principal food used. They use a little barley meal, skim milk, and rough fat and suet. The milk is bought up from farms; this costs about £10 per week, besides what they produce themselves. The rough fat is purchased in London at 2s. 6d. per 8lbs.; this is chopped fine and mixed with the meal into quite a soft substance (about the thickness fat pigs are fed on), so much so that it does not hold together when the birds peck at it. It is so soft the feeders have to put it in troughs with spoons, or pour it in out of the pail. They give neither corn nor water while put up to fatten. They are usually up from twelve to fourteen days, according to the condition of the fowls. They are fed morning and evening with as much as they can eat. Care is taken not to put too much in the troughs at once, then they soon clear it up and look for more. This is one of the secrets in fattening, not to put too much in their troughs at once; if so, they soon turn away from the food. If it is given them a little at a time each one of them eats so fast they entice the others to eat, as each one tries to eat it from the other. The last seven days of fattening they are crammed by machine; a gutta-percha pipe is put right down the throat into the crop, so that the birds have not even to swallow; one man turns the handle of a machine, while the other places the fowl on his knees and puts the tube down the throat of the fowl, while he holds the crop with one hand so that he can tell when it is full. The crop is filled as quickly as one can count one, two, three. Two men can cram 25 dozen in an hour; in the ordinary way they cram 20 dozen in the hour.

Some of the chickens are in sheds, and some out in the open air. These were all in pens of sixes. One large pen, size 10 feet long by 16 inches wide, is divided into three compartments, and six birds are kept in each. There is sand scattered underneath the pens every morning for the excrement to drop on, which is all swept up every two days. There is no smell, although there are over 2,000 fowls on less than 50 square yards of ground. The pens are about 2 feet 9 inches from the ground, and arranged so that there is just room to pass up between the rows of coops. Mr. Joseph Oliver and his brother are the sole proprietors of the establishment. I may mention it is close to Heathfield, in Sussex, about 16 miles from Hastings. There are hundreds more who fatten poultry, but not in such a large way. Fattening in these districts is a distinct branch of the business. I know a few who fatten their own, but these are few and far between. Almost every cottager in some districts in Sussex, Surrey, and Kent keeps poultry and hatches chickens all the year round. They keep a few old stock birds to lay, and many of them never think of selling an egg; they set them all, unless a few are consumed in their own family. I think the poor rates in those districts must be very low, as poultry-keeping is the means of keeping many poor old people out of the workhouse. When old people get beyond work they can keep poultry, and if they have been accustomed to it, it gives them great pleasure in their old age; more than that, it butters their bread, and enables them to put on a warm coat or a warm dress, whichever the case may be.

How different the whole country would be if this thrift and industry were carried out through England, Scotland, and Wales, or even throughout the world, wherever there is a race of people. I have not met with a man yet, either white or coloured who would say No to either new laid eggs or a good roast fowl if he only had the opportunity. I must say the cottagers of Surrey and Sussex are patterns to our English people for industry. Their gardens are full of flowers. I call them kings in their own castles. Many of the women are up at from five to six o'clock in the morning through the spring and summer. Some may ask what breeds Surrey fowls are. They are no particular breed, being all mixed crosses. The breeds vary a little in the different districts. The owners have not the slightest idea what breeds or crosses they are. The breeds are left in the hands of the higglers in most cases. They change the cock birds, and their choice is usually a good one, as far as the table qualities go. They pick good plump fowls with white legs and full in the breast, and in most cases they produce good table birds; but there are not many good layers amongst them, in the winter more especially. They lay fairly well in the autumn, as they have several rest during the spring and summer with bringing up young chickens. There are some hens bring as many as six broods up in a year. Many of them rear three or four broods; but the great difficulty is, they cannot get sufficient eggs in the winter; there are many of the breeders have to buy. There are some farmers who keep hens for laying only, and do not rear any chickens for market. They sell the eggs to the higglers, who distribute them among the breeders. Each higgler has regular customers; some supply them with the eggs and broody hens at the same time, and most of them are very fair-dealing men, unlike most poultry-dealers.

The old-fashioned Surrey fowls were principally Dorking with a little Game blood in them; there are but a few to be met with now. The principal breeds are Game, Dorking, Cochin, and Brahma. There are a few places where the Plymouth Rocks and Langshans are used. The two latter are a great improvement. Young fowls do better in those districts than old fowls do. I believe this to be owing to a deficiency of grit, as in some of those districts there is a kind of sandstone used for the roads, and sharp grit is almost out of the question; though there is grit, but not sharp. I keep fowls in Surrey, but send them sharp grit prepared from flints and pebbles. Many people buy what is called shingle from the sea-shore. There are some firms sell it, but it is of little use, as grit or stones that have been washed upon the sea-shore are quite smooth; the friction of the water and the stones together wears the edges as smooth as glass. The fowls eat it all right, but it does them very little good, as most of it passes from the fowls in less than 24 hours, but the sharp grit usually remains in until it is worn smooth. Sometimes it is weeks before it passes. When it is picked up by the fowls it is as sharp as a knife, and when it passes away as smooth as glass. It is most important to see that the fowls have a good supply of sharp grit, as this is the only means they have of digesting their food. Now for a word for the Surrey and Sussex people, how to improve their table fowls and have an increase of eggs at the same time. I have mentioned that their birds are bad layers. A Dorking cock may be used with fair results; but as there is already Dorking blood in the birds, a Plymouth Rock cock is much better to use. When he is mated with these large hens the chickens hatch out well, are very hardy, grow fast and fledge fairly well, especially the pullets. They make good layers, most of the eggs being brown. They lay much earlier, from a month to six weeks, and in some cases two months. Most of them make large hens, and are a better shape. The cockerels are considerably better, having more breast-meat; they grow faster, and many of them make 3s. per dozen more when they are from nine to ten weeks old than the ordinary Surrey fowl. The Langshan is a good male bird to use when the Sussex fowls are free from leg feathering. Care should also be taken not to breed from a Langshan with many feathers on his legs. The flesh of the half-bred Langshan birds is excellent, but many of them come with black legs. This is not taken so much notice of in the market as it was a few years since; black legs are but little to go by, as they do not alter the flavour o the fowl. The breed of the fowl is not so much to go by as how it is fed or fattened. Our Surrey and Sussex fatteners have fowls from Ireland. Hundreds come over at a time. They are fattened in the same way, and sent to the London market and other consumers. It would take a person with an excellent taste to distinguish one from the other when cooked. Most of these fowls are sold for Surrey fowls. It is the way they are fed and not so much the breed. They have some almost pure Brahmas and also Cochins, and they make them up to splendid table fowls. I hope many may take the hint on Surrey fowls and follow in their footsteps. I have referred to fattening in detail in the chapter on that subject. Some may say they do not live in Surrey or Sussex. This may be, but fowls may both be reared and fattened in other parts of England. Many say the Surrey soil is so much better than elsewhere. Perhaps it would be better if turned the other way about. The Surrey people can manage their poultry so much better than in many other parts of the country. I think that would be nearer the mark. There is much heavy, wet land in many parts where these birds are reared. In some places it lies low, a clay-loam soil, and in spite of all this they are successful in rearing fowls. Many of them place their young chickens under sheds in coops. There are but few use bottoms in these, not more than one out of ten. They use old sacks or bags at the bottom of the coops in wet or cold weather, and dry them by their large wood fires, so the chickens are kept as dry as possible.

POULTRY FARMING AND KEEPING

THE question is often asked: Does poultry farming pay? I have had a large pile of letters the past three years asking me this question. I will try and answer in my small manual for the benefit of the public, or rather, those who read this book. The first question that is usually asked is, How many fowls must be kept to bring in an income of a certain sum—it usually runs from £100 to £500 a year—and how much capital will it require to start and carry it on, and how and where could the produce be sold; and how should the chickens be hatched, under hens or in an incubator, and if the latter, which is the best and where can it be purchased? These are not easy questions to be answered at all times. In reply to most of my correspondents on this matter, the first question I put to them is, Are they well acquainted with the management of poultry, and how long have they kept the same, and about the number; and do they understand diseases and the different little ailments which poultry are subject to? In many cases my correspondents have never kept a fowl; in some they have kept a small pen and have not had any disease in their fowls, and seldom know there is such a thing as disease in poultry; and because half-a-dozen fowls pay well, they think that if they had a few hundred a fortune will soon be accumulated in this direction, and with so much pleasure combined. There are many who have started, and unfortunately have lost their little capital. I do not know more than one in fifty that has really started a poultry farm and carried it on five years. I have known as much as £4,000 to have been lost in one large undertaking in five years, and in small concerns from £200 to £1,000. The old saying in our country is, that poultry-farming will not pay. It will pay if started and managed properly by those who understand their business. Who would think of putting a sea captain to manage a linen-draper's shop; or would a farmer engage a confectioner from a town to manage his farm? The contrast is as great in respect to people starting poultry-farming without any knowledge of the same. It is more often tradesmen who have had a business in large towns who start. They think poultry-farming is so simple that anyone can manage it. It is simple to those who previously understand it; but it still remains a mystery to thousands who have not had experience in it. Reading poultry books is not practical experience, though they may help very much in many respects. I know nothing that requires practical experience more than poultry-farming, especially if in a large way. It is a business that can soon be picked up if the owner is fond of poultry and starts in the right way. In most cases a poultry-farmer just begins to understand it when his money is gone. He tells his banker, or it may be, his friends; he may have over-drawn his bank or borrowed a little from his friends, but they say no more, so his inventions fall to the ground for the want of capital.

He can see where the mistake was when too late. Most people have to pay dearly for their experience. In many cases where poultry farmers have started they have bought in several hundred stock birds, and, of course, they are purchased from different parts of the country, and often they arrive before proper house-accommodation is provided. Some have been well housed, while others have been accustomed to sleep in open sheds, or, it may be, in trees. When the new-comers arrive they are put into a house very thickly together. The owner soon discovers a few of them not eating, or, in many cases, the eyes of some of them are entirely closed, and from 300 newly-purchased hens he does not have 300 eggs in three months, This may seem a dark picture to draw; but, nevertheless, it is a true one. My advice to all who intend to go into poultry-farming as a business is to commence with a few stock hens or pullets, if it is in the autumn when starting; but if in spring, purchase a few good eggs. It is well in starting not to have too many, so that they can be well managed. It is by far the safest plan to hatch and rear as many of the stock birds as possible for several reasons. Firstly, it is cheaper; secondly, the owner gradually gets his experience and has more time to study his fowls, and becomes more acquainted with their habits, and soon discovers which breed suits his place best. If little ailments or diseases break out, there is time to attend to them, and the owner gets a knowledge of how to treat the different diseases, or, better still, to watch his poultry so closely that he sees a bird at once when anything is wrong, and takes it away and tries an experiment on it; and, if taken in time, they are usually well in a day or two. Another great advantage is that, in starting in a small way at first, a better market can be found for a little produce than a large quantity, for as the poultry increases it becomes better known and fresh markets keep opening, while, if there is a large number kept the first year, the owner cannot always find a fair market. This business in every branch requires to be worked gradually. Experience makes perfect. If a person commences in a small way he is usually successful. It is well to work up a fair stock of poultry where it can be done before a large place is taken. If a few small pens of good layers or well-bred birds are collected together there is a good foundation to build upon. It is not a matter so much of how much capital is required, but how it is managed. It is well to have another source of income, if possible, unless there is a good account at the bank. If the owner can use a hammer and saw, much can be saved in building the houses and coops, as these are large items where they have to be bought. If the owner has not time or cannot build them, it is better to buy the timber and employ a carpenter to make them, and also the gates. It is very easy to put up the posts and wire. If a poultry-man is employed, he should be able to use the hammer and saw fairly well, as if he does not do the building there are always things that require repairing and keeping in repair.

A poultryman should be industrious, or he will be but little good to his employer, as an extra pen is often required quickly, or a coop made for a sick fowl, or a perch may get broken, or the hinges of a door. All such little things as this get out of repair where a number of poultry are kept. The question rises now, What branch of poultry-keeping pays best? This greatly depends upon which way one's fancy runs. Some have a better knowledge of one branch than another. If there is a good sale for eggs this branch pays, and in fact every branch, if a good market can be secured. One cannot be done well without the other. If fowls are bred for laying eggs for the market only, a number must be bred every year; for instance, if only 100 pullets are required, there must of necessity be about the same of cockerels, and if it is 300 or 400, the young cockerels have to be sold at a very low rate, whereas if they are fattened they make half as much again. If good poultry are bred there will be many cockerels which are of no use for stock purposes; even if they were there would not be purchasers for them all. The fattening coop will come in very useful, as nothing need be sacrificed. If this is not used the cross-bred cockerels and the wastrels out of the pure, or I might say those which will not do for stock purposes, must be sold when young to make room for the pullets and younger broods coming on. If poultry-farming is to pay, these little things must be strictly attended to, as farthings make pence, and pence shillings. It becomes one to count the cost before the investment is made. There is no money to waste, especially in these days, when trade is so bad, and everything should be turned to good account. This is put down to the importation of different articles into our country. The importation of grain has considerably lowered the income of farmers. They say it does not pay to grow grain and sell it in the London market. This indeed is too true, and as most of the foreign corn makes about the same as the home-grown, there is not much inducement to farmers to grow at home. In poultry and eggs it is different, as one dozen of home-fatted fowls will fetch from 12s. to 18s. more than the same number of foreign. Ducks will fetch from 18s. to £1 10s. per dozen more; Turkeys and geese from £1 10s. to £2 10s. a dozen more than the imported. This, of course, is when they are well fattened. English eggs fetch from 2s. to 4s. 6d. per hundred when sold in the market, and from 5s. to 7s. per hundred retail more than the imported eggs. I have under-estimated rather than over. As I am frequently in the markets, I have good opportunities of seeing how things sell. Is not this an inducement for English farmers to consume their own grain, or a good part of it? Corn is cheap, and poultry and eggs make a fair price; but little attention is being paid by farmers to the enormous sum paid out annually by this country for eggs and poultry alone—over £3,000,000. These figures are rather startling, or ought to be, to the home producers.

I do not say the country should be all poultry farms, but most of the people should be poultry keepers. The words "poultry farming" are usually taken to represent nothing but eggs and poultry being the produce. Whatever it means it should not be so, as where there are a number of poultry kept there should of necessity be other stock, if everything is to be turned to good account. For instance, the poultry cannot eat all the grass in the summer months. It cannot well be made into hay, if there are a large number of poultry running over it, as if so, the cattle will not eat it. Then some other stock must be kept. Sheep are the best to keep if they are required to run where there is wire-netting, as cows are apt to upset the wire with their horns. Then if sheep are kept, a few mangold wurtzel or turnips should be grown to help them through the winter months. The same for the cows, as they should have roots of some kind. Where there are a large number of poultry kept, there ought to be cows kept, as the skim milk is so good for fattening purposes, rearing young chickens, and for laying hens. If a farm is taken with the intention of making it a poultry farm, fruit trees should be planted of the best kinds. When worked in this way, there is what may be called three crops growing at once, and yet one does not interfere with the other, but the contrary. The trees shelter the poultry from the hot sun, and the fowls manure the ground, thus improving it. Sheep or young calves may be kept in the orchard where the young fruit trees are planted. When worked thus it is not at all likely to fail, whereas, where only poultry are kept, the grassruns to seed, and then dies. Then all through the autumn and winter this long grass is trodden down by the fowls. It is not only a waste, but is not so good for the fowls, as while they are searching after insects on a wet or dewy morning, their plumage gets very wet, whereas if the grass was eaten down by cattle, the poultry would eat a large quantity of it, and be able to find the insects better. Poultry will pay if managed properly, either in a small or large way, but the former the best. A large farm will pay if managed in a practical way, but not if poultry only are kept. I know many who get a good living by breeding ducks only, and yet have not two acres of ground. They pay best when not too many are kept, as they get better attention. If one hundred laying hens are kept, and from three to four hundred chickens are reared, they will clear from £50 to £100 in a year, but this does not imply that if double the number are kept, the profit will be doubled. It is usually *vice versa.* Poultry should be kept much more by those who own land, and not too many in one place. Where poultry farmers have made the mistake is by commencing with little or no experience. Several pamphlets and books issued are very misleading to the public. One states that eggs can be produced for 1d. a dozen, and fowls for 3d. a lb.; another that the total on each hen is 16s. 6d. clear profit. It is all worked out in figures nicely. I need not say how misleading these glowing accounts are. I do not say that half-a-dozen, or even ten might not give a profit of 16s. 6d. each, or even more if the eggs can be disposed of at a good price, and the greater number of them produced in the winter months. Poultry profits are not like those in most other businesses—the more business done, the greater profit. It is usually the other way about; the less poultry the comparatively more returns. I have known thirty laying hens pay £29 clear profit in a year; while a neighbour of the same person had over 300, and lost about £30 a year. It is the management. I find nothing else in the way of live stock pay like poultry. Before I published my book I made my poultry pay over 300 per cent. per annum, but I put nothing down for labour and rent. I sold my eggs at 3s. and 2s 6d. a dozen in the winter (when the greater number were laid), and 1s. 6d. per dozen in the summer, and my old hens from 2s. 6d. to 5s. each. I do not make them pay 300 per cent. now that I keep a large number, but they pay very well. They require the owner's personal supervision, with a good practical experience, and then they cannot well fail.

I have made arrangements in different parts of the country to have fowls bred and reared for me from my own stock for the coming year of 1886, and have had large numbers reared for me this season. I introduce fresh blood in each breed every year.

Corn and land are both cheap, and farmers and cottagers ought to go in for poultry more than they do. Poultry and new-laid eggs should become a regular food and not merely luxuries.

I may mention that I have had so many orders for poultry during the last two years, that I have been unable to supply many of my customers, but I trust I shall not disappoint them next season.

FATTENING FOWLS

FATTENING fowls is a business comparatively few understand, though they may be acquainted with other branches of poultry-keeping. Owners of young fowls are usually dissatisfied with their young cockerels when they are killed, as their own fowls do not eat so tender as some that have been bought from the poulterer. From 13 to 19 days is long enough to have them up. The best meal to use is ground oats and a little barley meal with it. When ground oats cannot be obtained it is well to buy some fine oatmeal and mix it with the barley meal. French buckwheat, ground and the husks taken out, is a very fine meal for fattening. A little barley and pea meal may also be mixed with it. Oatmeal or ground oats make the flesh whiter than any other. The latter is rather difficult to obtain in some parts of the country. The fowls should be put in a coop on small round bars. They should be from 1 to 1¼ inch apart, and always put longways, so that the poultry can stand and eat out of the troughs. The bars in front of coop should be about 2 inches apart. One coop 3 feet long and about 16 inches wide is large enough for six fowls. It should be 18 inches high, otherwise the cockerels will injure their combs when crowing. For the largest fowls it is well to have the coop 21 inches high. Where small chickens are fattening a smaller coop will do. The fattening coops are best kept in a shed or outhouse where it is a little dark. The trough they eat out of should be fastened outside their coops, about 4 inches higher than the bars they stand upon, otherwise they waste the food. The trough should be made like a pig trough, narrow at the bottom and wide at the top, and should be from five to six inches across the top. The food ought to be mixed up soft so that it does not cling together when the fowls peck it up. In this way they cannot peck much up at once, so they peck away as fast as they can move their beaks. In this way one induces the other to eat. They do the best where two or more pens are together, as they eat one against the other. Their food should not all be put in the trough at once, but a little at a time, then they clear it up and look for more. Nothing sets fowls against their food more than giving them too much at once, especially when up to fatten, as they do not have any exercise to give them an appetite. They should not have a particle of food left in their troughs. It is well to let two or three fowls come in the house where the others are penned up to fatten, to peck up the few odd pieces that may have fallen down. This prevents any waste, and also induces the penned birds to clear theirs up. If their food is mixed with hot water in the winter and spring they fatten much faster. Skim milk is the best where it can be obtained. The last eight or nine days they should have suet or rough fat mixed in their food. An ordinary fowl should have from $\frac{1}{2}$ oz. to $\frac{3}{4}$ oz. in a day, but to large birds more must be given.

This helps to fatten the fowls, and also causes them to be tenderer and more juicy. If old hens are fed on a good proportion of fat the last three weeks before being killed, they eat much tenderer. If they are boiled gradually they cannot be told from young fowls when fed in this way. If for the market, it is best to cram them the last week, as a fat young fowl usually makes 6d. or 9d. more than one the same weight not fat. If crammed by hand the meal should be made into pellets from two to two-and-a-half inches long, and dip them into milk or warm fat, when they slip down easier. They should be worked down with the thumb and finger; if not, they are apt to get lodged at the bottom of the neck. When they have to be crammed by hand it is well to let them eat as much as they will first, and then give them a few pellets just so that their crop is well filled. They should have a little fine grit in their food about twice a week, but do not require any water to drink. My fattening powders are used very largely. After fowls have been shut up about four or five days they occasionally lose their appetite. When this is the case use a little of the fattening powders; they help the fowls when put up to fatten. When fowls are required to be large, weighing from 8 to 10 lbs., they require about five weeks' fattening, with very generous treatment; if not, they fall back the last ten days. When first put up they should be allowed a little boiled corn three or four times a week, and a good supply of green food cut fine the whole time. Give a good supply of sharp grit. A little boiled maize may be given the last week or ten days. They also require cramming the last fortnight. When there are many fowls fattening it is best to use a machine. This saves time, as a man and a boy can do twenty dozen in an hour nicely. These cramming machines can be purchased at Lewes, in Sussex. Fowls should always be killed fasting; if not, they usually turn a bad colour. There are different modes of killing. Some just break their necks and do not let the blood out of them; but it remains in their necks (draining from the body into the neck). I like to stun them and then put the knife up into the brain. In this way they bleed well, and it gives them no pain, as when they are stunned they do not feel it. Where there are only a few to kill at a time it is best to have a nail or nails knocked into a wall or beam to hang the fowls on. Their legs should be tied, and take hold of these in one hand and the wings in the other; hit them hard against a post and hang them on the nail at once and run the knife into the brain as quickly as possible. Another way is to dislocate their necks. This is easily done by holding the fowl's head between the thumb and finger; the back of the head should press against the forefinger and the thumb under the throat; press hard on the neck and it is out of joint in a second. The fowl should be hung head downwards to allow the blood to run from the body; if not, the flesh will be dark.

PREPARING BIRDS FOR THE SHOW PEN.

IT is not always those who have the best fowls that obtain the highest honours at Poultry Shows. On the other hand they are not mentioned where they ought to be, as there are so many people who know how to fake a fowl up for the show pen, and take the highest prizes with inferior birds. This has been carried on largely these last six or ten years. I am pleased to say the Poultry Club and its reporters are taking steps in the right direction to stop this fraud (such as dyeing, trimming and sewing). The paper *Poultry* has done the fancy a good service by detecting fraud. There would be more entries at shows if men would be honest and not fake their birds. Judges frequently have too many birds to adjudicate on in too short a time to find out the little defects. Sometimes they are not qualified to judge the different breeds. Frequently the first prize is awarded to a bird not worth its carriage home for breeding purposes. It is my opinion that a judge ought not to judge any breed unless he has had practical experience in breeding. There is no doubt judges do their best in every way as far as they know. Let it not be thought I am mentioning myself, as I always decline it; one reason is I have not time, and there are men more qualified to take the work than I am. It is certainly not right for any of the committee to be assisting the judges and telling them about certain birds. Each bird ought to stand on its own merits. I have seen them show favours and take care to keep in with the reporters and high-class people. They frequently tell them what to say in the reports. This sort of work will not keep pace with the times. Why should such be employed? Because their names are noted as judges. It is a pity when good birds are bred and not prepared in the proper manner for the show pen. I have known breeders of good-class fowls show at the highest shows year after year and gain no prize; but the birds they sold usually obtained first, or were highly mentioned.

In some instances I was invited to inspect a lady's poultry. They were first-class, but she said she never obtained a prize, and yet those she sold were usually in for the money. The secret lay here. She caught up her birds straight from the run, put them in a basket, and sent them direct to the show; whereas those which she sold were prepared in a proper manner. Those which are caught up direct from the yard and forwarded, when put in the pen at the show, usually fly up to the top of the pen to get out, and thus injure their combs by striking them at the top of the pen, and when the judge comes round to have a good look at them, and moves round the pen, they fly up to the top and try to get out; and even when they quiet down a little the feathers lie close to the body (as they are apt to when the bird gets frightened or put out), and the wing bars are spread out, and they are in such a confused state that it is quite an impossibility for the judges to do them justice, as they do not show their proper shape, and the owner cannot think why his or her birds were not noticed, and the judge gets blamed, whereas it is the exhibitor's fault (if it may be called a fault). A person cannot do a thing unless he has a little information on the subject, and it is very seldom that an exhibitor will tell his or her neighbour how they prepare their birds for the show pen, especially if they obtain a high honour. They usually think, "If I teach my neighbours what I know myself they may perhaps surpass me. This just suggests the old proverb to my mind, that "Giving does not impoverish." This may be true in many instances; but an old fancier who has won many prizes does not think it prudent to acquaint every one with his mode of preparing the birds.

There are some breeds which require different treatment to others; but all breeds should be put in a pen or large coop of some kind, placed about three feet from the ground, and be fed in front of the coop or pen. This induces them to step up to the front of the pen. A little food should be put in at a time, so that they have to wait for it a little time. At the same time the hand should be put in the coop very gently, so as to prevent the bird from being timid. If a little green food is taken twice or three times a day they soon begin to expect it, and will not get up into a corner when the feeder goes in to feed them, but will strut about and show themselves off to the best advantage. They should be penned from five to seven days previously to being sent to the show, and unless very tame should be put in in the evening or at night and handled very quietly. It is well to take them out and stroke them with the hand, especially down the back, a few times, then when they arrive at the show and are taken out of the basket they are not at all timid; and if so, they soon get over it, and are settled down nicely the next morning; and when the judge goes round to look at them, he has no difficulty in deciding which is to head the list, and does it with much more ease than when they are so wild. The preparation pens should be large, so as to enable the birds to walk and turn round easily without ruffling their feathers; they should not be less than 2 feet or 2½ feet square; even if larger they are much better, as it enables the birds to take exercise. The large breeds should have them 2 feet 6 inches high, and in a few cases a little higher than this, according to the size. The feather-legged tribes should have moss-peat or straw in the bottom of the coop. If anything else is used their foot feathers get broken off. When the clean-legged tribes are penned it is best to put a little perch in the pen—3-inch quartering answers this purpose. Length must be according to number of birds there are in the pen; if only one bird, 6 or 9 inches is sufficient. When required for the show they do not always improve if shut up by themselves. If they do not eat, another should be put in the pen to keep the other company, then they induce each other to eat. If the penned bird is a cockerel, put a smaller cockerel in with him, too young to show fight. The same with the pullets. Nothing should be allowed to go in that will be likely to fight. It is well to take the block of wood out in the daytime. Minorcas, Spanish, Hamburghs, Andalusians, Leghorn, and black rose-comb Bantams (and all breeds which have white ear-lobes) should be kept in a pen where it can be shaded from the light from 10 to 14 days before the show, such as a fine piece of canvas nailed in front of the coop; or, better still, if the coop can be placed back to the light, but not so that they cannot see to eat and drink. It not only whitens their ear-lobes but the combs come out much better and stronger. If the coops are in an outbuilding or any kind of house in which there is a window, a blind should be kept over it. At the same time there should be plenty of ventilation allowed.

Some exhibitors use artificial heat in their houses by running hot-water pipes through them. This makes the combs grow considerably larger; but it is running a great risk, as the birds usually take cold before they return home again. The purchasers of such birds have a great deal of trouble with them, as they are liable to take cold. Black fowls do not require washing for the show pen; but it is well just to wash their feet and legs. Houdans do not require to be washed all throughout, only the surface of the feathers, unless it is their crest. This requires well soaking if it is at all dirty, and will look all the better for it. The feathers on the body can be sponged over and made wet—just put in soak. A little soda and soap may be put in the water, but not on the brush, unless it is just for the crest, legs, and feet. If so, the soap does not always get rubbed out. If they are rather dirty, a nail-brush should be used. Hold the feathers on the left hand, and then they can be brushed. It is well to pour a little blue-water over them gently; then use a sponge to get the water out as much as possible; then a wash-leather, and rub them. Always take care that the feathers are rubbed the same way as they lie; finish them with a dry towel. The white, buff, or light fowls of any breed which really require washing to the skin, must be done as follows:—There should be a tub or bath of warm water about four or five inches deep, and the fowl should stand in the water, and well soak the feathers (a little soap and soda in the same). After they have been well scrubbed, they should be rinsed with the blue-water, and it should have the chill off. After this is finished they should be dried as described. Give them two roup pills; this usually prevents them from catching a cold. The room should be warm, and the birds should be put in a covered basket and set by the fire. They should always be washed two days before being sent to the show; if not, they may not be quite dry. When dry, it is well to brush the feathers carefully with a clothes-brush, each feather the way it lies, and then with a fine hat-brush; this brings each feather into its natural state. The fluff feathers should be held in the left hand, then they can be spread out and brushed properly. After the comb, face, and wattles are washed, they should have a little glycerine and rose-water rubbed on them; if not they are liable to crack or look very pale. I have known them to chap. Some people put oil on them to make them red and look bright. Birds with yellow legs, such as Plymouth Rocks, Leghorns, and Wyandottes, should have their legs soaked and scrubbed with a nail-brush. It is well not to put soda in the water; if so, it is apt to turn the legs a pale colour instead of improving them. After they are wiped there will be dark rims on the bottom part of their legs and toes. This dirt should be got out very carefully, if not the legs will be bruised; this makes them look worse than they were before. A small piece of wood can be cut into the same shape as a very small tooth-pick; the wood should be of a hard substance. They can be purchased ready made at a jeweller's; they are made out of box-wood. These little pieces of wood will fetch all the dirt out from under the scales of the legs. This dirt often prevents birds from taking prizes, as when the dirt is out they look much better, clear yellow, against those which have not been cleaned out. After they have been cleaned it is well to brush them again, as the brush fetches the loose pieces out; then they should be wiped dry. When the birds are in the pen, they should have a good supply of grit, green food, and water. If heavy-combed birds are rather weak in this respect, a little meat given to them causes the comb to grow very much. Brahmas,

Cochins, Langshans, and Plymouth Rocks should not have meat, or their combs will grow too much. When sent to a show, it is well to give a Roup Pill, as this often prevents them from taking a cold, andgives them a good appetite when they arrive at the other end. Many exhibitors use my Roup Powder for getting a gloss on the plumage; it also causes them to be livelier. When cockerels return from the show pen which have been accustomed to run with the others they should not be put with them, as they are apt to fight and injure themselves.

DISEASES.

POULTRY are subject to many diseases, and, as a rule, are much neglected when unwell, as they get much abuse from their own companions, and the owner often says they must take their chance, live or die, and, therefore, the poor sick bird or birds are left with the healthy, and driven about and pecked till they pine and die unhelped and uncared for.

All poultry-keepers should be acquainted with the different diseases fowls are liable to; if not needed, so much the better, while if the owner has sick birds it will often save pain to the fowls and loss to himself, as, if most diseases are treated at once, many valuable fowls may be soon and easily cured that would die if left alone, and also prevent the disease from spreading to the healthy fowls. One stitch in time saves nine. Just so with the sick fowls. If the first is saved there is little doubt about the remaining ones.

Where a large number of poultry are kept it is well to have a small house by itself, so as to isolate the sick bird at once, as most diseases are infectious. Any kind of house will do that is clean, free from draughts, and well ventilated at the top. The best thing for the floor is clean straw or moss peat, the latter having the preference, as it is a disinfectant, and also keeps the fowls warm and dry, and prevents any excrement from sticking to the feathers. The moss peat is invaluable for these purposes, and the house or coop can be cleaned out so much easier, as the peat absorbs all excrement. Some disinfecting lime and camphor should also be used in the house to prevent the attendant from carrying the diseases amongst the healthy poultry, unless the moss peat is used. This is the greatest boon to poultry-keepers of anything that has been used. It does away with all smell, and at the same time is such a comfort to the fowls. They dust themselves in it in the daytime, and if it is cold and wet they run into the house, and their feet are warm and dry at once. If it is put from three to four inches thick on the floor of the fowl-house, and turned over occasionally in the wet and damp weather, it is very comfortable, absorbing wet at once. If the fowls are very thick in the house in bad weather it is best to remove the excrement from under the perches about two or three times a week. In the dry weather there are rarely any droppings to be seen, as the fowls scratch them all about, and the moss peat absorbs them, so that there is no smell. Unless fowls are kept very thick in the houses, four times a year is often enough for them to be cleaned out. Sometimes it is necessary to add a little fresh moss peat on to the other. It is well to turn it all over occasionally, and when it is cleaned out it should be swept out thoroughly clean; if not vermin may harbour in it. I have kept it in a house six months as an experiment, and when it has heen removed there has not been a particle of smell. I kept birds in it and not allowed them to perch, and they kept very clean. I kept two pens of Hambughs on it this year without any perch, and they did remarkably well. I cannot speak too highly of it. In the first place it saves time in cleaning the fowl-house out, it keeps it sweet, it prevents the fowls from injuring their feet when they fly from their perch, it prevents the eggs from being broken when they drop from the roost, as they often do, as when they are broken the fowls usually start eating them at once. This is what often causes fowls to become egg-eaters, which is a very serious matter, whether few or many are kept. It is warm and dry to their feet, especially the feather-legged tribes, as their feathers get wet and cold. When it is taken out of the house it is very valuable for garden purposes, especially for flowers. Some florists will give 5s. for one barrow-load of it. It is much the same as our English peat for flowers, only so much stronger. I have tried it on vegetables, and find nothing to equal it. No poultry-keeper ought to be without it. For early chickens it is invaluable to put in the coops. It prevents cramp and crooked toes amongst them, and it is so reasonable it is in the reach of every poultry-keeper. Refer to advertisement, where full prices are quoted. When fowls are exported it is excellent for putting in the coops. I use it for all purposes.

The house is better not heated, as diseases are often traced to artificially-warmed houses. Poultry should be kept as much as possible in one temperature, and, therefore, if the house is heated, the runs should correspond, being made as warm and snug as possible. This may appear unnecessary, but to those who have tried and studied it it remains a fact; for when fowls come out of a warm house on a cold morning they stick about close together and look miserable, while if it is a mild morning, or a warm run, they will be busy picking about and enjoying themselves. Fowls roosting out of doors do not feel the cold nearly so much, and keep free from disease; but if roosting in a warm house the cold nips them very much, and they mope about and refuse to eat, which checks their growth and the production of eggs, and brings on diseases, and more especially cramp and roup.

One of the most important things to keep poultry in health is to keep their houses and runs perfectly clean. People who do not care for their fowls in this way often wonder why their birds do not lay, but the wonder is they live at all, and probably the only thing that saves their lives is the plentiful ventilation and pure air they get. In the country, about two people out of five keep their poultry in this way, but in the town it is different, as the sanitary authorities compel people to keep their birds clean, or otherwise they would be very offensive in a crowded neighbourhood. All excrement should be removed every morning, and the floor should be sprinkled with ashes or dry soil, and a sprinkling of Jeyes' Disinfectant once a week if the moss peat is not used, and the houses should be limewashed-out four times a year. If dry, dusty road-scrapings can be procured, they should be used to sprinkle the floor instead of ashes, as they prevent any smell arising.

I do not intend in this little work to go very scientifically into the matter of diseases, but only to mention the most common, and to give the remedies I have found most efficacious in a simple way, so that boys or girls may understand them, and treat their own fowls in a similar manner.

ROUP.

This disease is usually brought on by cold or a sudden chill of the blood, very hot days and cold nights, or sitting in a draught when the fowls have not been used to it, or the poultry-house door left open one night, or the ventilators left so that there is a draught through the house, or sleeping out of doors one night and in a nice warm house the next, getting wet and cold and then sitting in a draught. When fowls are accustomed to sleep in trees and are put direct into a warm house, or put in a covered basket and sent on a railway journey, especially when sent to a show after sleeping out of doors, they are almost sure to return with roup. When poultry are travelling by rail and are allowed to stand for hours on the draughty platform, especially when coming home from a show, after having been taken out of a crowded place where it has been very hot, and the railway companies allow them to stand for hours on the platform in the middle of the night, they are sure to have roup. I have mentioned a few causes of this disease. It comes in three different forms. The first symptoms appear quite distinct from each other. When a fowl first catches cold and the system is in good order, the first symptom is a little running at the nostrils. At first the discharge is clear water, but if neglected it usually ends in roup. If not taken in time and treated properly the fowl soon begins to cough and sneeze. The running from the nostrils may last for a long time. I have known this to continue for three months and not lay the birds up. This discharge from the nostrils goes harder with chickens than with old hens, and if they do not get good attention it stops their growth. When the first symptoms appear they should be examined to see if the mouth and throat are free from white spots or ulcers, and with no rattling noise in the throat. Their nostrils should be washed with a little alum and water. It is well to dip a feather in the alum solution, and put down the fowl's throat. If it is a little sore or inflamed the alum will do it good. Give one heaped-up teaspoonful of the Roup Powder to nine hens; chickens proportionately. The powder should be given in the morning meal. If they object to eat it then mix it with about two handfuls of meal and throw it down a small piece at a time. In this way of feeding they will usually all run after one piece and swallow it before they taste it. If they refuse to eat it when given in this way they must be pilled, as will be seen further on. As a rule there is no difficulty in getting them to take it. When there is only a running at the nostrils, and no offensive smell, they may be allowed to run with the other fowls without any danger of them infecting the others. If this cold is neglected there is a very offensive smell from the fowls' breath, and a discharge from the nostrils dried on all round the outside, often preventing them from breathing, also thick saliva in the mouth, and if this is not stopped it soon turns to a thick mucus, and corrodes very fast, spreads down the throat, and causes the fowls to breathe very hard. In very bad cases there is a thick cheesy matter forms on the tongue, mouth, and down the throat where their food passes. It grows very fast, so much so in bad cases the tongue protrudes out of the mouth, and they appear to be swallowing all the time. In a few cases the mouth is clear to all appearance, and the fowls look quite healthy and eat well up to the hour of their death. The only symptoms which appear are, they open their mouth to breathe, and if they are watched they may be seen to try to throw something up from their throat, but in vain. In such cases as these the fowl should be caught (a second person usually is required to hold open the mouth), the opening of the trachea (that is the windpipe) should be worked up and down from the outside by the thumb and finger. Hold the fowl's mouth wide open, if not the opening cannot be seen, and hold the head quite still for a few seconds, and when the fowl breathes the opening of the windpipe can be seen. Then dip a feather in the lotion. In this case do not strip the feather, and well saturate it with the lotion. It should be a small pointed feather, plucked from a fowl's wing. A tail feather will not answer this purpose. The opening of the pipe is small, so care must be taken to put the feather right down the windpipe and not the throat or swallow. It may be put from two to four inches down the pipe. Give two or three twists round and draw it out slowly, and in most cases there will be little pieces of fungus adhering to the feather, a kind of whitish-yellow matter. It crumbles like little pieces of cheese. In some cases it can be seen just at the top of the pipe; sometimes it is half as large as a small pea, and in other cases it may not be larger than a pin's head, but in all cases it should be well saturated with the lotion by another feather. Then use the quill end of the same to rub it off. In most cases it will peel off very easily; if not it will the next morning. If a sharp instrument is used it may injure the fowl if it makes a slight struggle. It usually bleeds a little when removed. In some cases it grows again; if so, treat as before, and it will gradually get better. Always take care to burn the feather which has been used. When the lotion has been used for a fowl's throat it is well to use a glycerine feather in the same way, or pour a few drops of glycerine down the fowl's throat, which saves time. Sometimes this scrofulous matter forms on the side of the mouth; in some cases it forces the mouth out so that from the outside it looks like a swelling. The lotion should be used in the same way, but it will require more of it. Sometimes it is necessary for a few drops to be dropped on or in, as sometimes when the fungus is removed there is a hole. In this case do not omit the glycerine, as stated previously. When the disease comes in the last two forms I have mentioned, or in a similar way, the fowls do not always have a discharge from the nostrils. It sometimes stops their laying, but does not appear to injure their health, unless in very bad cases. If neglected it usually ends in death to the fowls. What is called canker in pigeons is much the same thing, and can be cured in the same way. Roup shows itself in quite a different form at times, viz., with a swelling in the face and round the eye. The first symptom is usually a little white foam round the eye, and the fowl will frequently scratch her eye with her toe-nail. Sometimes before anything else is visible these symptoms will appear: at times the fowls' nostrils are quite dry, and at others there is a slight discharge with an offensive smell. Sometimes in the course of 12 hours the fowl's face has swollen to the extent that the eye is completely closed up. The face should be bathed at once with very warm water, using a sponge or piece of flannel. Bathe it for a short time, from two to five minutes, according to how bad it is. In all cases wipe the face quite dry; if not more harm than good will be done, as the fowl is apt to take a fresh cold again. A little alum may be put in the water used for bathing the fowl's face with advantage. A few camomile flowers boiled or steeped in boiling water and the decoction used for bathing the face is the best remedy I know of. They must be very bad cases that the last remedy does not cure. Bathe twice a day. After it is wiped quite dry rub a little lotion on the swollen part. This not only helps to draw the humour out of the face, but prevents the cold striking the tender parts of the face. The fowl or fowls should be kept out of the draught, and yet have plenty of air in a fairly warm place, but not a heated one, unless the fowls are very ill, when warmth is required. When they are recovering they should be hardened off a little at a time, first put in a snug outhouse, then in an open shed. The first time they are allowed to go in the pen should be in the middle of the day; if not they may take cold again. In some instances the swelling of the face does not go down, or only partly so, but becomes much harder. In such cases as these there is a hard, cheesy lump formed under the skin. It is much the same as that found in the mouth and windpipe, only that it is of a harder substance, and smells much worse, being under the skin, where the air cannot get to it. If it is just round the eye the fowls usually lose the sight of the same. In some cases when the scrofula has been got out I have known the eye come out with this matter. Of course it is very painful to the bird. There are some fowls get over it fairly well if the scrofula does not spread under the eye. When the hard substance begins to form round the eye the fowl or fowls should be killed, unless they are very valuable. If the owner wishes to persevere with them then a lance or very sharp penknife should be used. It is best to cut the substance in the centre, then the contents can easily be removed. The incision will bleed a little; then use a small piece of sponge to clear the blood away, and put a few drops of the lotion in. This will loosen the hard scrofulous matter so that it can be removed. Vaseline should be used on the wound. I do not recommend this to be done generally, but only where fowls are very valuable and the operator has a good knowledge of what he is doing; if not it may give the fowls a great deal of unnecessary pain. Roup comes in three different forms, and whichever it comes in it can usually be cured. My advice is if the fowl is not valuable kill it at once, or isolate the bird from the others, especially if there are many kept.

Treat the affected bird with roup powder, and add camphor to the water of the unaffected birds. If the fowls are free from liver disease, and inflammation can be kept from the lungs, not five in 100 will die if treated properly. It is always safe to give a teaspoonful of castor oil when a bird shows any of the symptoms mentioned.

If they are breathing hard, give a teaspoonful of glycerine an hour or two after the oil. If the rattling in the throat is very bad, dip a feather in glycerine, and put it down the windpipe. The fowl may be distressed for a few minutes, but this will perhaps help the breathing after. A few green leaves of rue are very valuable in such cases. These may be difficult to obtain, but linseed is in the reach of every person (as it can be bought at the grocer's or cornchandler's). This should be put in cold water, and put over a slow fire, so that it does not boil fast, but just simmer for half an hour. If a little lemon juice can be added, so much the better. Give the linseed as warm as the fowl can take it. A hen may have six teaspoonfuls; a cock eight or ten. If they have more it will not hurt them. The bird should be held under the left arm, in a position so that the feet cannot have any bearing; if so, the linseed cannot easily be given; or the bird can be held between the operator's legs, with the fowl's body resting on its thighs, the legs hanging down, so that they cannot catch against anything. A small piece of camphor, about the size of a pea, may be given after the linseed; and give two roup pills, and fifteen birds out of twenty are well the next morning, if treated when the first symptoms appear. It is always the best to go into the fowl-house in the evening, especially in the autumn and winter months, just to see whether the fowls are all right. I prepare roup pills ready for use; these are a convenience to have if the birds are a little out of sorts, but for bad cases I prefer the pills made from the roup powder, as it is useless to give patients medicine without a portion of food also (especially fowls). This is why I give the powders the preference. For one hen mix half a teaspoonful of the roup powder (if very bad, three-quarters may be given), one heaped-up teaspoonful of flour, one-and-a-half of fine oatmeal, and a little piece of fat, about a quarter of a teaspoonful of dripping, lard, or butter will do, and a little hot water, just sufficient to make it into a paste, so that it will hold together. For a cock, three-quarters of a teaspoonful of the powder may be given. If the fowls are very bad, give this quantity twice a day, especially the first day. If the fowls cannot eat any food, that is, if they do not pick it up for themselves, then an extra quantity of meal and flour can be used, that is to keep the fowls' strength up. In this case I cannot state exactly the number of pills to give each fowl; they should not have less than two or three at a time. I usually make them the size of the little finger to the second joint. If the fowls do not appear to swallow them, they should be worked down the neck with the thumb and finger. Should the fowls be blind in both eyes, they ought to have a little water poured down their throat with a teaspoon. If the fowls are treated as I have described, they will often be well in a few days. Even bad cases soon begin to recover if there is nothing but roup in their system. When they breathe very hard they usually have inflammation of the lungs. (Refer to paragraph on that complaint). If they only partly recover, and do not eat after fifteen or twenty-one days' treatment, they usually have liver complaint. If they are valuable fowls, it is well to give them two teaspoonfuls of cod liver oil.

It is well for those who are interested in poultry to try these experiments on common fowls, if time will permit, and especially if they think of keeping valuable poultry; if not, killing the first is usually cheapest in the end, especially if there are many birds left. The first symptoms of roup in young chickens are usually a slight running at the nostrils, roughness of the plumage, drooping of the wings, and loss of appetite. They usually drink a great deal of water, which makes them much worse, as it frequently gives them diarrhœa. It is well to put camphor in the drinking-water, only allowing them about half the usual quantity for two or three days; then discontinue water altogether. If it is hot weather, soak the corn in water. Use soft meal in the morning with the roup powder in it, and in ten or fourteen days the chickens will be in a healthy state again. When the chickens' throats become sore, they usually open their mouths very much, and many people put it down as gapes. When there is a sign of gapes discontinue the water, and give sharp grit, soft food with roup powder mixed in, and boil the corn for a week or ten days. These simple remedies will work wonders, bringing health and vigour to the chickens very quickly. Under any circumstances do not overcrowd chickens, and give them ventilation, but not draught.

LIVER DISEASE.

There are many fowls suffer and die with this complaint while their owners are quite unaware of the cause of death, and often put it down to consumption or cramp unless they happen to open the bird and find an enlarged liver.

Fowls in confinement appear most liable to this complaint, and this is often for want of some necessaries, such as green-food, grit, &c., and I have found birds that have suffered in confinement recover from this disease when let out to run on a grass field, and this, I think, was on account of their eating dandelions, which will often effect a cure.

When the birds are not valuable they should be killed at once, as this disease often sticks to them all their lives ; but if persons wish to save their birds they should be supplied with tonics, such as the advertised powders, and treated with the same remedies that human beings use for this complaint, viz., gentian and horehound.

The symptoms of this disease are rather difficult to describe. In many cases there is lack of gloss on plumage ; the feathers look rough, and the fowls seem to have lost all energy. First thing in the morning they go to the drinking fountain, but do not drink very much, as they do in many other diseases. They eat but little soft food ; many of them will not touch it, and usually eat fairly well of hard corn, especially maize ; of this they eat very greedily If allowed to have it, they will eat this until the hour o' their death. There is usually a yellow cast about the face, especially round their eyes. Their face appears sunken in. It can be noticed better if put beside a healthy bird. The eye is rather dull. There is often a peculiarity in their walk, appearing as though they were rather stiff, and were afraid to shake their bodies. If they are made to run, they usually go a little lame on one leg. It is the heavier breeds which are the lamest. It is seldom the smaller breeds show any tendency to be lame. Their food does not digest, and their crops are seldom empty. There are several causes for this complaint. In-breeding in the heavy breeds is often the cause. I have traced this in many poultry yards, and, in some cases, nine out of twelve have died. Insufficiency of sharp grit, to help digest the food, is one of the greatest enemies to the liver. Fowls cannot keep healthy long unless they are supplied with sharp grit. Cayenne pepper should be avoided. The liver is usually the first organ to suffer. Sometimes it brings on consumption and roup. When the liver is not acting properly, the fowl is much more susceptible to other diseases, as when this is out of order the blood is very hot, and at other times very low in temperature. Insufficiency of green food is very bad for the fowls. This frequently affects the liver. The more they can have of it the better they are. Another cause of liver disease is over-feeding on hard corn, especially maize. This should be avoided ; a little does not hurt them, but feeding heavily on it is ruinous to the liver, especially when the fowls are in confined runs, and do not get sufficient exercise. When fowls have liver disease, very hot weather will carry them off very quickly. They will stand any amount of cold. Sudden changes upset the liver very much; such as roosting in a warm house one night and in a tree the next, or anywhere, causing a sudden change. This brings on congestion of the liver. The bird should be kept in one temperature as much as possible. When fowls have the disease badly, their excrements are very yellow. In bad cases, the fowls waste away, so there is scarcely anything of them left, with the exception of skin and bone. In such cases as these it is an impossibility to effect a cure, as the liver is scrofulous (covered with white spots or streaks). At first the liver becomes enlarged, usually through some of the causes I have mentioned, and then followed by these scrofulous spots. When they first appear they are not larger than a pin's point; and if the fowl or fowls are not treated at once, they grow very rapidly. Some of them grow as large as horse beans, in which state they become like a fungous matter, and spread to the other organs of the body, especially the entrails. The passage leading from the crop to the gizzard is rather more liable to take them than the other parts. When this matter commences to form there, the excrements are green and very thin. When they get to this stage, the scrofula spreads very fast in other parts of the intestines, and in some cases entirely blocks the passage up, so that even a liquid cannot pass. After this occurs, death ensues in a few hours. In many cases the fowls waste to a skeleton. In a few cases I have found on post mortem examination in male birds a kind of tumour formed of this scrofulous matter encased in a skin in the abdomen, just in the same way as the eggs in a hen. I have found them various sizes, weighing from half an ounce to nine ounces. I have taken them out as round as a cricket ball, and in other cases they have been the shape of a hen's egg. The liver disease is indeed a thing that ought to be avoided as much as possible. A preventive is better than a cure, though it may not be thought much of. When a fowl is really bad with the liver disease it is waste of time and money to attempt to cure it, unless it is for an experiment. This disease is found much more where exhibition birds are kept or the offspring from them. In-breeding and too high feeding to obtain size, or chickens that have been bred from hens that have been fed chiefly on maize, are the causes. I have known more than half the chickens die from this disease where the parents have been fed entirely on maize. As hard corn, do not give more than one-third of maize ; less, if anything.

Remedies.—As herbs, nothing are better than dandelions, watercresses, and horehound. The two former can be cut up in small pieces, and given to the fowls. They eat them up greedily, and enjoy them very much. When horehound is used, it is best to boil it for about fifteen minutes, and give them the decoction. About two sprays are sufficient for from twelve to fifteen fowls. The best way of giving the liquid to the fowls is to mix the soft food with it in the morning. Use as much water to boil the horehound as will mix the food. A little gentian root (powdered) is very good. It is strong, and should be used carefully. My powders (especially the roup), as advertised in this book, are prepared to act upon the liver. This is the remedy I use myself for my own fowls. I use the poultry powders twice a week; but if it is a cold or wet morning I substitute the roup powders. I use the poultry from August to March or middle of April. I give it from three to five times a week, according to the weather. If it is very cold I give it every day. If the weather is milder I discontinue it for a few days, sometimes for a week. In sudden changes—such as a cold, wet morning, or a sharp frost—I give the roup powders. With this treatment my fowls keep in perfect health, even through their moult. Many of them do not lose their redness of comb. I have had some hens lay up to eight years of age. The powder strengthens every organ of the body. When fowls are in confinement, and do not get much exercise, it is well to boil their grain occasionally; also give boiled rice for a change for the evening meal, and finish them off by giving a little hard corn or stale soaked bread. If fowls are treated properly, liver disease would soon have but little effect upon poultry. If care and proper treatment are given to them they will fully repay their owner.

LEG-WEAKNESS.

Sometimes young cockerels that have grown quicker than the others are taken with this disease, the symptoms of which are much the same as cramp, viz., tumbling over when attempting to stand up, dropping down quickly and frequently, sitting down to eat their food, as though they had no strength. The best remedy is to feed on stimulating food, such as meat, bone-meal, &c., and to give a tonic in the water. The birds should not be allowed to roost, but should be put on straw, hay, or moss-peat for a time. They are best killed for table and not kept for stock birds.

GAPES.

This disease is mostly confined to young chickens, and requires different treatment from any other, as it consists of small worms in the windpipe which cause the chickens to gape and run backwards, and if some remedy is not applied immediately they live but a very short time. There are many thousands perish annually of this disėase, more especially among farmers, and I have known as many as 300 to die on one farm in a year. How the worms get in the throat is a mystery, but some scientific writers tell us it is from eggs deposited by a kind of tick often found on chickens; this may be possible, but it is also very plain to me that chickens reared in the country appear more liable to this disease than those in the town, and the only reason I can find for this is that country chickens often drink dirty, stagnant water, while those in town generally get clean, fresh water. I tried the experiment of giving a few chickens water from a tub that had stood some time and found that many of them had gapes, while those with fresh water were quite free. I may also mention that there are many wild birds in the country die from this disease.

These worms may be extracted from the chicken's throat by inserting the stem of a hen's feather stripped of the downy part, except just at the end, down the windpipe, and when withdrawn after being properly twisted round two or three times there will sometimes be as many as half-a-dozen worms on the end of it.

Another good remedy is Jeyes' Disinfectant. Use one teaspoonful of the liquid to one tablespoonful of water; the gullet should be worked up by the thumb and finger so that the windpipe is within easy reach. Dip the feather in the solution and put it down from two to five inches, according to the size of the chicken. Twist it round two or three times, and if the chicken is very much distressed put a salad oil feather down its windpipe and then a teaspoonful of water. This is a sure and easy cure. It is also inexpensive. as a 1s. bottle would cure 1,000 chickens.

Another good remedy is to give the chickens a few small pieces of camphor, about the size of a pea, at intervals, or if many are attacked at once they should be put in a box with a little disinfecting lime and a little common lime, and when the box is shaken the chickens will flutter about and breathe the lime dust, which is an immediate cure. They should be left in about five minutes, and after shaking the box the lid should be left open a little way to observe them, so that if any appear overcome they may be taken out at once and relieved, which may easily be done by blowing down the throat, when they will soon recover. If the eyes are closed they should be opened and gently wiped (not washed) with a silk handkerchief. It is always best to feed on meal only for a day or two after any operation.

The best preventive I know of for gapes is plenty of clean water and clean and dry runs and coops, but a little camphor added to the water often prevents any disease of this kind.

Camphor is the best purifier to the body I know of. It is worth a guinea an ounce to poultry-keepers. There would not be half the disease among chickens, turkeys, and pheasants there now is, if it was used in the water. It should be put in the drinking vessels. A piece as large as a walnut will last twenty chickens from three weeks to a month. It dissolves very slowly. Every time the water is changed the piece of camphor must be replaced in the drinking vessel. My Lotion, as advertised, will cure the gapes, used in the same way as Jeyes' Disinfectant; but as every poultry-keeper has not it by him, I have mentioned a few remedies which can be obtained at once if required.

CRAMP.

Early chickens are often subject to this disease in the cold weather, when from one to six weeks old. The result is that the toes are contracted, and the chickens fall down in trying to walk, and shuffle about on the joints of the legs. When this is the case the foot and leg should be rubbed with turpentine, and a little vaseline rubbed well in, and a piece of stick should be obtained with three prongs, the same shape as the chicken's foot. The toes should be bound round with cotton wadding, and each toe strapped with wool or worsted separately to a prong of the stick, the chicken being put in a box on wool or flannel, and kept warm for a few hours. If very bad they should be kept away from the hen for a few days, but should be put under at night, being removed first thing in the morning and replaced in the box. When the wood cannot be obtained, get a piece of cardboard. Wrap each toe in cotton wool, place them on the cardboard, and sew them separately on to it with worsted,putting the stitches over the toe and through the cardboard, so that they cannot be moved.

Some chickens never get over cramp, but are always shaky on their feet. These should be killed for table, and not kept for stock birds. Cramp in chickens is usually caused by their being on hard floors, either boards or flagstones. It is for the want of circulation in the blood.

The symptoms in laying hens are: they sit down on the ground; their feathers are rough just across the rump, *i.e.*, at the top of the back. When the hen is disturbed she holds her wings out, flutters, and falls over. She appears to have no use of her legs and feet. She is still very red in comb, is bright in the eye, and also eats well.

They are very subject to cramp in the winter and spring

months, and these are usually the best layers. They use up carbon too fast, and the blood gets chilled, and does not circulate in their legs properly. Their legs are quite cold, and the hens lose all the use of them, and cannot stand upon their feet. This so very often happens to good layers; it causes them to lay soft eggs. If the hens are not noticed when they are in this state, and taken from the male bird, they often lose their lives. They should be taken from the other fowls, and their legs held in hot or warm water, just so that the finger can stand it, with a little mustard in. It is well to rub the legs with a nail brush. When taken out of the water they should be rubbed quite dry; then a little turpentine rubbed in, and a little vaseline applied after. This keeps the skin from drying and cracking. Then wrap the legs round with cotton wool or flannel, put on warm. Then place the bird in a basket quite out of all draughts, in a moderately warm place if possible. This usually cures them the first dressing; if not, repeat the same.

They should be kept on moss peat, or straw, and then there is a warmth arises to their legs, and the blood circulates freely again.

EGG-EATING.

Some hens are addicted to egg-eating, and as they clear away all traces of the eggs so neatly it is difficult to find them out, and if not found out and stopped at once the other hens soon learn the bad habit. If there is a suspicion of any eggs being eaten, an egg should be laid in the run and the fowls carefully watched. If some of them turn the egg over, but do not eat it, it proves they are not egg-eaters, but if any of them do commence eating it the egg should be at once taken away, and after removing the white a quantity of mustard and ammonia or some other hot substance should be mixed with the yolk and replaced in the run. In most cases the taste of the mustard, &c., proves a cure at once, but it may be necessary to repeat the operation with another egg treated in the same way. If this proves ineffectual the egg-eater should be killed at once; if not she teaches the others. Egg-eating is generally caused by soft-shelled eggs being broken, or eggs dropped from the roost and broken. The birds all rush to them at once and clear them up. Peat moss is a good preventive as it is soft to catch the eggs should the hens drop them from the roost. Another cause is the want of materials for shell-making, and if the birds are to be cured they must, of course, be supplied with these necessities, such as oyster, shells and bone-meal. I do not have one egg eaten in two years. If egg-shells are given they must be broken up very fine, or this will teach them egg-eating.

Egg-eating is a very serious matter. I have known people sell their hens because they said they did not lay whilst almost every hen was laying at the same time, but the birds ate them all. I have had several gentlemen complain to me this last year, saying their fowls did not lay. I asked them to watch the birds, and in every case they were in full lay, but ate all their eggs. At one place they ate about 15 a day, and yet the trace of an egg was never to be seen. If there is only one hen which eats the eggs it is best to kill her at once.

EGG-BOUND.

This a not a complaint, but rather a misfortune, to which pullets and young hens are more susceptible than old ones. The cause of these accidents is that the egg-passage is too small to admit the egg passing through: Symptoms :—The fowl is often on the nest, and in walking the tail will touch the ground, while the head and breast are reared straight up. If they are not extra valuable and quite young, it is best to kill at once, as they are then in excellent condition for eating.

The best remedy is to dip a feather in castor oil and pass it up the egg-passage, and this generally causes the egg to be laid; care must be taken so as not to break the egg inside the fowl, as when this happens it is generally fatal. Sometimes the egg breaks of its own accord, and the skin remains in the fowl. This should be attended to at once; if not, it causes her to rupture herself by continually straining, and the egg-passage comes right out. If the fowl is seen at once, and attended to, she may be saved. The passage should be rubbed with a little castor oil, and then gently put back again. The hen should be held head downwards, then the egg-passage will fall into its proper place. The hen should then be wrapped in a bag or thin canvas, so that she can easily breathe through it. She should be laid with her head about six inches lower than her tail. If the hen lies in this position for about six or eight hours the egg-passage will fall back into its proper place, but if she is allowed to stand upon her legs it causes her to strain herself, and the passage falls out again.

The eggs hang round in a cluster, something like a bunch of grapes, and at times they get out of place, and so press very hard one against the other, thus causing deformed eggs. This is more especially the case with Cochins, the reason, I think, being that they are generally very fat about the egg-passages, and so have less room for the eggs to pass.

Fowls, after being egg-bound, should only have a little soft food for several days. If they are not attended to at once, inflammation takes place, and the hen suffers very much pain. When this is the case the birds should be killed at once.

CROP-BOUND.

This is a common complaint, generally caused by careless or over-feeding, and sometimes for want of sharp grit. It generally occurs when the birds are in full lay, but if treated at once, it seldom stops there. The first symptoms noticed are that the fowl mopes about, often taking up the food and laying it down again, and drinking a great quantity of water. The crop turns hard, and the passage from it to the gizzard gets stopped. The best thing is to give the fowl two teaspoonfuls of castor oil and a little warm water, and some time after to gently rub the crop with the thumb and finger, so as to remove every particle of its contents. If the crop is not softer in three or four hours, the dose of warm water should be repeated, rubbing the crop as before; and if, in another four hours, the crop is still hard, the warm water, oil, and rubbing should again be repeated, and if ineffectual, the only remedy left will be to open the crop and remove the hard contents.

The best way to do this is to get some one to hold the fowl on its back, and then to part the feathers down the centre of the crop, taking care not to pull any out if it can be helped, as they keep the cold from the wound. The incision should be made at the top of the crop with some sharp instrument or small penknife, taking care not to cut any of the large blood-vessels in the outer skin. The hole should be about an inch long, or just long enough to remove the contents of the crop with the end of a teaspoon. The crop should then be washed out with a little warm water, and a little neatsfoot or castor oil put round the inside with a feather. It should then be carefully sewn up with silk or horsehair, each skin being sewn up separately. A little alum and water applied hardens it very much. Wipe the wound as dry as possible, and then put a little lard on it.

The fowl must not be exposed to the cold for several days, and no water must be given for thirty hours, or it will find its way through the stitches and wet the hen's feathers, and cause her to take cold, especially if in cold weather. The diet should consist of soft food given warm, and in two or three days the fowl will be quite recovered. Care should be taken in removing the contents of the crop, as sometimes there are pieces of glass, bone, or cinder inside. Very often, when fowls are crop-bound, they drink such an enormous quantity of water that the crop becomes full and remains so, hanging down like a bladder. When this occurs, the best remedy is to hold the fowl's head downwards, and press the crop so as to force all the water out, if not the crop will fall. The under skin gives way and lets the crop down, and when the hen walks it is in her way of stepping. This is what is termed a ruptured crop. Alum and water is the best outward application. Bathe it twice a day. If this is done in time it can usually be cured. When the crop is empty, give the bird three-quarters of a teaspoonful of castor oil and feed sparingly on soft food only for a day or two, giving no water during this period.

SOFT EGGS.

Poultry-keepers are often troubled with fowls laying soft eggs. There are several causes. It may be for want of shell-making material, but not this in all cases. Sometimes when hens have been laying a large number of eggs, they make eggs faster than nature can shell them. I have had fowls lay one perfect and one shell-less egg in twelve hours. I have frequently had them lay one shell-less egg in the night and a perfect one early the next morning. This is not an exception, but often occurs where good layers are kept. I have had as many as six soft eggs from thirty fowls in one night, some years since, so that I was obliged to put straw underneath the perches to catch the eggs. I thought it was impossible for a fowl to lay two perfect eggs in 24 hours, or rather to shell them in that time; but I have proved it is not, having had them do it—pullets under eight months old. Fowls are not always out of order when they lay shell-less eggs, as many think they are; that is, if they are supplied with everything necessary to form the shell and to keep the egg organs in a healthy state. A fowl often lays double-yolked eggs. This weakens the egg organs, and often causes soft eggs to be laid. When fowls are over-fed and become very fat internally, they often lay soft eggs; also when they have been laying a long time without a rest their egg organs naturally get weak, especially if they lay large eggs. Their oviduct, or egg-passage, is wonderfully constructed. It is attached to the ovary (this is where the eggs first form). They hang much the same as a bunch of grapes, and can be seen by a microscope when not larger than the point of a pin. They are so constructed that the largest ones are at the bottom of the ovary, or rather they are encased in a skin, and as they grow they lower themselves into the top of the oviduct. After the egg is severed from the ovary it has to pass through the oviduct or egg-passage, which is from 12 to 19 inches long. I have found it 7 inches longer in some fowls than in others. In some it has been known to measure 23 inches long. It is while the egg is passing through this pipe, or passage, it is shelled. The egg-passage does not lie in one straight line, but is constructed much the same as the entrails of a fowl are, rather more of a S or pothook shape. If an egg is examined in a fowl before it leaves the ovary there will be found some small blood veins upon it. These pass from the egg before it passes into the oviduct. Should a hen be startled or very much frightened, or over-reach herself, the little blood-vessels become ruptured. This is the cause of small, dark spots being found in a new-laid egg; they are usually found at the large end of the egg, not in the yolk, but at the top of it, just between the yolk and white. Sometimes it is caused by the male birds being too heavy. When these spots are found in a boiled egg people think they are not new laid, and that they have been sat on. In some cases they are as large as a pea. After a hen has been very frightened, sometimes a shell-less egg breaks in the egg-passage. When this is the case the fowl may be seen standing very erect with her tail down and head up. The feathers are usually wet behind, while the other part of her plumage looks very rough. If not attended to, fowls often die when this occurs. They are usually found dead on the nest, and the cause of death is frequently put down as egg-bound, when it is really the skin of the soft egg left in the egg passage. This irritates the fowl and causes her to strain, as she cannot pass it. This causes a rupture of the egg-organs, and often of the body, too, and is often the cause of the laying-hen being so large and down behind. When any of these symptoms appear, the hen should be caught and examined. The skin of the egg can usually be found just inside the egg passage, occasionally it is already protruding; if so, it can easily be withdrawn by gently pulling it when the hen endeavours to pass it. It must be done very steadily, if not, it will break inside. When it is broken inside it can be withdrawn by tweezers; a small piece of linen rag should be tied on the end of the tweezers and a little oil put on the rag. When this is done, it is not so likely to break the skin or hurt the fowl. If this precaution is not taken, inflammation follows. This is partly caused by the hen straining herself. She should have a teaspoonful of castor-oil and a little warm water given her, also a little soft food (not much), so that she does not lay any more eggs until the oviduct is strong again. If so, it causes irritation, and the fowl becomes very ill. Ground oyster shells are excellent things for laying-hens, as they answer two purposes, viz., supplying material for making the shell, and helping them to digest their food. Old mortar and cinder-ashes are useful for them to pick up. When all these remedies fail, bone-meal puts them right. I find nothing to equal this. In the spring and summer I use it with a little ground oyster shell mixed in the soft food every day, in the autumn and winter three or four times a week. One single handful is sufficient for twelve fowls. Since I have used this meal I scarcely ever see a soft egg with all my fowls, and rarely have any ruptured birds—not more than three out of 400. A very small quantity will keep the egg organs in good order. If only given them three times a week it helps them very much. Some people give laying hens lime water. I always find if it is something to help them digest their food it is better for them.

COMB DISEASE.

This disease is rather a peculiar one, or perhaps I ought to say it comes in various forms and from various causes, and is very troublesome when it attacks the fowls. I cannot say what it arises from in the first place, whether it is a chill of the blood or overheat. When a fowl is killed and the disease is well developed, the blood is almost black, but at the same time the cause cannot always be traced, as in some cases when the fowls have diphtheric roup very badly the comb disease comes on. Of course this is when the blood is very much out of order, and at other times when fowls are to all appearance in good health. I have known them lay when they have been almost blind with the comb disease. In many cases it does not affect the fowls' appetites if taken in time. If the fowls have a touch of liver disease death is almost certain, but if free from this they can be cured and the disease stamped out. The symptoms do not always show themselves in the same form, but in most cases it appears in little white spots on the comb, sometimes on the eye and wattles, and in a few cases on the neck, but the latter is very rare. It should be attended to at once, as it is very contagious. The affected birds should be removed quite away from the others. As these white spots develop they become much the same as warts in appearance, and as they get worse they come like a fungus and spread rapidly if not checked. When they appear round the eyes they entirely close them in about three days. I have tried many things for this disease. As an outward application I have found nothing better than Jeyes' Disinfectant. It is a liquid. (Refer to advertisement at end of this book.) I have found it a certain cure if the fowl has no other disease. A feather should be stripped within half an inch of the end, so that it does not hold too much, and just touch each place, so that the liquid does not run down too far, as it is very strong. Should it run on the fowl's face or comb where there are no spots it should be wiped off with a piece of linen rag. Each spot should be touched with oil; either sweet or salad oil will do. Each bird should have not less than half a teaspoonful of Roup Powder in one day; in bad cases three parts of a teaspoonful is not too much, especially if the affected bird is a cock. It is well to mix the powders with a little flour and oatmeal, not less than half a tablespoonful of each. If the patient is very ill, and cannot eat, a double quantity of meal may be used, as food they must have. Give the fowls one teaspoonful of castor oil each for the first two or three days. When the fowls are taken ill it is advisable to dress them twice a day, and also give the pills above-mentioned. After they reach the turn once a day is sufficient. If the above remedies which I have mentioned are given, the spots will come off like scales, quite clear, so that the comb and face get quite well again, and nothing can be traced. If neglected it is almost certain death, and will become a fearful epidemic, as it is so contagious. If fowls have anything the matter with their livers, followed by this complaint, they fall victims to it. In such cases some may think it is scrofula breaking out outside the skin. I have heard this remark, but do not think it is so. Where there are many fowls kept it is best and safest to kill the birds which are affected with it at once, in case of it breaking out in other pens, or take the birds quite away. It is well to purify each bird in the house in which the disease broke out. The best way of doing this is to add one teaspoonful of Jeyes' Disinfectant to one pint of water, and sprinkle in the feathers; or a better way is to rub part in with the hand, and sprinkle the other about the fowlhouse. Give the unaffected fowl some Roup Powder. Proportion: One teaspoonful to six hens. When treated in this way it seldom spreads any further, if taken in time, and a preventive is better than a cure. I cannot say how long this disease has been in our country, but it did not come under my notice until the past two years. It has broken out in many parts of the country, and many fowls have been lost through it, although it is comparatively little known. It is well for all poultry-keepers to acquaint themselves with the symptoms of diseases, and then if any disease appears in their poultry they know how to treat. If they keep clear so much the better. I have known £50 worth of fowls die of this disease for the simple reason that their owners did not know how to treat it.

FEATHER-EATING.

This habit is very common with fowls that are confined in small runs, and if not checked early becomes very serious. I have seen fowls quite naked about the neck, breast, and back, and in the summer they will peck each other until the blood runs. I cannot always account for feather-eating, but neglected fowls are most subject to it. A good supply of green food and oyster-shells, and a little corn scattered in the runs with soil sprinkled over it, are excellent modes of giving the fowls exercise and keeping them employed. Of course this is a good thing, but it does not always stop them from feather-plucking. I have never known so many feather-pluckers as there are in this year (1885); even on farms they do it. I had not had a single feather-plucker in my yards until this spring, when I had two. I killed them as soon as I detected which they were. The best way of finding them out is to stand some distance away, out of their sight, when the sun is shining, and the fowls are cleaning themselves; then the feather-plucker does her work. They generally commence in the spring on the feathers about the head, and this is caused by their pecking at the nits from vermin, which are generally found round the head and upper part of the neck. The fowls persist in pecking at the nits until the feathers come out, when they at once swallow them and repeat the operation. In a few days the quills begin to grow, and the feather-pickers observing the quills with the moisture in them, which consists principally of glutinous matter, peck them out also, and therefore keep the fowls quite bare if left with them. The first thing to be done towards effecting a cure is to remove the feather-pluckers at once, and place them in a coop by themselves for a fortnight, and, as a rule, this will stop them. If, however, they persist in feather-plucking after they come out, they should be put with a hen that has had the feathers on her neck cut short and covered with mustard mixed stiff with vinegar, or other hot substance. The taste of mustard will cure all but the most inveterate feather-pluckers, and if it fails the best thing is to kill them at once. Steps should, of course, be taken to rid the other hens of the nits on their feathers, as described in the paragraph on vermin. I have prepared powders especially for poultry and all dumb animals, to destroy all insects, and at the same time harmless to the fowl or animal it is put on. If a small piece is cut off the end of the top beak and the sharp edges of the sides of the same and the edges of the bottom beak also, they cannot pluck the feathers, as when they go to pick them they slip through their mouths. This is a certain cure. It does not prevent them from eating their corn. If any one will bring a hen to my office I shall be pleased to cut the beak and show them. Care should be taken not to cut too deep, and then it does not hurt the bird in any way.

CONSUMPTION.

There may often be noticed two or three chickens moping about with long beaks and pale faces, while the wings appear too long, often drooping to the ground, and the chickens are sometimes too weak to walk. Dorkings and Hamburghs when bred-in too much are very liable to this disease, and when other birds are affected it is often for want of fresh blood in the poultry yard. If taken in time the chickens may recover, but as they are seldom of much good, and take up the room of healthy birds, it is the wisest plan to kill them at once, as it saves much time and trouble. Cod-liver oil, sulphate of iron in the water, and other strengthening tonics, are the best things to use for those desiring to try and effect a cure.

Roup Powder will be found very efficacious in this complaint.

DIARRHŒA.

The cause of diarrhœa cannot always be traced, as it arises from various causes. Sometimes it is debility; at others it is a thunderstorm. Very stale meat will bring it on, or corn or meal that have been lying by for a long time, and the mites have taken their share out of it. Corn that is full of small holes should not be given to poultry; if it is, other good corn should be mixed with it, as what are commonly called mites have made these holes, and taken most of the nutriment out of the corn. If fowls are short of sharp grit, the liver does not act properly, and this brings on diarrhœa. The excrements are of a yellowish colour when this is the case. If fowls are fed irregularly (*i.e.*, half starved one day, and the next a quantity of food allowed to lie by them), and also kept short of water, they become very thirsty, and when they have the opportunity they drink a large quantity of water. This brings not only diarrhœa, but also ruptures their crops. Too much soaked bread given to young chickens will bring it on. They should have a little meal mixed with it. This will prevent diarrhœa. If this complaint is not stopped, or rather something given to the birds to relieve it, they become very thirsty, and lose their appetite, and their plumage looks rough, and at the same time they move about very stiffly as though hurt in some way. Broody hens are very subject to this complaint, as they usually drink too much water, and do not have sufficient grit to digest their food. The hen leaves her nest, and in many cases dies. This is not only the loss of the hen, but also the eggs, and disappointment of losing the prospect of chickens for the want of knowing how to treat her. Very hot weather will bring diarrhœa on in chickens. When this is the case, they ought not to have water, but the food must be nice and moist, and the corn boiled occasionally. When a hen has the diarrhœa she ought to have a teaspoonful of castor oil given her. A cock should have one teaspoonful and a half (chickens in proportion to their size). Also give one heaped-up teaspoonful of powdered chalk, and half ditto of ground ginger. In addition to this I give a quarter of a teaspoonful of Roup Powder a few hours after to each bird. I have not known this remedy fail yet. It is very seldom it has to be repeated, unless the fowls are very much out of order. If a fowl will eat, the ginger, &c., can be mixed in the soft food; if not, it must be made into pills with a little baked flour; not oatmeal. Sometimes if a fowl is neglected dysentery sets in. In this case use about five drops of chlorodyne for a hen and seven for a cock. It is best given on a piece of loaf sugar; sometimes it requires two pieces. A teaspoonful of water should be given after; not quite cold, just tepid. When fowls have had diarrhœa, it usually leaves them in rather a weak state. They should not only have a tonic, but also a stimulant. The Roup Powder will be found one of the best things to get the fowls' strength up again. It brings them along quickly, and they are usually in full lay in a week or two. For a day or two the patient should not have much corn, but chiefly soft food. A little corn should be given, as that does not pass through them quite so quickly, and it helps to stay the other food. I have not found the chalk and ginger fail for young chickens. A brood of ten from a fortnight to three weeks old can have about the same quantity as prescribed for a hen. It can be given according to age. If they have a little overdose, it will not hurt them.

DROPSY IN THE ABDOMEN.

This disease is not often found in the poultry yard, not one out of every hundred that is kept. The symptoms are, the fowl stands about very much by herself, and does not care about eating soft food; is very inactive, and large behind. In bad cases they are very large, and sometimes a little lame. The comb does not usually lose its redness; they look very much like a fowl which is ruptured. The abdomen is very soft when examined, and the bird is usually rather heavy. When they are in this state they should be tapped. This can be done by making an incision about an inch and a-half or two inches from the passage, that is, the underneath part of the abdomen. A small incision should be made with a lance or sharp pen-knife. The first skin should be cut through carefully, and the second skin looks very much like a bladder, that is, with the water pressing against it. After this skin is cut through the water will spirt. I tapped a hen this summer of 1885, and took over a pint and a-half of water from her. She soon recommenced laying, and is now quite healthy; the water did not accumulate again. (The water I took out of her can be seen at my London office.) The hen should be held for a few minutes for the water to drain out; then let her stand upon her legs, and hold her by her wings, and in the struggle to liberate herself she forces the water from her inside. The feathers should be wiped as dry as possible, and a little oil put on the incision. Then it should be sewn up with a fine needle and silk.

There may be a few drops of water drain out after it is sewn up, but it will soon cease. Two or three teaspoonfuls of cold water should be poured down the hen's throat, and a Roup Pill should be given. This acts as a stimulant to the bird. Put it in a basket or coop for two or three days: longer if in cold weather. If free from liver disease, the bird will be quite right in a few days. A fowl that suffers with liver disease is very subject to dropsy. If the bird is only a common one it is not worth the trouble.

The affected bird can be brought to me. I will do it, and show the owner how to perform the operation; or any other case of the kind should an operation be necessary.

INFLAMMATION OF THE LUNGS.

This is a complaint fowls are subject to more or less, though fowls may be kept for twenty years, and yet not one may fail with it. At the same time, there are many fowls die with it. I have tried many remedies for this complaint, and have found warm stewed linseed one of the finest remedies. Give a few spoonfuls as warm as the fowls can take it, and keep the affected bird in a warm room. One teaspoonful of glycerine should be given them once a day. I have been trying an outward application for this, and also when there is a little cold on the lungs, and have found it answer well—a little mustard and vinegar mixed thin, rubbed on under the wing well up against the base of the wing, about an inch from the joint It is usually bare, as it is very seldom feathers grow there, being just over the lungs. Tincture of arnica can be used in the same way. The symptoms are—the breathing is very bad, and at the same time the mouth is usually open, and they appear to be in great pain, and usually drink a quantity of water if not very bad. If not relieved they frequently close the eyes. It is not always inflammation, but a cold, and the bronchial tubes are a little stuffed with fluid I have found them full of coal-dust and soot when I have made a post-mortem examination, especially fowls which have been bred in a town. I have mentioned the remedies which may be used, whether it is inflammation or a cold. Fowls after having recovered from this complaint should be taken care of, and not be allowed to run out into the cold air.

Fowls which are handled frequently open their mouths and breathe hard. This is from fright. They should always be handled as gently as possible, both the old and the young ones. When they are being treated as I have described, they should be fed on soft food.

VERMIN.

When vermin prevail fowls never thrive, and I have referred to this subject several times, as it is most important that poultry should be kept quite free from them. When the chickens do not thrive without any apparent cause, the best way is to examine them for signs of vermin about the head and neck, as it is on these parts that the nits or eggs mostly appear. If any should be found, oil and turpentine mixed together are the best remedies, and these should be rubbed well into the feathers round the head and neck. This destroys the nits. The Insect Powder is a safe remedy for destroying these pests. It can be used on chickens of all ages, and is a certain cure. It does not injure the fowls as many other things do, such as lime, snuff, &c. These are apt to blind the birds.

The fowl should also be laid on its back, and the whole of the body, and especially the under part of the wings, should be thoroughly dusted with the powder, all the feathers and skin being entirely covered. The fowls should then have plenty of clean ashes to thoroughly clean themselves.

When fowls have a plentiful supply of ashes or dust to clean themselves in, they are rarely troubled with vermin, especially if a little sulphur or common lime be added to the ashes occasionally.

It is when hens are sitting they usually breed these. Dust them well with the powder.

DUCKS.

DUCKS are often kept, and as they are frequently mismanaged, loss is the result instead of profit, but if looked after properly they are very profitable and pay well when reared for killing, as they are little trouble and grow very fast. The Aylesbury breeders, who consist not only of farmers but also of cottagers, are the most noted rearers of ducks in this country, and many tons weight are sent to the London markets.

It is more natural for ducks to have a pond in the breeding season, and the eggs can be better depended upon for sitting; but there are many who are very successful although their ducks have no water.

Ducks are good sitters but bad mothers, as they leave their nests before all the eggs are hatched, taking the ducklings that can walk to the nearest pond they can find, the result being those left in the nest perish, while the others get the cramp. It is, therefore, better to let a hen hatch ducks, as they require a mother for a very short period, and one hen will take charge of twenty to forty ducklings at a time. Ducks' eggs cannot always be depended upon, and should therefore be examined when they have been sat on for eight days, and those clear removed. A very good plan, when chickens are kept, is to substitute hens' eggs for those taken away, and as ducks' eggs take twenty-eight days to hatch, another hen set on hens' eggs at the time the unfertile eggs are removed will hatch the same date, and can therefore take all the chickens, leaving the first hen set to take charge of the ducks alone.

The best varieties to keep for domestic purposes are the Aylesbury, Rouen, and Pekin.

Duck-keeping is very profitable when carried on by those who understand it. Much more might be done and still pay well, leaving aside the market question. If families would rear them for their own consumption it would pay them, as they are so hardy and but little trouble to rear, much less to fatten. There are but few who dislike roast duck, and but few who are able to have it unless it is a foreign duck purchased in the market at from 1s. 6d. to 2s. 6d. These are very tough, and not to be compared with home-fed ducks. I think that in a few years duck-keeping will become a more general thing. *It ought to.* If cottagers were to rear them for their own consumption it would pay them; but a better way is to sell a few to pay for their food, and the remainder is the profit. Ducks ought to be food for thousands, whereas they are only for hundreds now, as duck-food is cheap. They are ready for the table very quickly; the largest are ready at eight weeks old. If more than one brood is reared it should be at different periods; if not, they all come in together. If ducks are not killed when from nine to eleven weeks old they lose weight in their duckling moult. It is not every one who can keep stock ducks for laying; this is quite another branch. There are many who would keep them if they could dispose of the eggs. There are those who live outside towns or in farm-houses who have water; these can keep stock ducks. In fact there are many who do, but have to sell their eggs for a penny each for eating purposes. This is what I call a waste of good food. Stock ducks can be kept without a pond of water, but the eggs from them do not hatch so well as when they have water. A tub or a zinc bath will answer this purpose if there is no pond. The bath or tub can stand in the run with a plank put on the top of it. The length of the same must be according to the height of tub or bath, and just laid so that the ducks can walk up it. Then a small piece of board should be nailed on to the end of the plank, and small laths across it; this should go from three to six inches into the water, so that the ducks can go down into the water and get out of it without slipping. I do not recommend ducks to be kept in a run with the fowls, as a rule, but if they are, the ducks' water should be put in this way and the fowls' water upon something, so that the ducks cannot reach it. It should be put eighteen or twenty inches from the ground, and one or two perches put for the fowls to stand on to drink. One perch can be six or nine inches from the ground and the other about sixteen. The water should be first put on something so that the fowls can reach it from the ground, and raised a few inches each day until it is in its proper place. If it is done in this way there will be but little difficulty in the fowls drinking, and, at the same time, the ducks cannot reach it, as they will not get on the perches. There may be one or two of the fowls drink out of the ducks' water, but this is very seldom. If it is a zinc bath that is used for the ducks, there should be a round hole cut in the side of it near to the bottom. It can be either the end or the sides. The hole should be well soldered round to make it strong, and a round wooden plug should be cut not less than from four to six inches long, so that there is a good handle to pull it out by when required. The end of the plug should have a piece of strong linen or fine flannel round it; this prevents any water from running out, and can be easily withdrawn when required. When it is constructed in this way the stale water can easily be emptied out.

A small house from 3 to 4 feet square is quite large enough for a drake and four ducks.

Ducks differ very much in laying. Some have been known to lay 150 eggs each per annum, and others not more than 25 in the same time; but 80 eggs each per annum is a very fair average, though many of them will lay more.

Drakes can be distinguished from the ducks by one or two curly feathers in their tails. These appear when about fourteen or sixteen weeks old. If noticed when quite young, they can be distinguished from each other as soon as they lose their squeaking duckling noise. The young ducks will have a clear and a loud voice and the young drakes a very faint noise—a kind of scraping—quite distinct from the ducks. It is well to notice this when only ducks are required to be saved for stock purposes, so that the young drakes can be killed off early. I find young ducks thrive much better and grow much faster if they do not have water to run in. Those I breed for killing I do not allow to go into the water at all. There are many people who would rear young ducks but think they cannot because they have no pond of water. However, this is quite a mistake.

HATCHING AND REARING DUCKS.

Duck eggs take twenty-eight days to hatch, but if the hen or duck does not sit close the first two days of incubation, they often go over twenty-nine days. If they are set very fresh, especially after just having been laid, before they are cold quite through, they will frequently hatch at twenty-six-and-a-half or twenty-seven days. There are often a few weak ones, which are much later than the others in coming out, sometimes twelve hours after the first. In some cases it is necessary to assist them, especially if the shell has been cracked for some time and does not get any more forward. The beak of the duckling usually lies near the large end of the egg; sometimes it is quite at the end. If it is just in the centre of the egg the duckling frequently gets suffocated. This can be partly remedied by freshly lining the nest two or three days before the period expires for them to hatch. A little fine sweet hay I find the best. The eggs should all be removed out of the nest and the hay well beaten down tight, so that it does not prevent the eggs from rolling when the hen or duck returns to her nest, or when they are turning their eggs. It is well to take part of the eggs out of the nest when the hen is returning to it, if time will permit, especially about three days before the time expires for them to hatch, as one or two of them frequently get broken. The ducklings should not be taken away until they are dry, unless a very warm place is provided for them. It is always advisable to take the first hatched away; if not, they are apt to get out of the nest and, consequently, disturb the hen.

I usually feed young ducklings on hard-boiled eggs chopped fine with a little biscuit meal or bread crumbs just made a little moist, and after they are from fifteen to twenty-four hours' old they will usually eat nicely, unless it is a few of the weak ones. Care must be bestowed upon them, as it is rather difficult to get them to eat, as they cannot be fed like young chickens (by the hand). I find it best for the weak ones to have a little flat tin or saucer. Put a little water in it and then sprinkle a little coarse oatmeal in it (small groats will answer the same purpose). Dip their little beaks in the water, and as soon as they can taste it they begin to drink, and as the oatmeal swims on the top they are obliged to swallow a little. In the cold weather I use warm milk in the same way. This past year I have given them a shallow vessel with a little water in it, and then sprinkled a few groats (the inside of oats) in it. This saves any waste, as not a particle can be wasted when done in this way. I have not given any water except thus, as the oatmeal sinks to the bottom, and sparrows, rats and mice are all deceived. A little fine middlings, with barley, buckwheat and maize meals may be used, and make very good food. In the cold weather it is well to give all the food as hot as they can eat it, as then they grow so much faster. A little boiled corn is excellent for them after they are a month old. Change their food from the mixture of meals mentioned to biscuit-meal, which should be scalded with boiling water and be given to the ducks quite warm. If the ducklings' soft food can be mixed with milk they grow much faster. I always give my ducklings as much as they can eat of the mentioned foods up to six weeks old, and the last twelve or fourteen days I use a little of my Fattening Powder. Rough fat or any kind of meat is very beneficial mixed in the soft food, if it can be procured reasonably. It should in all cases be quite sweet. At farmhouses where there is plenty of skim milk and good warm outhouses, a good business could be carried on, as ducks are so much less rouble to bring up than chickens, requiring less attention and room.

If ducks are kept over nine or ten weeks old they usually lose weight after that age, as they shed out their feathers; this is called the ducklings' first moult.

White ducks should be bedded down on straw, as the moss-peat stains their plumage. Stock ducks after they have laid and are going through their moult, usually take a long rest. They should not be over-fed, and should have little or no maize, as if they do they become very fat internally, and this prevents them from laying as early as they otherwise would.

Where many ducks are kept it is well to use brewers' grains. Mix them with good middlings; if these are not good use a little barley-meal with them. In some districts small potatoes can be purchased cheap (farmers usually have some of their own). If these are boiled and mashed up when hot and mixed with middlings or meal of some kind, they make a cheap food, which is very good to bring the young ducks on. A little salt should be given in their food, especially when potatoes are used. Turnips, mangold wurtzel, or any kind of vegetable refuse can be boiled up in the same way. It not only makes a cheap food, but is much better for them than all meal and corn.

In the winter, when ducks' eggs are so valuable, great care should be taken in feeding and management, as they pay well for it. They should be put in a fairly warm house, well ventilated, and have warm water given them to drink in the morning, and their food as hot as they can eat it. If tripe, liver, or paunches are purchased and boiled and cut up they help very much. The water they are boiled in can be used for mixing the soft food for the morning meal. A little bone-meal and Laying Powder should be mixed in it. Meat should be given at midday, and corn in the evening. Ducks can be fed after it is dark in the winter months when eggs are required. It is well to feed them about seven o'clock at night. If the corn is boiled and given to them as warm as they can eat it, say three or four times a week, it helps them very much. The best grains for ducks are good oats, nothing less than 40 lbs. to the bushel, and 42 lbs. or 44 lbs. if they can be obtained, and good wheat, about 60 lbs. to the bushel. Barley and French buckwheat may also be used, making a change. Maize should not be given until they lay, then a little will not hurt them. Boiled rice is also good for a change, and is cheap. Where there is not plenty of sharp grit, it is well to put a little ground oyster shells in a small drinking vessel for the laying ducks. When offal meat cannot be obtained, granulated meat or greaves can be used. It can be scalded with boiling water and then mixed with the other meat. Some boil it, but this is unnecessary. It is well to give them a little green food.

If ducks are treated as I have described they will lay all through the winter months.

AYLESBURY.

This breed is celebrated for table purposes; in fact they are the best that can be kept for that purpose, especially if required for the London markets, as there they command a better price than any other breed. They thrive much better at Aylesbury than any other place in England; whether it is their practical management or not I cannot say, for indeed Aylesbury ducks are bred nearly all over the world, and yet those which are bred at Aylesbury are usually first in all the leading show pens wherever they are shown. They also command the longest price in the London markets. The old saying is they will not thrive unless they have the Aylesbury sand or grit; in other words, they will not thrive so well anywhere as at their original place. This I have proved to be only a saying as regards ducks for the table, but in respect of breeding them for the show pen they still remain unrivalled as regards my own experience, although I intend to test them thoroughly. They grow quickly where they have good attention. I have had them weigh over six pounds before they were nine weeks old. Of course these were the largest. Aylesbury breeders are what I call wise people, as they usually keep the largest ducks they breed for their own stock purposes, which of course pays them in the end. Some of them are remarkably fine, larger than any I have before seen. A pure Aylesbury duck cannot always be distinguished from a cross-bred one. When an Aylesbury drake is allowed to run with either Pekin, Rouen, or Cayuga ducks there will be a few come exactly the same as the pure breed to outward appearance, and are sold as the pure; but when bred from the fraud is discovered, as the offspring come coloured. If bred from the Rouen cross they throw brown feathers, if from the Cayuga cross black feathers, and if they have Pekin blood in them they usually show it in their beak, which will come yellow. This the pure Aylesbury should be free from. There are some breeders use a little Pekin blood so that the progeny may look larger, as their feathers do not lie close, and consequently make the ducks appear much larger than they really are. The description of a pure Aylesbury duck is: Plumage quite white, and free from a yellow tint; bodies long, they should not be erect; their backs should be straight; beaks large, and of a pale tint, what is usually termed a flesh colour, quite free from yellow; the legs should be a pale yellow. If well bred they are very large. It is only a few attain the size of those seen in the show pens. I may here mention why this is. It pays to breed Aylesbury ducks much better than most other prize stock, as those that are required for the show pen must be hatched early, and these fetch the longest price in the markets; hence the large breeders hatch out hundreds, and only the very largest are selected for stock. They are fed well and taken great care of. In some cases persons have as many as from 50 to 100 reserved. Then they select the best for exhibition. There is another advantage the Aylesbury breeders have. They go round to farmers and cottagers and pick the very best out of thousands that are bred, perhaps one out of a flock of from two to three hundred. These large breeders give from £1 to 30s. each for them. Mr. Weston has some very fine ducks, and is one of the most practical men on ducks I have met with. Mr. Fowler's name has stood very high on the list of Aylesbury breeders for many years. I think I am right in saying he has exported more Aylesburies than all England put together. He has a very fine stock this year. Ducks are hatched out all through the winter, spring, and summer in Aylesbury. They only appear to be without eggs, that is the larger breeders about two months in the year, which is from the middle of August to the middle of October. Ducks differ very much in laying, and cannot be depended on like hens. Some years they will lay double the number they will another—the same strains and often the same ducks. Sometimes they will commence to lay when from five to six months old, and at other times not before nine or even ten months old. Where ducks have the advantage of water they should not be let out too early in the morning, especially when they first commence to lay; if so, they will save their eggs and lay them in the water, and when once they have acquired the habit of so doing they will hold their eggs for 24 hours, and then when they are let out they will lay two eggs in the course of two hours. If there is a grass field for them to run over to catch the worms, and they are let out before it is well daylight, they often get half their food in the early spring months if they have a good range. This, of course, applies to all ducks. If there is a pond it is well to run a piece of wire netting round it, so that they cannot get into the water before a certain time in the day; this is when they do not lay before they go out. Ducks usually lay early in the morning, from two to six o'clock. It is a very bad practice to leave them out in the water all night as many farmers do. Ducks usually lay every day until the whole batch is laid, and then take a rest. They have been known to lay over 50 days in succession. They will frequently lay 20 and 30 days without intermission. They should have a good supply of grit and shell-forming materials while they are in full lay, if not the egg shells will be very thin, and many will break during the period of incubation if under hens or ducks. The Aylesbury sand contains all that is required for making the shell and digesting the food at the same time, that is if it is of the right sort. I have not analysed it, but can see it contains a great deal of lime. There are also small pieces of shell in it, and little pieces of bone, much the same as the backbones of fish. I have not met with anything like it with the exception of one place, which is Chislehurst, in Kent, and this in most places is 10 feet below the surface of the ground. It is well to use a little of it in their soft food; the large pieces should be picked out previously. The Aylesbury people usually put it in their water, that is where they are deficient of it. Duck eggs are very dear at Aylesbury in December and January. In these two months they do not study whether they are from good bred ducks or not so long as they are from large ducks. They give 12s. a sitting for rearing them for the London markets, as ducklings fetch a long price from the middle of February to the end of April. When it has been a sharp winter they have realised from 18s. to 26s. a pair. Of course this price is only given for the best and the first in the market. This price is handed to the breeders, after the salesman has taken his commission. In 1881 the best realised the highest price mentioned (for the pair), and the small ones 18s. per pair. They are usually sold when from seven-and-a-half to nine weeks old. In the winter months there are many ducklings hatched and brought up entirely indoors. Some have much better accommodation than others—such as small barns and stables. Doubtless some of them were built for the purpose. Most of them are thatched, to secure warmth in the winter and coolness in the summer. They have windows and good ventilation to give when it is needed. They will keep from thirty to forty in a place from 9 to 10 feet square. In the spring and summer they turn them out in the daytime in what the Aylesbury people call "day sheds," just for an airing. These little sheds or pens are made with boards from 12 to 18 inches high all round, with four or six posts, whichever is necessary, and a few pieces of rough wood laid on as a roof. In some cases they are nailed, and a little loose straw put on to keep the sun from the ducks. They do not let them stop out long as a rule, that is, according to the weather. Three-day sheds have to do sometimes for six or seven lots—let out alternately. Barley meal is the principal meal which they use for fattening purposes, with fat and granulated meat mixed with it. No doubt some have little secrets of their own which they do not reveal to the public. My way of rearing, feeding, and fattening will be found in the chapter on this subject.

PEKIN.

This breed is often taken for the Aylesbury ducks, because they are white in plumage. Their beaks and legs are different from the Aylesburies, as they are a bright orange colour ; the shape of their body is also quite different. They carry themselves much more erect, in very much the same position as geese. There is a yellowish hue on their plumage. It is sometimes spoken of as a yellowish cast.

Their feathers are also longer and do not lie so close, which gives them quite a different appearance to the Aylesbury. They look much larger than the latter breed, but in reality they are not. There are some excellent layers to be found amongst this breed.

As a rule they are the best layers of any breed; but at the same time there are some inferior layers to be found amongst them; but taking the average they are the best layers. If an amateur desires to start keeping a breed of ducks for the table, that is, requiring to breed from them again, and wants hardiness combined, have the pure Aylesbury, and then they can be crossed with either Pekin, Rouen, Muscovy, or Cayuga. The largest ducks I have bred were from a cross between Aylesbury ducks and a Muscovy drake. At eight weeks old, three young ones turned the scale at 18½ lbs., at ten weeks old the same three weighed 23½ lbs. They were not shut up one day; they were running about in an orchard and fed just the same as the fowls. They were hatched late in the season, viz., the 29th of August. That is the time of the year when many say young ducks do not thrive. This is one reason why I tried the experiment so late. I also have some this year hatched about the same time, and they are doing just as well as last year. They sleep out in the open and do not have an open shed to go in. I find all young ducks much hardier when crossed, although there is no difficulty in rearing the pure ducklings. Pekin and Aylesbury make a good cross both for laying and table purposes. All come white in plumage. When the Rouen is crossed with the Pekin or Aylesbury a few come all white, and one or two may come all brown. If the Cayuga is crossed with any other variety many of them come black, especially if a Cayuga drake is used. I do not recommend this cross, as they do not grow quite so fast as the other crosses, unless it is early in the season, as they fatten so quickly. One Pekin drake may run with four ducks, or, if they have a good pond of water, five are not too many.

ROUEN.

This breed are brown, and do not show the dirt when they have no water to wash themselves in. They can be kept in a town with advantage in this respect. They are very hardy. The colour of the plumage (in the duck) is brown, pencilled with a darker brown. The head and upper part of the wing are rather lighter, the centre of the wing being a dark green, edged with white. The drake has a dark green head, and about half the neck is the same colour. They ought to have a white ring round the neck, just at the bottom of the green. . The lower part of the neck is a reddish brown. The breast and lower part of the body is of a light drab, the back dark. Their beaks are dark. This breed thrive more in the North of England, or it may be they get better care. I do not like them for laying when in their pure state, as they are bad in this respect. I do not find they lay so well as the other mentioned breds do. When crossed with either the Pekin or Aylesbury they make good layers, and also good for table. This breed is a great favourite with some breeders. The drakes are very handsome.

MUSCOVY.

This breed is rather peculiar both in colour and formation. The drake is very much larger than the duck, weighing almost as heavy again. The colour of them is black and white, not variegated, but in large patches ot each colour. The head of the drake is very large, the side of the face is naked, and a scarlet fleshy space round the eye, and on the top of the beak is also a red fleshy substance; a part of the beak is dark. The drake is devoid of the curly feathers in the tail which most other drakes have. The male sex is rather spiteful to fowls and to the ducks if he does not take to them. These ducks will at times kill chickens.

The duck is the same colour as the drake, but not so bright in beak and face. The ducks are not such good layers as other breeds. I like the Muscovy drake to cross with Aylesbury ducks. I have bred these for two years and am very pleased with them, as they are a good weight at an early age, heavier than any other ducks I have kept. I saw one this summer which weighed 9½ lbs. at fifteen weeks old, which was not shut up to fatten but ran with the hens.

The flesh of the Muscovy when in their pure state is rather dark, and not the best of flavours, but when crossed with the Aylesbury they eat splendidly, with an excellent flavour, and the size is marvellous, as they look more like geese than ducks. There is one drawback with them: there is rather a large proportion of the eggs unfertile, but those which are fertile make up for the others, as they grow so quickly and attain such a large size.

CAYUGA.

This variety is little known in comparison with other breeds. Their plumage is black, some call it a dark green on account of the lustre on their plumage, which is very glossy, being of a dark green tint, more especially the drake. Both sexes are the same colour; the drake is a little larger. This breed are very fair layers of rather small eggs, as the ducks are rather small. They fatten quicker than any breed I have yet kept. They are of splendid flavour, although rather dark in flesh. They are often kept as a fancy duck. When crossed with the Rouen they attain a fair size, and look very nice; they grow fast, and are a good cross for table. Some of the cross come black and others much the same as the wild duck. They also fly similarly if kept a little away from the homestead.

FATTENING DUCKS.

THIS is a small item as regards trouble. If the ducks only have the food, and at the proper time, they are sure to get fat. The following is the best food : Barley-meal and sharps, with a little granulated meat or chopped greaves mixed with it. When they are five weeks old give a little sulphur and common salt, one teaspoonful of each, about four times a week to six or eight ducks. This helps them very much, and their feathers grow much faster. These are to be given when they are from five to seven weeks old. Give no sulphur a week or ten days before the ducklings are killed ; if so, their flesh will taste. It helps them very much to give a little rough fat and skim milk. If they do not get on well, a little of the fattening powders, given about six times the last twelve days, gives them a keen appetite, and helps them to put on fat. In cold weather they require keeping warm, and then they fatten much quicker.

HOW TO MAKE A DUCK POND.

THERE are many who have a good space at their command, and yet have no pond for a pen of breeding ducks, There are several ways of making a duck pond, but it depends very much on where it is to be made and for how many ducks, and also on the soil. I have known duck ponds which have been made that require repairing every time there is a sharp frost, which cracks the cement, letting the water through. This pond, though cheap in the first instance, is very expensive and also unpleasant. When it freezes sharp the earth swells, and in this way raises the cement up and causes it to crack. These cheap ponds are made by simply cutting the earth out basin-shape and then putting a layer of cement about an inch thick. This is not sufficient, and having them made in this way is only a waste of money.

I will describe the best way I know to make a duck pond (a substantial one). They can be made any size and depth. A pond about 6 feet by 4 feet is large enough for ten ducks, but if there is likely to be more it is best to make it larger. A pond of this size is large enough for two pens of ducks. If they are of two different breeds the pond should be divided in the centre by wire netting. When there is a pond ready for use now, it can be divided by wire netting, and several breeds kept. Of course, they must have separate runs.

Some people prefer a deep pond, but a shallow one is much better in one respect, viz., it can be drained out better, and it takes so much less water to fill it. About 1 ft. 6 in. or 2 ft. is as deep as ducks require.

Whatever size the pond is to be, it should be cut or made about six inches larger than intended to be. If it is to be 4 ft. wide and 6 ft. long, it should have the outsides a little on the slant, viz., the top should be cut 6 ft. 6 in. and the bottom 6 ft.; this is the measurement from end to end. The sides should be cut in the same way, 4 ft. 6 in. at the top and 4 ft. at the bottom, this to be measured from side to side. When made in this way it is a little on the slant, and the sides are not so liable to fall in in case any weight or pressure should be brought to bear upon them, such as a horse, or cow, or a cart wheel.

After the pond is cut in this way, the bottom should be concreted three or four inches thick. The concrete can be made with lime and gravel, or any kind of stones, only they should not be too large. It is well to break the largest, as then they bind so much better. Any kind of brick rubbish or hard clinkers will answer the same purpose. Cement, of course, can be used, but it is more expensive. It is rather more substantial, but the lime makes a very good pond. A little sand or road scrapings should be mixed with the lime, as this acts as a binder. If cement is used for the bottom, 2½ inches will be thick enough; if lime, 3½ inches. A pipe of some kind should be let into the bottom so that the water can easily be drained out when required. It is well to have an iron pipe laid in so that the bottom part of the pipe is one inch lower than the bottom of the pond. Have a good-sized pipe, either four or six inches, then it does not get blocked The water will all run out easily, together with all the sediment. It is well to brush and stir it up with a broom while it is running out. If the water has to run far, a clay pipe can be used; this is much cheaper. It should be a little on the slant, then the pipe keeps clean, as the force of the water clears it. The posts should be put in before the bottom concrete is laid. They do not require putting in deep, as there must be some cross-pieces to keep the sides firm when the concrete is put in. The boards should be placed three inches from the sides of the pond (according to the thickness intended for the walls), then the concrete should be put in all round. These boards form a mould. Let it lie a few days before the boards are taken down, then it will have set hard. When the boards are taken down and the posts drawn out, the holes should be filled up with cement or good concrete. After the boards are taken away the surface of the concrete is rough. It should not be left thus; if so, the stagnant dirt will cling to it, and then it cannot be cleansed. It is best to plaster it over with clear cement, thus giving it a clear and hard surface which will stand both water and frost, and can easily be cleaned.

The pond can be filled by means of a gutta-percha pipe fastened to a tap. A better way, of course, is to have the water laid on so as to have a tap to run into the pond. In some places there is no water laid on. In this case it is well to connect, so that the water from the outbuildings runs into the pond. Then it requires to be emptied occasionally. This cannot well be done by a tap, as the grit gets in and spoils it, so that it leaks, whether it is wood or brass. I find the best and easiest plan for this purpose is to have a piece of wood about a yard long, a little larger than the pipe quite round, sharpened a little at the end; then wrap a piece of strong linen or flannel round it. Just knock it in gently, so that it is firm. This usually acts splendidly, and is no trouble to repair, only to put another cloth round it occasionally.

As ducks require both sand and grit, it should not be put in the pond; if so, it will get washed away when the pond is cleaned out. A trough can be placed at the side of the pond, or it can be so constructed that the trough is in the pond, just underneath the surface of the water. This can be done by putting some iron rests into the concrete wall for the trough to rest on. When constructed in this way it is very convenient for the ducks, as corn can be put in as well as grit. In this way Aylesbury sand and grit can be given them.

If fowls are not allowed to run with the ducks, the pond may be made so that there is a sloping place for the ducks to walk down into it. If fowls are kept with them, it is best to have a little plank ladder (a board with little pieces of lath nailed across it). This prevents the ducks from slipping. It should reach 3 in. or 4 in. in the water. Then the ducks will usually get on it when they want to leave the pond.

If an ornamental duck pond is required, it should be made a little deeper, and not filled up to the top. In this way tree roots, old stumps and pieces of rough wood can be embedded in the concrete in a rustic manner, and then the large common ferns planted, such as break fern and nest fern. Both these ferns grow up very large, and spread out, partly covering the rustic work. A few rushes may also be planted. These are very hardy, and grow fast. It not only gives the pond a nice appearance, but makes it nice for the ducks to shelter themselves under. It gives the pond quite an ornamental appearance. It can be done in one year. If planted before March they will grow up beautifully the same summer.

TURKEYS.

TURKEYS are not bred so largely as geese, as they are not so hardy. They are to be found more generally in Norfolk. They are like most other things, they thrive best when well looked after. They pay well, but are rather delicate, and require generous treatment when young, as they pay for the extra trouble bestowed upon them. Inbreeding is very fatal to Turkeys. Some of the young ones droop their wings and die before they are two months old. It is a very trying time for them when their feathers are growing, especially the breast feathers. Young turkeys require more attention than chickens do, being more delicate when hatched. When hatched they should have hard-boiled eggs, boiled rice, and oatmeal, all mixed together. After they are two days old they should have a little onion cut up and mixed with it. A little ground ginger is a fine thing to mix with their food. Soaked biscuit meal is also an excellent food for them. It should not be made too wet. After they are a week old any of the below-mentioned herbs are good for them: Docks, chickweed, dandelions, and young nettles. Onions can always be used with advantage. If a few leaves of rue or hyssop be chopped up and mixed with their food it gives them a keen appetite. Potatoes and swede turnips boiled and mixed with their meal can be given in the spring. When the mornings are chilly they should have their food as warm as they can eat it, as they require so much heat when young. They should not have any food left by them, as it turns them against it. For the first seven or ten days they should have groats, not the split, but the whole ones, given dry. After this they can have a little wheat and barley, and after they are six weeks old a little round maize is good for them the last feed at night. They thrive better if their food is varied. Barley, buck-wheat, and maize meals mixed with sharps and small potatoes, boiled, I have found form a very cheap food for them, and it also suits them. They thrive very fast if they have plenty of potatoes. It is well to mix a little common salt and sulphur in their food about twice a week. Half a teaspoonful of each is sufficient for eight or ten turkeys a fortnight old, and more in proportion according to age. If fed well after they have all their feathers they grow fast. Where turkeys are reared there should be some open sheds, so that the young ones can be kept in on wet days and early in the mornings while the dew is on the grass. If allowed to run in long grass on wet mornings many are apt to succumb to an early death. Young turkeys should be reared where sheep are kept, if possible, as these keep the grass short, the long grass being sure to be fatal to the weak ones. As large turkeys sell so much better than small ones, they are usually sold at Christmas. Many breeders make a great mistake, as the largest birds should be kept for breeding, as they are much stronger and will produce stronger offspring. They are much easier to rear when bred from strong birds. It is a great error to sell the largest young ones, although they will often fetch 5s. a head more in the market. The foundation for the succeeding year should not be forgotten. Where they are very fine turkey cockerels they ought not to be killed, but sold for stock purposes, or exchanged for another similar for breeding purposes. This should be done amongst turkey breeders. Fresh blood cannot be introduced too often, as the young ones grow so much stronger, and good fat turkeys fetch such a good price, especially if they are large. When well fattened I have known them to weigh from 19 to 26 pounds each, sometimes over this if attended to well when young. They fatten much better if put in large sheds, not in coops, as some do. The shed or building should be rather dark, and if there is a window a curtain should be drawn before it to keep it shaded. When fed it should be removed, as then they must have good light. Give plenty of ventilation, and keep them fairly warm. The house should be bedded down with moss peat or straw. Short straw is the best. Rough chaff will answer the purpose where it is on a farm, and there is plenty of this without any outlay; but if it has to be purchased I prefer the moss peat, as that is more durable, and keeps them sweet, and does not require to be cleaned out once the whole of the time they are up to fatten if it is put about three or four inches thick on the floor. They should have some perches from two to three feet high. Many of them perch part of the day, and plume themselves. They are very fond of a dust bath to roll in. Moss peat answers this purpose very well. They should have a large trough to eat out of; length according to number fattening, the width about seven inches. It can be made of wood or galvanised iron, and should be small at the bottom and large at the top. It should be placed about six or nine inches high, and then there is no waste, as they cannot throw the food out so well. The best meals for fattening are ground oats and barley meal, with small potatoes boiled and mixed with it. The last fortnight they should have a little fat also mixed with it. A little of my Fattening Powder helps them very much. They can have boiled corn, either maize, wheat or buckwheat, given for the evening meal three or four times a week for a change. They do not require any water. The question is often asked which breed is the best to keep. The Cambridge speckled is a good bird to keep. The male bird is of a bronze colour, and grows to a very large size, but is delicate, unless fresh blood is introduced frequently. When turkeys are only required for table purposes, it is much the best to cross these with the Black Norfolk. The produce are much hardier, grow faster, and usually make much heavier birds. Size is the principal thing to obtain in turkeys, as they are usually sold by weight. The Black Norfolk are rather hardier than the Cambridge Bronze, and are less trouble when young. Turkeys are of a different nature to most other feathered tribes, as one male bird is sufficient to run with from thirty to fifty hens. However, it is wise to have two male birds in case anything should happen to one of them, or he may fall ill just in the breeding season, and time will then be lost, and especially if in the early part of the season. When this occurs it is a serious loss to breeders. It is much the best to have two turkey-cocks, and if they do not agree, one should be shut up, and let out on alternate days. In this way the fertility of the eggs is guaranteed. On the other hand, if they disagree, and are not parted, the greater part of the eggs will be unfertile. After the hens have laid, and the eggs have been set, one of the male birds can be disposed of. Where turkeys are bred, there ought to be a large cross of fowls kept, such as P. Rock-Dorking or P. Rock-Brahma, as it is a loss of time to allow the turkey-hens to sit. When one comes broody, she should be penned up and fed well for a few days, and she will soon re-commence laying. The eggs should be taken out of the nest every day, and one or two chalk eggs left remaining in. As they are rather timid, it is best to make them a nest in a dark corner. However, if they do not take to that, the one they choose must be made comfortable; if not, they are apt to lay their eggs about where they are not likely to be found. A turkey will usually lay from thirteen to seventeen eggs before she will come broody, but if they are taken away each day, and she is fed on warm stimulating food, she will lay twenty-five, and even thirty before coming broody. Feed them on warm food in the morning, and a little flesh meat with their food, or granulated meat is very good. A little of the Laying Powder mixed in the meat will help them very much if it is a cold morning, and give hot-boiled corn in the evening in the spring months. Some people say this is forcing them to lay, and is not natural. It is rather assisting nature to do her work, and the results prove what is best. Turkeys' eggs take twenty-eight days to hatch, but if the hen sits very closely they sometimes hatch n twenty-seven days. On the other hand, if she does not sit very closely, they will frequently go twenty-nine and even thirty days. Turkey-cocks are sometimes very spiteful to young chickens. They will frequently jump on them and kill them. I have had them do this when the chickens have been half-grown. It is well to keep the chickens separate as much as possible. Turkeys should not be reared unless time can be given to the young ones, as they require good attention the first few weeks, and are like most other stock, they pay for it. A dry and warm situation suits them best. They require shelter from the cold east winds, especially the first six weeks.

GEESE.

GEESE are but little kept in many parts of the country, as the majority of farmers think they are very unprofitable. They have paid me as well as any other poultry I have ever kept. There is one disadvantage (or annoyance), they make so much noise. I may say geese answer the same purpose as a dog, for if there is a stranger about they will let it be known. In this respect they are better at times than dogs, as they are very quick of hearing. If they are out at night or sleeping in an open shed they make a very loud noise. A country resident should keep a few geese where possible, as they are great enemies to burglars, as they cannot entice them to be quiet as they sometimes do dogs. A fox cannot face them; he will seldom stop to take anything when he hears their noise. They will run after a fox or dog, especially if it is a moonlight night Geese should be kept in large numbers where land is cheap They pay better than sheep, although the latter can be kept at the same time. Geese-returns are much quicker than sheep; the early-hatched ones realise a good price. The retail price is 10d. per pound when picked. I sold my early geese at 7s. 6d. and 10s. each when eleven weeks old; this was retail. Goslings are but little trouble to rear in comparison with most other stock. Stock geese require water, if not the eggs will not be very fertile. A small pool of water will do, but it must not be shallower than 18 inches or 2 feet. One gander to four geese is about the number. If he is active five are not too many for him, but it is best to be on the safe side and only allow four with him. It is best to shut the stock geese up at night, especially if it is frosty weather; if not they will not lay so early in the season They can be fed on warm stimulating foods the same as other poultry. Give the food as hot as they can eat it. A little meat, greaves, granulated meat, or any kind of offal meat mixed in the food is very good for them. Give them boiled corn at night, as hot as they can eat it. Maize and oats are very good grains for them; wheat and barley for a change. When this attention is bestowed on them they lay from a month to five weeks earlier, and more eggs The young goslings can be hatched earlier. Geese treated in the manner I have described will lay more eggs than if treated in the ordinary way. When the goslings are hatched they ought not to run with the old gander; if so he will take such care of them that he will forget to pay attention to the geese, and the eggs will be unfertile. This happens more particularly to the Toulouse. When geese are only required for table purposes I prefer them crossed, as I find they grow faster and fatten quicker. The Toulouse are a splendid breed. They usually go by the name of "Grey Geese" with most farmers. They are very upright in appearance, the lower part almost touching the ground. I crossed the Toulouse geese last year with a

Chinese gander, and the results were very good; the young ones were ready for table at 11 and 12 weeks old, weighing from 9 to 12 pounds each. They eat splendidly; all geese do if well fed. There is not much difference in flavour of pure breeds and crosses. The flavour and quality depend on the feeding. When well fed they eat so very differently to those which are bought, as those are usually from 15 to 20 weeks old. The Embden Geese are larger and rather better layers than the Toulouse, though there is not much difference if fed the same. The Embden are pure white, with yellow beaks and legs. When crossed with the Toulouse they make very large geese, grow fast, and fatten well, and lay much better when crossed, though of course if pure they make much more if sold for breeding purposes. Why many people do not succeed with their geese is that they breed from such very small stock, and their offspring do not grow much larger than a good-sized duck. This class of course does not fetch anything in the London markets. The secret in breeding geese is to have fine stock. It is not so much the breed, but the size. It is best to have a good large gander, and also a pure-bred one. Cross-bred geese can be bred from with good results if they are fine large ones. There is a breed called Italian Geese. They are principally white, with a grey head. They are not large, but broad and very compact. Their plumage is rather peculiar, much the same as that of a Silky hen, between feather and down. There appears to be no quill to the feather. This, of course, gives them a very short appearance. They are remarkably hardy, and are excellent layers. I intend to try this breed. A gentleman kindly sent me the results of three geese of this breed for the spring and summer of this year (1885), viz., 240 eggs from the three, and they had no special attention to induce them to lay this number. I hope to give a full account of these geese in the paper *Poultry*, which every poultry-keeper ought to take in. It is only one penny per week. I believe it to be the best paper of the kind, both for practical information and reports of all the shows. I am told they eat very mild, more like a young duck. This breed ought to be cultivated more in our country, as they possess such marvellous laying qualities, and at the same time are excellent for the table. The egg table in geese is rather low, as if they lay from 35 to 50 each in a season it is considered good. A few may go over this number, but it is more often under. This is one disadvantage, so few eggs, and this is the more reason the Italian should be cultivated, especially for crossing with the large breeds. I trust the readers of this book who are interested in geese will endeavour to cultivate this breed. The young ones are as hardy as those of other breeds. I have not met with a delicate breed of geese yet. When young goslings are hatched they can have a little boiled egg or groats put in a little water in something rather shallow, and a little biscuit meal soaked. After they are two or three days old they can have a little barley meal and middlings. It is best to give them a little biscuit meal and groats for a fortnight. When done well by the first few days they are no more trouble. There are many geese have nothing but grass from seven or eight days old until they are put up to fatten. If size is the object they should have a little meal twice a day, and they will grow very quickly after they are six weeks old. They can have a little corn at night; any kind will do, but they appear to do best on maize and oats when they have sufficient grass. Geese are not like most other feathered tribes in eating green food. After the old stock geese have finished laying they can be turned out to grass just the same as a flock of sheep or any other cattle. They do not require corn until the winter comes on. Then they may have a few oats and not too much maize, if so they get too fat internally. Brewers' grains mixed with a little meal or middlings is a very good food for them. By feeding in this way they keep in a good condition, and do not get too fat. When December sets in they should be fed on good meal and boiled corn, given as warm as they can eat it. When fed in this way they will commence laying four or five weeks earlier than if fed in the ordinary way. Some geese do not lay until the end of February or beginning of March. It is a waste of time keeping them in this way. There is also another peculiarity in geese, viz., they usually lay better after the first season up to eight or ten years old; they have been known to lay up to 18 years of age. Another advantage farmers who keep geese have is they can drive them to the cornfields after the corn is carried, and after they have been in for about a month or five weeks they weigh nearly as heavy again as when first turned in. The best of them should then be fattened and sent to market. When fattening they should not be allowed to go into the water, and are the best shut up in a shed or outbuilding, and should be so that they cannot see the others which are running at leisure. The best meal is barley meal with fat mixed in, and maize put in their water as grain. Geese pay well, and it is a pity to see so much waste land in our country. Thousands of geese could be kept where there is not one kept now. I went through a village this spring where hundreds of acres were lying idle, and not a goose kept in the whole village, and yet many of the families were almost wanting for bread. It is a great shame to our country that we pay foreign breeders millions of pounds for poultry annually, which is received by industrious and thrifty people the other side of the ocean for what might be produced in our own country, and improve the working classes.

TO PRESERVE EGGS.

PUT into a tub or vessel one bushel of quicklime, two pounds of salt, half-a-pound of cream of tartar, and mix the same together with as much water as will reduce the composition or mixture to that consistence that it will cause an egg put into it to swim with its top just above the liquid ; then place the eggs therein. Half the quantity will do three or four hundred eggs. The eggs preserved in this way will keep twelve months if required.

Another way is to butter the eggs as soon as they are laid, and lay them in tissue paper and set them on the small end. If buttered when warm they will keep four months quite fresh.

Another way is to put them into sawdust as soon as laid On the small end they keep two months in this way

VARIOUS.

THERE may be some who think I have treated too much on cross-bred fowls, or described too many crosses, as the same thing appears so repeatedly. If persons read the chapter on crosses and they happen to keep birds which were not described there, they would be disappointed. Some may think I have not treated on exhibition fowls sufficiently. This would be almost impossible in this small manual, and where there are fifty who keep fowls for egg-production, there is only one who keeps them for exhibition. Some may say they keep their fowls without any condiment, and yet have eggs through the winter. This of course can be done; but the way that answers best must be proved. Refer to testimonials on the subject; they will prove which is the best. I must apologise for not putting all the testimony in. This was impossible in such a small book. I feel sure that 19 out of 20 of my Powder customers speak well for its use. I trust purchasers of my Powder will examine the tins to see they have my name and *full* address on, as I have found several persons tampering with it. The reason why poultry spices and medicines get such a bad name is, that if they do the birds any good they leave them much weaker than before. When medicines are prepared by such a man as Professor Woodroffe Hill the purchasers may be sure they are having good value for their money. His book on the *Diseases of Poultry* will show this. It is published at 171, Fleet-street, E.C., at 2s. 6d. It treats on diseases in a scientific manner, and is, I believe, selling well. Poultry-keeping is becoming a leading feature in our country, and, I am sure, will do so even more. In 1884 I sent out over 1,100 sittings of eggs for hatching, and this year, 1885, over 2,020 sittings. This shows an increase.

When small chickens are found dead, and there is no apparent cause, the water should be taken from them at once. They can be reared without water. I know breeders who never give them any, and they are very successful in rearing them. I always give a good supply and find it answer, but do not condemn the no-water system.

With the rapid increase of poultry-keeping there is a great demand for poultry appliances, and I have been asked to manufacture houses and all appliances, which I have done on an improved style. Refer to advertisements for particulars. I have been selling a poultry fountain made with zinc, similar to other makers. This metal is not safe for poultry and pigeons to drink out of where sulphate of iron, salt, or any other acid is put in the water. There have been both poultry and pigeons killed through putting these different acids in the water. Drinking the water from zinc if no acids are put in it does not affect the birds in any way. To save any risk I am now having them made of galvanised iron. I have the drinking fountains and feeding troughs made of the same materials. I have also a pigeon fountain which can be taken to pieces to be cleaned the same as the poultry fountain. It is what pigeon-fanciers have needed for some time, for the birds have a good supply of clean water, and they cannot drop their excrements in.

If there is any little thing I have omitted mentioning, I shall be most pleased to give any hints and advice on receipt of a stamped and addressed envelope. I give information gratis at my London office, 105, Queen's Head-yard, Borough, S.E., on Saturdays from 11 a.m. to 8 o'clock p.m., and on Monday from 2.15 p.m. to 6 o'clock. From February to the first week in June I am at home every Wednesday afternoon, and am pleased to show visitors round my pens of poultry, and give a little advice on poultry management if required. I have so many birds sent to me for post-mortem examination, that I shall have to charge a nominal sum of 1s. They must all be carriage paid. I only dissect poultry, not cage birds or rabbits. I give the full particulars of cause of death, and how to treat the remainder. If sick birds are brought to me, I attend to them (the days I am in town). I shall be pleased to give advice to poultry-keepers, both in laying their places out, and stocking it, and inspect farms before they are taken for poultry. My fee is £1 1s., and travelling expenses. Where I give lectures, I am most pleased to visit gentlemen in the neighbourhood to give advice. In lecturing, I endeavour to make poultry keeping as plain as possible, and how they can be kept profitably, and am pleased if any of the audience will ask any question during my discourse. I frequently lecture at working men's clubs, and to those committees; and in some cases, a gentleman hires a room for the benefit of the working classes, to encourage them in poultry-keeping. I send all my poultry out on approval, and if not satisfactory, I wish them returned to me. I do not get one returned in a hundred. I guarantee eight eggs fertile in every sitting up to the first of March, and after that date ten in the sitting. The unfertile must be returned to me carriage paid, and I make them up to the respective numbers—viz., eight and ten. The unfertile eggs should not be shaken at all; then they can be held before a light in a dark room, and the owner can see whether quite clear or not. If they look quite clear they are unfertile; if dark they are addled, or have dead chickens in them. I hope my customers will remember this, as it will save the expense of sending them back. When an unfertile egg is broken, and it has not been sat upon more than three weeks, there is no smell.

I have cross-bred pullets for disposal all the year round, from 4s. to 5s. 6d. each, and cross-bred hens in the autumn at 2s. 6d. and 3s. 6d. each. Broody hens from 4s. to 5s. 6d. each, according to season and quality. Pure-bred birds from my good laying strains from 6s. 6d. to 10s. 6d.; and those which are bred from my good laying strains, with exhibition points combined, from 15s. to £5 each. I can usually supply really good birds from £1 to 30s. each. It is the best time to buy stock fowls about June or July. I sell them much cheaper then to make room for my young stock. Stock ducks run from 6s. 6d. to £2 each. I export fowls in large numbers, and always endeavour to give good value for the money, Cockerels for crossing from 6s. 6d. to 12s. 6d. Every basket is charged for, and allowed for when returned. Remittance to accompany all orders. P.O.O. payable at Orpington and the Borough.

SINGLE-COMB BLACK ORPINGTON COCK.

NEW BREEDS OF FOWLS.

SINGLE-COMB BLACK ORPINGTON.

SEVERAL new breeds of fowls have been produced in the last few years, but this has been done principally by our American cousins. The Plymouth Rock and Wyandotte are of American production; the former breed has proved very useful, and has spread more than any other in our country. The Wyandotte is also a nice fowl, but looks best on paper. English poultry-fanciers have paid from £2 to £30 a pair for both of these breeds. To me this seems a folly. English breeders sit with their arms folded, content to pay such exorbitant prices for fowls which they might produce themselves, and with a certain amount of pleasure, and thus keep thousands of pounds in this country. I have frequently wondered why our English breeders did not take it up. The Plymouth Rock was made with three breeds, but since it has been in our country it has had another added to these (by a good many breeders) viz., Scotch Grey. The Wyandotte is made with two breeds, and those who like the colour must be pleased with the shape of the fowls. The neat rose comb gives them a very nice appearance, in fact, they are superior birds in head properties. They are spreading well, but do not take so well as the Plymouth Rock. I had both breeds almost as soon as imported into the country, and have bred them ever since, and have found them useful birds, especially the Plymouth Rock. My endeavour has been to produce a breed which combines all the good qualities found in several breeds. The Plymouth Rock have yellow skins, unless the stock are selected to avoid this. A yellow cast on the skin is only natural to them. The same with the Wyandotte. They both lay brown or tinted eggs, and are winter layers; but it is difficult to produce true specimens from them, even when the greatest care is bestowed. To breed good-coloured birds it is necessary to have two breeding pens, one for pullet and the other for cockerel breeding (and this is also the case with several other varieties if well-marked fowls are desired, and to be fit for exhibition). This makes it very difficult for those who cannot afford to keep more than one pen. A fowl which has more than one colour in it is much more difficult to breed true than a self-coloured bird. The Black Orpington will fill up the vacancy there has been in the poultry world. The Plymouth Rock has come the nearest to the requirements; but this breed has several disadvantages where the Orpington has the advantage. They have white skin and flesh, the latter being very fine; they eat much the same as the Dorking; feather and grow faster the first six weeks, and are easier to breed true to colour; are shorter on the legs, lay rather more eggs, and are not so liable to become fat internally; neither are they such inveterate sitters as the Rocks. I have been asked by many to bring out a breed which would make a good table fowl and lay brown or tinted eggs, free from feathers on the legs, and plumage a colour that will not show the dirt, for town use, one that will stand confinement and lay

SINGLE-COMB BLACK ORPINGTON PULLET.

through the cold winter months. The Orpingtons possess all these qualities, and I feel sure that in time it will become a very popular breed as an all-round fowl. I have not a strict account of the laying of each hen; a few have laid over 200 eggs in a year; one laid 315 in 12 months, and some of them have only averaged 125 eggs. The Americans have been well repaid for their trouble in producing new breeds, the sums that have been paid by English fanciers to them having been enormous. I have done what is unusual with poultry-breeders, made known through my monthly publication how I have raised the breed. They must commend themselves to anyone who has studied the qualities of the various breeds. They combine the blood of Minorca, Langshan, and Plymouth Rock. The Minorcas are noted for their excellent spring and summer laying; but if they have good attention and are well sheltered from the cold winds, they will frequently surpass the other so-called hardier breeds when the snow is on the ground. Their combs are large and occasionally get frost-bitten.

The Plymouth Rocks are good fowls, especially the black variety, although these should not be used to produce the Grey Rock; if so, it brings them a smutty colour, although they are usually the best layers. Then there are the Langshans. These have such a splendid gloss upon their plumage, and they are extraordinary layers, especially in autumn and winter. They will often lay while going through their moult, which is unusual for any birds to do. It is always much easier to breed good pullets than cockerels in any new breed. Many of the leading fanciers are taking up this breed, with the full intention of having classes at many of our leading shows—Dairy, Crystal Palace, and Birmingham. Being black, they are easy to breed; they are very hardy as chickens, and feather and grow fast; they can be reared in confined spaces, and do well in an open run; they answer every purpose. If kept for show purposes, they will pay well, as they are such good winter layers; or, if required for table purposes, they are very satisfactory, being of an excellent flavour, and the breast-meat white. The eggs are brown and tinted, not large, but a good average size—eggs very salable in town or country.

The birds fatten up very quickly for table when young. A few of the cockerels may come a little splashed in the hackles and saddle feathers. This is liable to appear in all black breeds, more or less, and especially in a newly-raised breed. Sometimes there is not one chicken in a brood which shows a coloured feather.

The plumage is very glossy in both sexes, but more particularly in the cock. The sheen should be much the same colour as that of a good Langshan; single combs, evenly serrated in both sexes, standing erect in the cock, not large but neat; red face and ear-lobes, black or dark legs, not too long, white toe-nails, four toes on each foot, well spread out from each other. The hen's comb may fall a little to one side if it is evenly serrated and without folds in it. The large comb in many breeds denotes good laying qualities. This also means that the best laying fowls have to be done away with because their combs are large, and a judge passes them over. This in a great measure destroys the utility of poultry, whereas it should be *vice versâ*. The poultry clubs and societies should award prizes to those which are capable of laying the largest number of eggs in twelve months. If judges would but study the laying qualities and general shape of the fowls, and not spend all their time on judging the plumage, it would be more beneficial to poultry at large. The proper feathers would soon follow if the other matters were attended to as they should

ROSE-COMB BLACK ORPINGTON PULLET.

be. In three years our poultry would be much improved both in laying and table qualities. The birds would be a better shape, and, in many cases, the plumage would be better.

ROSE-COMB BLACK ORPINGTON.

In the fourth edition of my Poultry Breeder and Feeder I gave an illustration of a cock and hen of a new breed of fowls, named the Orpington. I brought this variety out for the public in the autumn of 1886, and it has spread more rapidly throughout the world than any other breed of fowls has ever done. They are in nearly every part of the world now. I have exported a great many, and several other breeders who have taken them up have done the same. They have become very popular in England. They are not only taken up as a variety for exhibition, but many people have purchased them on account of their useful qualities. They are excellent winter layers of a fair-sized, brown egg, and are first-class table birds, having very white flesh and a fine white skin. Independently of the above qualities they are possessed of a beautiful appearance and handsome carriage, which cause many lovers and fanciers of poultry to take them up. They are everywhere most highly spoken of as a good all-round fowl, and their appearance recommends them, as they are such beautiful birds. I have not been able to supply the demand for eggs or birds this season. During the last two years and present season I have sent out over 600 sittings of eggs in England, besides a large number sent abroad. I thought, when I brought the Orpingtons out, that they would be well taken up, but I had not the slightest expectation that the demand for them would have been as great as it has been. Some people think they are too much like the Langshans. These people should try them, and they will find the Orpingtons will grow away from the Langshans from chickenhood, and plump up as table birds in a shorter time. All who have tried them are more than pleased with them.

In this fifth edition of the POULTRY BREEDER AND FEEDER I give the plates of a cock and hen of another new variety, viz., the Rose-comb Orpingtons. They are very much like the Orpingtons in shape and colour, but they have a rose comb; the Orpingtons being a single-comb bird. I do not hesitate to say that this new variety stands right away from all other breeds in appearance. It is the only breed out which is black in colour that has a rose comb, except the Black Hamburgh, this latter being a small bird with white earlobes. The Rose-comb Orpingtons are free from white in the earlobes, and, being large birds with rose combs, the demand for them is very great. There are always a number of people to take up a fresh variety of fowls, more especially if it is likely to be a profitable one. This last variety I have brought out will well repay those fanciers who speculate in it. It is my wish to be plain in writing of this breed, and not to lead people astray, and, as I have referred to their good qualities, I will point out their failings. Most writers point out the good or bright side of a thing, and leave the dark side to be found out by experience. The question which will be asked by most of my readers is—Is the new variety really any better than the Orpington, and, if so, where does the advantage come in? Firstly, a fancier or lover of fowls usually likes something different from his neighbour, more especially if eggs can be collected daily during the winter months for breakfast, and this can be done by those who keep the Rose-comb Orpingtons, for they stand far before other varieties as winter layers. Their eggs are rather small, but are brown in colour. A really good specimen of the Rose-comb Orpington is much more difficult to breed than the Orpington, but will make more money. I told my readers how I raised the latter, so that those who felt inclined might set to work and breed them, and I will now show how the rose-comb variety was formed. Many years ago there were some Langshans with a rose comb imported into this country; their having a rose comb was merely a sport of nature in the first place. I very much admired them, and began to breed from them. Whenever there was one imported I immediately bought it. In a few cases our English breeders of Langshans have produced the same sports of nature, and these have usually fallen into my hands, and I used them in forming this new breed. I mated them with the same two breeds in the same way as I did by the Orpington, only I used these sports of nature, —the Langshans that came with the rose comb. These birds were not a recognised breed, and, had I not utilised them, would have had their heads cut off. I have four different strains of this new breed, and, at the end of the season, 1889, I shall have five strains; so I have fresh blood to go on with for some years. The pullets breed very true to colour. I have not had more than two mismarked ones in every hundred the last two years. Occasionally one may come with feathered legs. The cockerels do not breed so true, as they often throw coloured feathers in the neck, hackles, and saddle. Therefore, good marked cocks are scarce. Sometimes not one cock or pullet in three or four broods will come without the rose comb, and then you may get two come with single combs in one brood. I mention this so that those who may go in for them may not be disappointed by finding all the birds do not come like the illustrations given. (I am breeding from 120 stock birds this season, 1889.) Although the eggs are rather small they are very salable on account of their brown colour. The birds are not non-sitters. They make excellent sitters and mothers; at the same time they are easily put off from broodiness if shut from the nest, and come on laying again in a few days. As chickens they are very hardy, and can be brought up in cold and damp places, and many of them will lay when they are six months old. They fledge well, and rapidly grow into good table birds, their flesh and skin being whiter than any other breed of fowls. They stand confinement well, both as chicks and grown-up birds, and they cannot be put in the wrong place. As layers they have beaten all other breeds in the autumn and winter months. Their colour is right for a town, as they are black. They always look nice, as they do not show the dirt. I can strongly recommend them as the best all-round fowl in regard to the number of eggs laid, whether they are kept in a confined town run or a grass field, and at the same time one of the handsomest fowls in existence. It is not necessary for me to dwell long on the different points. Their plumage should be black throughout, both cock and hen, both with rose combs set close to the head, with a small peak at the back, and the neater it is the better; red face, red earlobes, black or hazel eyes; black, nicely-curved beak, black legs, and white toe-nails. The cock's tail should be made up with very fine hanging feathers on each side, with a brilliant metallic green on them. The tail should be carried fairly well back; carried too near the neck is a fault. A brilliant gloss should always be aimed at in mating these birds. If a cock have a large comb mate him with hens that are deficient in size of combs, and if the hens lack gloss mate them with a cock that has a few red feathers in his hackles, as this will bring the gloss up very much in the pullets. When first hatched the chickens should be black on the back and white underneath, and are usually pale in the legs, which darken as the birds grow and fledge.

During the last twenty years I have spent much time on poultry, and especially so the last twelve years. I have had a new breed of birds on hand for thirteen years, but it does not please me yet, therefore I have not brought it before the poultry world. I shall try it for two years longer, and then, if I can really recommend it to the public, I shall bring it out; if not, I shall drop it, as I have done many other experiments. I have, however, a breed of birds almost ready to add to the already long list of varieties of fowls. They are quite different from either the Orpington or Rose-comb Black Orpington. At the same time I think they will take the public fancy almost as well; but they are white in colour, and, therefore, not so well suited for towns as a black bird, on account of their showing the dirt so much. Some people say they do not see the need of any more varieties of fowls. Many fanciers do, however, see a necessity, and I am one of these. Take, for instance, the White Leghorns. These birds are admitted on all sides to be the king layers of all breeds, and yet they do not as a breed thoroughly please the people who keep them, as their yellow legs and skins are objectionable, and they are poor table birds. I have been trying to produce a fowl that will suit those who keep White Leghorns, and have every reason to believe my efforts will not be in vain. This variety will be a white fowl with a rose comb, white legs and skin, and a larger bird than a Leghorn, combined with the laying qualities of the latter breed. They are in my opinion a nicer-looking bird, will be much better table birds, and quite as hardy; but a few of them will want to sit. They are very quick growers, and will lay at six months old, and I have tried them side by side with the Leghorns and they have passed them as layers, taking the year through, as they lay more eggs during the winter. As chickens they grow and fledge quickly, and will stand any climate, as I have had several pens in different parts of the country to try them in this respect. They lay white eggs chiefly, but a few of them come cream-coloured. They do not, however, breed so true as a Leghorn ; a few of them throw dark feathers, and a coloured leg sometimes will appear, also a single comb. Some of my readers may think that these defects spoil the whole thing, and it may appear so on the surface. If I buy a sitting of eggs, and the seller tells me the chicks will all come alike, I expect them to do so, and, if they do not, I am disappointed. If, however, he tells me I may breed some not so good as most of the others, I naturally expect to get some of the chickens inferior ; but should, however, all of them come right so much the better. I would also inform inexperienced breeders that many old-established varieties do not breed true, but throw different-coloured offspring. For instance the Plymouth Rock is a speckled bird with yellow legs, and yet in breeding them many come black in colour with dark legs. Wyandottes are a black and white fowl ; they will throw some chickens black. Andalusians are a blue or slate colour, and yet breed many black and many white chickens. Hamburghs, Wyandottes, and Red Caps are rose-comb varieties, yet often come with single combs. I mention these examples to show how old breeds vary, and do not breed all true to colour, as all varieties are likely to throw back. This new variety is the White Orpington, as they should be white throughout, white beak, white legs, with four toes (not five toes like the Dorking) on each foot, rather large comb, not on one side, with a nice peak at the back. I do not expect them to become valuable as show birds. They may, however, do so ; that depends very much upon how they

ORPINGTON.
GOOD LAYER.

ORPINGTON.
BAD LAYER.

are taken up when I introduce them to the poultry-fanciers

The Orpingtons are evidently appreciated as a good and useful breed of fowls, for a club has been formed for them, and is called the "Orpington Club." There are already nearly one hundred members. The Orpingtons are recognised as a distinct breed in all the leading shows, and cups and other good prizes are offered for competition.

LAYING QUALITIES.

Laying qualities in hens! Some people try and turn this subject into ridicule, and say it is all nonsense. So it may be to those who say it is, but not to those who have made the subject a study. Many people say it is impossible to tell a good laying hen from a bad one by its appearance. It is not at all impossible; it is as easy as *a*, *b*, *c* to many people who have studied it. I have given my attention for many years to the laying qualities in hens, and I am able to pick out good layers from bad ones, simply from study and observation; and I can prove to poultry-keepers that this is a fact, and not a farce.

In visiting poultry-keepers, I frequently ask them to allow me to pick out from their stock those birds which are the best layers, just to see if there is any truth in it or not. People who keep but few fowls, and take an interest in them, usually know their best layers, and in many neighbourhoods where I have lectured I have been able to tell poultry-keepers their best laying hens, and some hundreds of poultry-fanciers have found the benefit of my advice on this subject. There is far more in picking out the best layers, and only keeping those hens, than many people think.

Most poultry-fanciers are pleased when they have learned

to select a bird fit for exhibition out of a number of fowls. This can only be done by a practised eye after careful observation and study, and yet for one poultry-keeper who keeps birds for exhibition purposes there are twenty who keep fowls for profit. Therefore, it is far more important to make a study of laying qualities than of exhibition points. If the former were studied more it would save a great deal of expense and disappointment to fowl-keepers. For instance, many people keep 20 to 30 fowls during the winter months, and often get but very few eggs, perhaps 5 or 6 eggs from 20 birds, or 8 or 9 eggs from 30 hens per week, and the fowls that do lay are kept back by their brethren. If only 7 or 10 birds, all good layers, were kept in place of the 30, more eggs would be the result, and these few birds would be kept at a third of the cost, and the income from them would be considerably increased.

When I kept hens for laying only, I never kept any but those that would lay in the winter months, and November, December, and January were usually higher with me as regards number of eggs than any other three months of the year. I had 30 pullets one season that laid in the three months mentioned 1873 eggs, or about an average of 21 eggs monthly for each bird. Some, of course, laid more, whilst others laid fewer. Some of them laid 15 and 19 days together without missing a day. Most things that have been done can be done again. I have known many instances where only 6 to 10 birds have been kept and the egg return has averaged 25 eggs per bird a month.

I often visit people who keep 10 fowls, and who get more eggs than their neighbours who keep from 40 to 50 fowls during the winter months. It is not the number of birds kept, but the quality and the management of them. I visit over 2,000 poultry yards a year, and travel about 15,000 miles, so I have good opportunities of seeing birds kept

PLYMOUTH ROCK.—GOOD LAYER.

PLYMOUTH ROCK.—BAD LAYER.

under different treatment. I have often picked out the good laying hens from the bad ones, so that their owners could judge for themselves. This book may fall into the hands of poultry-fanciers whom I have not visited, therefore a few hints to them may not be out of place, especially if my remarks may keep the corn bill a few pounds lower in the year, for a pound saved is a pound gained. It is not always what can be gained from good laying fowls, but the convenience of having new laid eggs when they are scarce, and also avoiding being laughed at by other members of the family, who often crack jokes when eggs are expected, but do not come.

Selecting the best layers is not a new study with me, for I have been doing it for the last 15 years in my own yards. I did not begin to give the public lectures on the laying qualities until the autumn of 1888. Since then I have had a great many applications from all parts of the country, and this induced me to write a few pages on the subject in this fifth edition of my book. I am only too pleased wherever I visit or lecture to point out the laying qualities of fowls, and it is easy to point out the difference to my audience by having some bad and good layers brought to me; but it is rather difficult to make this plain in print, as it is not possible to convey the expression of the eye and face to paper. But one can point out these to people in the live bird. What induced me to take up laying qualities as a study was the idea that as I was able from observation to pick out a good milking cow from a herd, why should I not be able by observation to find out the points in a fowl which would denote a good layer?

This study has well repaid me in my own stock, and hundreds of poultry-keepers have reaped a part of the benefit with me, as I have sent out many thousands of sittings of eggs to all parts of the world, so that many poultry-keepers have shared a small percentage of my observation and study by having had some of my laying strains. I may say that if a hen is not in good health and condition the laying qualities do not show to advantage, and it is also very necessary to study age and the breed of birds, as birds of some breeds look much older than they really are. An extraordinary good-laying hen of any breed will look younger when she is four years of age than a bad-laying hen does at two years old. Those who are anxious to pick up the good laying points in hens should watch their own birds very closely, that is if they have one or more which lay better than the others, and this is usually the case when even only six or seven hens are kept. If the owners will observe the heads of these birds they will find they differ in shape from those which do not lay so often. The heads of the good layers are much finer, not nearly so thick and heavy looking, the eye is bolder, and they have generally a far more intelligent look than a bad layer has. The observant fancier will also notice that the good layers are more active, and generally on the move, and scratching about, that they are the first birds out in the morning, and the last to roost at night, and they usually have the fullest crops.

Some people say that a good-laying hen can be told by the size of comb; this depends a great deal on the breed. For instance, Brahmas have a very small comb in most cases, and a good layer of this breed has a very small comb; but in the Cochin this differs very much, and if a Cochin has a large comb she is usually a good layer, but if she have a very small one that is not a reason that she is a bad layer. It is the formation of the head and eye that is the best guide to go by. I have given a variety of heads of good layers and bad ones, so that my readers may compare them. These heads were photographed by the winner

LIGHT BRAHMA.
GOOD LAYER.

LIGHT BRAHMA.
BAD LAYER.

of the Crystal Palace gold medal in 1889, Mr. E. Davy Lavender. The photographs will help you to study your own fowls. There is nothing like practice, so study from live birds as much as possible. A good-laying hen has usually a very pretty face; perhaps, in the heads of Brahmas and Cochins this is more noticeable than in any breed, as they have rather thick heads, and are heavy over the eye; therefore a good layer of either of these breeds stands right out from the bad ones.

There is a difficulty in judging the laying qualities of Houdans, Polands, and Creve Cœurs, as they have feathers on the top of the head, which overhang the eyes. By study it is also quite easy to detect a cock that has come from a good-laying strain. I can do this quite easily, and so can many of my friends and pupils. I have not given portraits of any male birds, for the simple reason that those who by study can tell the laying points in the hens, will be sure to observe merits in the cocks. I may mention one thing as regards the cockerels. If they are bred from a good-laying hen they are usually more precocious, and do not grow so large. They begin to crow much earlier, and are much more active. This is noticeable in all varieties, and very much can be learnt in this way by selection of cocks, as if a cock come from a good-laying strain, and he is turned down in a poultry yard, he may prove a great boon, as a good-laying hen can only lay a certain number of eggs. If a cock is used with eight or ten hens every chicken comes from him, and good results may be expected in the young pullets the following year.

If the points for layers are taken up and studied in the same way as the points are for exhibition it will be a great boon to poultry-keepers, and I have every reason to believe fowls will pay twenty-fold more than at present, and I shall be much surprised if prizes are not soon offered at shows as much for laying qualities as they now are for purity of feathers. Our judges of to-day laugh at the idea, but they will find in the course of a few years that if they do not study the laying points in poultry their services will not be in demand as much as they are at the present day. If they do not move with the times they will be left behind. It is useful poultry that is required for the million. Not half of the old hens carted from show to show, perhaps, lay 30 eggs in a year. In fact, many of the cup birds of to-day have not laid an egg in two years. Is this the way to improve poultry? No. It is the way they have been ruined as layers and table birds. Many poultry-fanciers of to-day have a horror of prize strains on account of the few eggs they lay.

My intention is not to run down prize-bred poultry, but to try and improve them, and produce a bird to win prizes and yet have laying qualities. Exhibition points and laying ones can be combined, and when they are the birds are much nicer-looking, and that is why I brought out the Orpington fowl, just to show the public that it is possible to have a very handsome breed, good layers, and table-birds combined.

The remarks on the laying points may be criticised by our judges and fanciers of to-day, but I am quite prepared to prove my statements before any public audience, either in town or country. I never put a statement in print unless I have proved it first. The study of keeping poultry profitably is only in its infancy at the present day, though I am pleased to say it is steadily advancing, and will do more so as time goes on, and committees of shows take up the laying points and useful qualities of fowls, and gentlemen who support these exhibitions see that their money is put in the right channel for the improvement of our poultry. Most exhibition breeders admit that their birds are nothing like

CROSS-BRED HAMBURGH-BRAHMA.

GOOD LAYER.

CROSS-BRED HAMBURGH-BRAHMA.

BAD LAYER.

as good layers as they were ten years ago. This is not improving poultry, but is going in the wrong direction, and is one reason why I use my pen for the public to support me in the right thing. Why should our poultry deteriorate in their useful qualities year after year? They ought to improve, and will do so before long. Why should we pay the millions yearly that we do to foreigners for eggs and fowls, when we might in England produce all we require, and have a surplus of eggs, &c., to send to the foreigner, if poultry were only attended to as they ought to be, and will be ere long? Landlords, farmers, and cottagers can all do with more money, and can easily increase their incomes by giving more attention to keeping profitable poultry.

LECTURES.

I GIVE Lectures on Practical Poultry-Keeping and Management throughout the country. My object is, as fully expressed in my Book, to draw the attention of the labouring classes to this easily-attained means of adding to their income and increasing their present limited sources of Home Comfort.

It is necessary that Secretaries or other persons making the engagements should correspond with me early, as I am continually making arrangements for Lectures in various parts. In many cases these could be arranged so as to fit in with others in neighbouring districts, and expense of travelling lessened.

Fee, £1 1s. and travelling expenses, or within a distance of 12 miles of London, free.

Address all letters and orders to W. COOK, "The Waldens," St. Mary Cray (late of Tower House, Orpington), Kent, or Queen's Head Yard, 105, High Street, Borough, S.E. (three minutes' walk from London Bridge).

ADVICE AND CONSULTATIONS.

I give information free to all poultry-keepers on the management of poultry, also answer any questions by stamped and addressed envelope. All communications concerning this should be addressed to "The Waldens," St. Mary Cray (late Tower House, Orpington), Kent. I also travel to all parts of the United Kingdom for the purpose of planning-out poultry farms and runs, mating breeding birds, &c., for the nominal sum of 21s. and travelling expenses.

NOTICE TO VISITORS.

The Breeding Pens and Stock Birds are open for inspection any week-day. Mr. Cook is at home on Wednesdays from 1.30 p.m. till evening, to supply every necessary information concerning the birds and give advice. For the benefit of the working classes, the place is open for inspection on Bank Holidays. "The Waldens," St. Mary Cray, is 2½ miles from Orpington Station on the South-Eastern Railway, and a little over a mile from St. Mary Cray Station on the L.C. & D. Railway, and 2 miles from Swanley Junction, on the same line. Any-one who cannot conveniently walk can be met by my trap at either station by appointment. Address all Telegrams:—"Cook, St. Mary Cray."

W. COOK'S

PRICE LIST OF EGGS FOR SITTING.

EGGS of the following breeds supplied from strong healthy birds, carefully mated. Birds can be inspected on any week day. Broody hens supplied at reasonable prices.

PRICES PER SITTING OF 12 EGGS (PACKING INCLUDED).

	s.	d.
Plymouth Rock	10	6
Black Minorca	10	6
White Minorca	10	6
Partridge Cochin...	10	6
Buff Cochin	10	6
Black Spanish	10	6
White Leghorn	10	6
Brown Leghorn	10	6
Langshan	10	6
Wyandotte	10	6
Black-breasted Red Game	10	6
Indian Game	10	6
Silver-Grey Dorking	10	6
Light Brahma	10	6
Dark Brahma	10	6
Silver-spangled Hamburgh	10	6
Gold-spangled Hamburgh	10	6
Black Hamburgh...	10	6
Houdan	10	6
Andalusian	10	6
Scotch Grey	10	6
Redcap	10	6
Coloured Dorking	10	6
White Dorking	10	6
Black Rose-Comb Bantam	10	6
Silver Sebright Bantam	10	6
Golden Sebright Bantam	10	6
Black-breasted Red Game Bantam	10	6

These are all prize birds with laying qualities combined. Hundreds of birds have been successfully exhibited, bred from eggs supplied by W. Cook.

Orpington - - -	10/6 and 21/-	per sitting.
Rose-Comb Black do. -	10/6 and 21/-	,,

This breed, which W. Cook has brought out, combines a handsome appearance with good winter and summer laying, and excellent table qualities.

The birds have fine white flesh and lay brown eggs.

The following are Pure Birds, but bred especially for laying qualities:—

		s.	d.
Plymouth Rock	per dozen	6	6
Black Minorca	,,	6	6
White Minorca	,,	6	6
Partridge Cochin	,,	6	6
Buff Cochin	,,	6	6
Black Spanish	,,	6	6
Andalusian	,,	6	6
Langshan	,,	6	6
Dark Brahma	,,	6	6
Light Brahma	,,	6	6
Black Hamburgh	,,	6	6
Silver-spangled ditto	,,	6	6
Gold-spangled ditto...	,,	6	6
Brown Leghorn	,,	6	6
White Leghorn	,,	6	6
Redcap	,,	6	6
Coloured Dorking	,,	6	6
White ditto	,,	6	6
Black-breasted Red Game	,,	6	6
Silver-Grey Dorking	,,	6	6
Houdan	,,	6	6
Indian Game...	,,	6	6
Scotch Grey	,,	6	6
Silver Sebright Bantam	,,	6	6
Black Rose-Comb Bantam...	,,	6	6

Guinea Fowls' Eggs - - - 7s. 6d.

FIRST CROSSES.

		s.	d.
Langshan-Minorca	per dozen	5	0
Houdan-Minorca	,,	5	0
Plymouth Rock-Minorca	,,	5	0
Houdan-Dorking	,,	5	0
Gold-spangled Hamburgh Cochin...	,,	6	0
Houdan-Cochin	,,	5	0
Minorca-Brahma	,,	5	0
Houdan-Brahma	,,	5	0
Leghorn-Brahma	,,	5	0
Leghorn-Dorking	,,	5	0
Leghorn-Cochin	,,	5	0
Indian Game-Dorking	,,	5	0
Houdan-Plymouth Rock	,,	5	0
Leghorn-Plymouth Rock	,,	5	0

		s.	d.
Plymouth Rock-Dorking	per dozen	5	0
Langshan-Plymouth Rock	,,	5	0
Indian Game-Plymouth Rock	,,	5	0
Cuckoo Leghorn-Plymouth Rock	,,	5	0
Plymouth Rock-Brahma	,,	5	0
Plymouth Rock-Game	,,	5	0
Houdan-Leghorn	,,	5	0
Andalusian-Brahma	,,	5	0

DUCK EGGS.

PER SITTING OF 11 EGGS.

	Up to March 1st. £	s.	d.	After that date. s.	d.
Prize Aylesbury	1	1	0	15	0
Aylesbury		7	6	6	6
Muscovy		7	6	6	6
Rouen		7	6	6	6
Pekin		7	6	6	6
Cayuga		7	6	6	6
Black East India		7	6	6	6
Rouen-Aylesbury		6	0	5	0
Muscovy-Aylesbury		6	0	5	0
Pekin-Aylesbury		6	0	5	0

GEESE EGGS.

	Each. s.	d.	Per Sitting 11 Eggs. s.	
Italian	1	6	14	6
Italian and Toulouse Cross	1	3	11	0
Embden and Toulouse	1	3	11	0

TURKEY EGGS.

	Each. s.	d.	Per Sitting of 11 Eggs. s.	d.
Black Norfolk	1	4	15	0
Cambridge Bronze	1	6	15	0
Norfolk and Cambridge Cross	—		11	0

Special quotations for large orders and Incubators. After the 1st of June the price of Eggs is reduced.

ALL EGGS GUARANTEED FERTILE.

Unfertiles replaced if returned per Parcels Post to "The Waldens," St. Mary Cray (late of Tower House, Orpington), Kent.

ame and Address of sender to be enclosed in each box of returned Eggs.

EGG TESTIMONIALS.

Lancaster, February 10th, 1889.

DEAR SIR,—The Langshan eggs you sent me have been very satisfactory, ten having produced strong chickens, which is excellent at this time of year.

Yours, etc., FRED NORRIS.

Brighton, February 7th, 1889.

SIR,—I thought I would let you know I have eleven chickens from the thirteen eggs you sent (Orpingtons). I am most pleased.

Yours, truly, WM. JONES.

Manchester, March 1st, 1889.

SIR,—The three sittings of eggs have turned out as follows:—Langshans, eleven chicks; Minorcas, ten ditto; White Leghorns, eleven. I am well satisfied.

Yours truly, F. MARCHANT.

Lewisham, March 3rd, 1889.

SIR,—The eggs I obtained from you have been satisfactory having produced eleven strong chickens.

Yours, etc, F. F.

Ewell, Surrey, March 5th, 1889.

SIR,—The eggs have produced ten strong chickens.

Yours truly, FANNY WATCHORNE.

Manchester, March 9th, 1889.

SIR,—I am pleased with result of Wyandotte eggs, twelve eggs containing strong chickens.

Yours faithfully, W. THOMAS.

Liverpool, March 11th, 1889.

MRS. JACKSON is pleased with result of eggs, as she has obtained thirteen lovely chickens from the same number of eggs.

Camberwell, S.E., February 19th, 1889.

SIR,—I am delighted with the results of eggs obtained from your London office, as I have twelve beautiful chicks. The thirteenth was crushed in nest, unfortunately.

Yours, etc., F. WILLIAMS.

Old Kent Road, S.E.

DEAR SIR,—I have ten chickens from the Plymouth Rock eggs purchased from you, and the other three were also fertile. I am very pleased.

Yours truly, A. MACDONALD.

Wyboston, St. Neots, March 20th, 1889.

DEAR SIR, I have twelve chickens from the Minorca eggs received from you.

Yours, etc, W. MANWARING.

Lancaster, March 30th, 1889.

SIR,—I have a lovely hatch of thirteen chickens from your Plymouth Rock eggs, and am more than pleased.

Yours, etc., F. WARBEATON.

Macclesfield, March 2nd, 1889.

DEAR SIR,—I have fourteen chickens from fifteen Langshan eggs you supplied. Yours truly, ANNIE WARING.

Newark, Notts, March 2nd, 1889.

DEAR SIR,—I have ten chickens from the thirteen eggs supplied, and two dead in shell. Yours faithfully, M. MARCHANT.

Lozells, Birmingham.

SIR,—I am pleased to tell you I have thirteen Orpington chickens from eggs supplied by you. Yours truly, T. WARREN.

Caxton, Bridgwater.

SIR,—The eggs are very satisfactory, having produced thirteen chickens; the extra egg you kindly sent was addled. Yours faithfully, A. MERRIE.

Pinxton, Derbyshire.

SIR,—The eggs have proved satisfactory; fourteen out of the fifteen have produced healthy chicks. Yours, etc, F. FARQUHAR.

Lancaster Road, Lancaster.

SIR,—The eggs you sent to Scotland for me have hatched ten strong chicks. The others were broken on journey. Very pleased. Yours truly, A. M.

Dublin, Ireland.

SIR,—The eggs are very satisfactory; twelve of the Minorcas have hatched, eleven of the Orpingtons, and thirteen of the cross bred.

Yours, etc., J. MURPHY.

Highwood House, Mill Hill, December 7th, 1888.

DEAR SIR,—I think you may be interested to know that a cock and hen, hatched from eggs bought of you in 1887, gained First Prize and a Special at a local show held at Barnet, December 6th. I shall be glad if you will book me a sitting of Black Minorca eggs for next spring. If you have two prices I should like half a sitting of each. I thought it would be well to sit them the first week in March. Yours very truly, M. LOCKET.

Eastbourne, April 18th, 1889.

DEAR SIR,—I am very pleased to tell you that out of the sitting of eggs you sent me I have ten fine chicks. If the majority should turn out cockerels could you tell me the best market at which to effect either a sale or exchange?

Believe me to remain, yours truly, H. EVENDEN.

[Advertise them.]

Kingsbury House, Shortlands, Kent, April 13th, 1889.

DEAR SIR,—Three weeks ago I had a broody hen and sitting of Black Hamburgh eggs from you. I write to say that the hen has sat very well indeed, and yesterday morning brought off twelve chicks; the thirteenth died during hatching, I think through my own mismanagement.

Yours very truly, N. DENCE.

Brannocklie, Airdrie.

SIR,—I am pleased with results, eleven eggs having produced good chickens. Yours faithfully, T. JONES.

136, Brecknock Road, N.W.

DEAR SIR,—The hen (and sitting of Black Hamburgh eggs I bought of you on the 2nd March, 1889), hatched them all to-day; that is to say 12, as she broke an egg on the second day of her sitting. The chickens are all in good condition. Yours truly, E. SONDHEIM.

North End, Kirby Stephen, April 19th, 1889.

DEAR SIR,—I thought that I would tell you my luck this time. I set a hen with fourteen Orpington eggs, and I have got fourteen chicks, strong and healthy. Yours, etc., J. THOMPSON.

W. COOK'S

IMPROVED SITTING COOP.

THIS Coop will be found very useful by poultry-keepers, as timid hens often refuse to take to a nest when it is placed in a strange house.

The Coop can be placed in the house, close to the position in which the original nest was situated, and the hen will scarcely notice the difference. After the hen has taken to the nest, it can be removed to any convenient spot.

It is made so that it can be closed up to prevent rats or other vermin getting at the eggs, and will be found most convenient for sending broody hens by rail. It is also arranged so that, although the hen cannot get off the nest, sufficient light and air are admitted by means of a sliding door.

Strongly and Substantially Made, 6s. 6d. each.

W. COOK'S

IMPROVED POULTRY HOUSES

(*MOVABLE*).

Put together with Bolts; and free on rail.

SIZES.					PRICES.		
LONG.		WIDE.		HIGH.	£	s.	d.
7 ft. 0 in.	×	5 ft. 6 in.	×	6 ft. 0 in.	3	10	0
6 ft. 8 in.	×	5 ft. 3 in.	×	6 ft. 0 in.	3	5	0
6 ft. 4 in.	×	5 ft. 3 in.	×	6 ft. 0 in.	3	3	0
5 ft. 6 in.	×	4 ft. 6 in.	×	6 ft. 0 in.	2	19	0
4 ft. 6 in.	×	3 ft. 6 in.	×	4 ft. 8 in.	2	5	0

CHICKEN AND BROODY COOPS OF ALL SIZES.

W. COOK, "THE WALDENS," ST. MARY CRAY

(LATE OF TOWER HOUSE, ORPINGTON), KENT.

BIRD TESTIMONIALS.

Woodland Villa, Birkbeck Road, Enfield, N.
April 27th, 1889.

DEAR SIR,—The birds came to hand safely, and I am well pleased with same. Hamper returned. Yours truly, H. G. RAMSDEN.

Heywood, Lancs, March 21st, 1889.

DEAR SIR,—The fowls (Orpington cockerel and six pullets) arrived safely. I am very much pleased with them. Yours faithfully,
WILLIAM BOOTH.

Cheap Street, Frome, March 22nd, 1889.

DEAR SIR,—I enclose cheque for brown Leghorn cockerel you sent me, with which I am highly pleased. He has been very much admired by all who have seen him, and it clearly shows that anyone living in the country can safely leave the selection of their birds to you. Put in the run with some of my best pullets, together they make a splendid picture.
Respectfully yours, S. BAILEY.

Whitegate House, Halifax, March 20th, 1889.

DEAR SIR,—The two Orpington pullets have arrived, and I am very much pleased with the same. Yours faithfully, J. W. TILLOTSON.

Linton Rectory, Skipton, Yorks., March 17th, 1889.

MRS. BRERETON encloses cheque for Langshan cockerel and hens, and begs to say she likes them very much.

Dove Holes, by Stockport, March 2nd, 1889.

SIR,—I am in receipt of Langshan cockerel, and am well satisfied with your selection. Yours, &c., ALEX. FROGGATT.

Chapel Lane, Hoghton, March 20th, 1889.

DEAR SIR,—The Plymouth Rock pullets arrived safely. I am exceptionally well pleased with them, and shall certainly introduce your birds to poultry keepers here. Yours faithfully, J. MALLEY.

114, Abel Street, Burnley, February 26th, 1889.

DEAR SIR,—The Minorca cockerel you have sent me is a grand bird. I am well satisfied with your dealings. Yours, etc., J. WILLIAMS.

Ocean Road, Grangetown, February 22nd, 1889.

DEAR SIR,—White Leghorn cockerel received safely. I am well pleased with him, as I think him a good bird. Yours truly,
THOMAS E. MILLER.

Badsworth Hall, Pontefract, February 18th, 1889.

SIR,—The Leghorn cockerels you sent me are nice birds, and I like them very much. I enclose cheque. Yours faithfully,
R. HEYWOOD JONES.

Clayton Hall, Accrington, February 13th, 1889.

MISS NICKSON encloses cheque for the six pullets, which are very satisfactory.

Perry Barr, Birmingham.

DEAR SIR,—The Plymouth Rock cockerel you sent me is a cheap bird, and gives me every satisfaction. Yours respectfully, W. BRADFORD.

Wortley Hall, Sheffield, February 19th, 1889.

DEAR SIR,—Langshan cockerel received. I like him very much.

Yours truly, J. ROULSTONE.

Roundwood Park, Greystones, Wicklow,
February 24th, 1889.

MR. JAMES GOWER has received the two cocks, and is very pleased indeed with them both.

Skirbeck Parsonage, Boston, February 9th, 1889.

MRS. SEDGWICK is very pleased with the two Minorca-Plymouth Rock pullets received from Mr. Cook.

Fairchilds, Warlingham, February 8th, 1889.

MR. A. S. DANIELL encloses cheque for the seven Langshan pullets supplied by Mr. Cook. Mr. Daniell is much pleased with the birds.

Rosegarth, Dunoon, Scotland, February 16th, 1889.

MRS. CAMPBELL has received the two cockerels and pullet, and is much pleased with their appearance.

Chesterfield House, St. John's Hill, S.W.,
February 7th, 1889.

DEAR SIR,—I enclose cheque for the nine fowls, with which I am very pleased. Yours truly, G. FITZGERALD.

Eggington, near Leighton Buzzard, February 6th, 1889.

DEAR SIR,—Cockerel safely to hand. I am very pleased with the bird.

Yours truly, F. MEAD.

The Beehive, Reigate.

DEAR SIR,—Birds received. Accept my thanks for the handsome way in which you have treated me. I shall not forget you when I want birds or eggs. Yours truly, G. T. BASSETT.

23, Walpole Street, Birmingham, January 2nd, 1889.

DEAR SIR,—The bird arrived safely, and is in excellent condition. She suits me well. Yours truly, J. MORGAN.

Flixton, near Manchester, January 25th, 1889.

DEAR SIR,—I received the pullets safely this morning, and am much pleased with them. Yours sincerely, T. TAYLOR.

Newbold, Rugby, January 25th, 1889.

DEAR SIR,—My friend has received the pen of Brahmas and thinks them very good value for the money. Yours &c., W. DANIELS.

Hensall, Snaith, February 26th, 1889.

DEAR SIR,—Cockerel received. I am highly pleased with him.
Yours faithfully, W. LEE.

Earls Cottage, Maldon, January 23rd. 1889.

DEAR SIR,—Birds to hand. I am very pleased with them, especially the Langshans and Minorcas. Yours faithfully, H. M. BEART.

Clayton Hall, Accrington, February 15th, 1889.

SIR,—I enclose cheque for the Rouen drake and ducks. They are splendid birds, and I am well pleased with them. Yours, etc., A. NICKSON.

Attaryn, Newport, Mon., January 21st, 1889.

DEAR SIR,—I enclose £1 for the Langshan Cockerel, with which I am much pleased. Yours truly, W. C. COLLIER.

Helmcroft, Manchester, January 21st, 1889.

MRS. DEAN is pleased with the birds received from Mr. Cook yesterday, especially the Minorca cockerel. The Rose-combed Orpington cockerel is a very nice one.

2, Lubeck Villas, New Barnet, January 22nd, 1889.

DEAR SIR,—I am much pleased with the Silver Grey Dorking cockerel. But you always do your best for your customers.
Yours truly, ETHELBERT R. HUTCHENSE.

Manchester, January 4th, 1889.

SIR,—I am greatly pleased with the splendid pen of Aylesbury ducks you have sent me. They do you credit. Yours faithfully, A. MASON.

Redditch, February 9th, 1889.

SIR,—I am most pleased with the birds you have sent me.
Yours, etc., A. F.

FOR many years W. COOK has had applications to take Pupils to learn Poultry Farming, and the management, &c.; but had refused to do so, until about two years ago. He has taken a few, who have been much pleased with the knowledge gained. The fee is 10 guineas (which is very reasonable). The Pupils can stay one or six months, as they wish. Every branch of Poultry Keeping is taught practically. As his house is large enough, he can board the Pupils, if they wish (this being extra). He will be glad for gentlemen desiring to learn the business to come down and see the place—

"THE WALDENS," ST. MARY CRAY, KENT.

testify. I have not been without eggs for more than sixteen years, even in the most severe weather. The same Powders are used for bringing up young chickens, turkeys and pheasants, and this year they have been used with great advantage for young ducks; they have a good effect on all young poultry, assisting them in their growth, getting their feathers, and giving them health and vigour.

The quantity to be used is a full teaspoonful for eight full-grown fowls, and chickens proportionate to age, given from 3 to 5 times a week, with the morning meal of soft food; it is best to mix the Powder in the dry meal previous to adding the water, or it can be mixed in any kind of soft food. When the fowls are in full lay, or the weather mild, the Powder may be omitted for a week or so. A change does them good. I cannot state exactly the time to give it to young chickens, but early-hatched ones require it oftener than later-hatched, as the former suffer most from cramp, cold, &c., according to the weather. The use of it must depend upon the feeder's judgment.

These Powders are sent to all parts of the world. They help the fowls to produce eggs in the coldest weather, and also when kept in close confinement eggs are produced in abundance. Where many did not get an egg for three months together, since using the Powders they are never without them.

Sold in 6d. and 1s. tins, post free, 8½d. and 1s. 3d.; or 5s. tin for 5s., carriage paid; 12s. tin for 10s., carriage paid. Cash to accompany all orders.

SPECIAL QUOTATIONS FOR LARGER ORDERS.

POULTRY POWDER TESTIMONIALS.

Bridge Street, Tadcaster, March 26th, 1889.

DEAR SIR,—Please send me two 1s. tins of Laying Powders. My hens are now laying well, and I give the Powders credit for the increase in the number of eggs laid. I am, dear Sir, yours truly,

MR. W. COOK. E. PAYNE.

Fauldhouse, Scotland, March, 1889.

SIR,—I am pleased to inform you that the Poultry Powders I had from you have made a great improvement upon my poultry. When I began using the Powders the birds were laying very badly, but after the first week things began to mend rapidly, and within a fortnight I had abundance of eggs; therefore I can recommend it with confidence to all poultry keepers, as I have found nothing like the Powders for making eggs. I have recommended them to others, and you will know by their repeat orders that they also have found them as above. I am, yours truly, DAVID NELSON.

Hail Weston, St. Neots, Hunts, March 6th, 1889.

DEAR SIR,—I have had a great increase of eggs since I have used your Powder, therefore can testify to the great qualities of the Powder. I am trying to spread its fame amongst poultry-keepers of my district.

Yours truly, EDWIN W. ALLEN.

49, Hamilton Road, West Norwood, March 22nd, 1889.

SIR,—I have had very beneficial results from the use of your Poultry Powders, and can recommend them strongly to poultry keepers.

Yours truly, W. J. CLEAVER.

204, Wetmoor Road, Burton-on-Trent,
March 7th, 1889.

SIR,—I have pleasure in asking you to send me 27s. worth of Powders; the others have sold wonderfully well. People have come miles for them, and several have offered testimonials as to the efficacy of the Powder.

Yours truly, A. BOOTH.

Westfield, Beverley, March 19th, 1889.

SIR,—I find your Poultry Powder of great advantage to my hens. We are now, and have been for a long time, getting a large number of eggs from them. Yours faithfully, W. GRAHAM LEES.

London, S.E.

SIR,—Allow me to testify to the value of your Poultry Powder as an egg producer. Yours, etc., F. MARTIN.

Bearnett House, near Wolverhampton, April 24th, 1889.

MRS. GEORGE WARD will feel obliged by Mr. Cook sending her 28 lbs. of his Poultry Powder and 14 lbs. of his Roup Powder. Mrs. Ward has much pleasure in informing Mr. Cook of her thorough approval of both Powders. Since using the former, which she has done for many months, her egg supply has been nearly doubled, and she has found the latter a most efficacious preventive in all cases of threatened disease. Mr. Cook is at liberty to make any use he pleases of this letter.

Islington.

SIR,—I have used your Poultry Powders and Grit, of which I cannot speak too highly. I think them a great boon to anybody that keeps poultry. I also had a bag of the Moss Peat, which is excellent. So if you will forward the list of cross-bred pullets, etc., I shall feel greatly obliged.

I am, dear Sir, yours respectfully,
H. GILL.

March 7th, 1889.

DEAR SIR,—Please send me some more Poultry Powder. I enclose postal order to cover cost. At first I thought all fowls required was stimulating, and it would be cheaper to buy cayenne and hemp seed, but I soon found I was overdoing it, and concluded to give your Powder a trial, and speedily arrived at the conclusion that it was going to have the same effect as the wonderful Yankee nest, that caused fowls to lay themselves to death. I found I was wrong again, for as time went on the supply of eggs still kept up, and the birds began to look better; and now you could not find a lot that looked bonnier or brighter, or that do their duty better. Allow me to acknowledge the utility and efficacy of your Powder. Yours, etc., H. B. VAUGHAN.

Gee Farm, Motham in Longdendale, Manchester.

DEAR SIR,—I enclose P.O., value 1s. 3d., for Roup Powder, which came duly to hand. There is a very great improvement in my poultry since I began to use it. I am, Sir, yours faithfully, THOMAS HALL.

204, Wetmoor Road, Burton on-Trent.

SIR,—Please send me a five shilling tin of Poultry Powders, as I find my fowls are doing well (as regards laying) by the use of them, and for which I enclose P.O.O. for 5s. I beg to remain, yours, etc., A. B.

South Yorkshire Asylum, Wadsley, near Sheffield.

DEAR SIR,—Will you please send me three tins of your Poultry Powders, at one shilling per tin, for which I enclose 3s. 9d. I think I shall be able to get you a few orders, as we are forming a poultry club here; it is the best thing I ever used. Yours, D. C. A. KIRBY.

Kirby Stephen, Westmoreland.

DEAR SIR,—I have been using your Poultry Powder, and I find it the best thing I have ever tried. I would advise all poultry-keepers to use it. It produces plenty of eggs, and keeps the poultry in good health.

Yours faithfully, JOHN THOMPSON.

Skirbeck Parsonage, Boston, July 21st, 1888.

DEAR SIR,—I must tell you that since I have used your Poultry Powder I have literally had double the number of eggs. I wrote to you two months ago, when I was getting only four or five eggs from fourteen laying hens. Now I have had eight, nine, and ten eggs every day for the last month from the same number of hens, and they seem in splendid condition. I had almost made up my mind to give up fowls, as I thought I could not make them pay in my small run. Yours truly, NORAH SEDGWICK.

76, College Street, Dumbarton, November 17th, 1888.

DEAR SIR,—Please send on twelve tins, six of Roup Powder and six of Condition Powder. I find it fulfils all you say of it. Enclosed will find postal order for amount. I am, yours truly, ALEXANDER CAMERON.

DEAR SIR,—Please send me 1s tin of your Poultry Powders for laying, by return of post. I should also be glad of a small sample of fowls' and chickens' grit. I find a marked improvement in my hens, laying only since using a small tin of Powders. 1s. 3d. enclosed. Yours truly, M. M. HARRIS.

Elm Grove, Steyning.

SIR,—Would you oblige in sending one box of Poultry Powers at 5s., and one box of Roup at 1s. I must say a word in praise of your Powders. A few doses soon began to work wonders. I have twelve laying fowls. The last three weeks I have taken an account of the number of eggs, viz., 53, 51, and 64. I have not used it all myself. My neighbours have seen the result, my fowls averaging double the number of eggs to theirs; they were induced to borrow, and now they are co-operating with me for more, as it has benefited their fowls as well as mine. Yours, C. GREEN.

Coton Hall, Sudbury, Derby.

MRS. KEMPSON would be much obliged to Mr. W. Cook if he would send her, as soon as possible, a 12s. tin of his Laying Powder, which he puts in his book is 10s., carriage paid Mrs Kempson used Mr. Cook's Powder last year, and found it quite wonderful. Mrs. Kempson encloses a P.O. for 10s.

Hope Villa, Springfield Road, Bexhill,
August 13th, 1888.

DEAR SIR,—Please send me as under. Your Powder is a thing no one should be without who requires an abundant supply of eggs. I have sixteen young hens fifteen months old; they have averaged 118 each since 1st January, not bad, thanks to the Powder. Twelve 1s. packets, carriage paid, for 10s. Postal order for 10s. Please send off at once, and oblige.

Yours truly, A. WICKHAM.

INSECT POWDER.

W. COOK'S Improved Insect Powder has been proved to destroy all insects on poultry, pigeons, cage birds, dogs, and cats; also destroys black beetles, and is used largely for household purposes; its use is indispensable in keeping the nest and sitting hen free from insects; is perfectly harmless. Should be freely used just before hatching, both on the hen and in the nest, as it is impossible for chickens to thrive when covered with vermin. Sold in tins, 6d. and 1s.; by post, 8d. and 1s. 3d.; or 5s. tins, carriage paid.

INSECT POWDER TESTIMONIALS.

London, S.E.

SIR,—I have found your Improved Insect Powder most efficacious—not only in killing the vermin on my poultry, but in my dwelling house. When I came here it was infested, but by using your Powder I have destroyed them all—small vermin, blackbeetles, and also bugs. Yours faithfully, W. W.

Redcar.

SIR,—I cannot speak too highly of your Insect Powder. My birds were not thriving, and on examination I found they were covered with insects, but by a few applications I have succeeded in getting rid of these pests.

Yours truly, W. JARVIS.

South Lewis.

SIR,—Seeing your Insect Powder advertised, and being tormented with insects, I procured some, and am glad to say that by its occasional use I now keep quite clear of them. I recommend it to all my friends.

Yours, etc., M. THOMAS.

W. COOK'S

ROUP POWDERS.

PRESCRIPTION FOR MAKING UP THE PILLS.

FOR three hens.—Two heaped-up tea-spoonfuls of the Powder, 2 ditto of flour 2 ditto of Oatmeal, 2 ditto middlings or any kind of meal, with a small piece of fat of some kind, about the size of a walnut; mix with a little warm water into a paste, so that it does not stick to the fingers. The Pills should be made about the size of the little finger to the second joint. Give 2 Pills night and morning. If the fowls have the disease very bad, a little extra Powder can be used without doing any injury to the fowl in any way. Though very strong, it is not poisonous. If the invalids cannot eat, they should have something nourishing, such as bread and milk or stewed linseed, given warm. Always let them have as much food as they can digest. When the fowls first show symptoms of Roup they ought to have a teaspoonful of castor oil given to them, and half a teaspoonful of glycerine; even when they show signs of a cold they can have this given them. Isolate affected birds, and add camphor to all drinking water. Give the unaffected birds the Roup Powder in their morning meal—one heaped-up teaspoonful to 10 fowls. This will often stop the malady from going farther. On a cold or damp day a little of it is most valuable. When fowls are going on a journey, a Pill or two will often prevent them from catching cold. Many exhibitors use it and find it most beneficial. A preventive is better than a cure. It has saved the lives of thousands of fowls all over the world. In many cases it has cured them when all other advertised remedies have failed. If fowls are suffering from lowness, or their liver out of order, it soon puts them right and brings a bright lustre on their plumage, which improves them very much for the show pen. When a fowl has a rattling in her throat and difficulty in drawing her breath, give her a teaspoonful of glycerine, and when convenient stew some linseed and give from 6 to 8 teaspoonfuls warm. Keep the affected birds on straw, or moss peat; the latter is much the best. When the birds have swollen eyes bathe them in milk and water with a little camphor in it. Always wipe the face and eyes dry; if not, they catch a fresh cold. When a fowl has a thick discharge, called mucus, which corrodes round the tongue and throat, write me for lotion, 9d. per bottle, per post 10½d. Directions for use of same:—Take a feather, which dip in lotion, apply to the bird's mouth and throat, turn the feather well round the mouth—in this way it will bring much of the thick slime away. In bad cases it requires a second feather to repeat; then it is well to take a feather and dip in glycerine and also mop out mouth with that. This heals the wound. If this treatment is continued night and morning, the reward will be the bird's recovery. Price:—2s. tin, by post 2s. 4½d.; 1s. tin, by post 1s. 3d.; 6d. tin, by post, 9d.; or 5s. tin, carriage paid, 5s.; 12s. tin for 10s.

SPECIAL QUOTATIONS FOR LARGER ORDERS.

Can be had at any corn chandler's in the United Kingdom. Special arrangements made with Agents for sending it abroad.

CASH TO ACCOMPANY ALL ORDERS.

ROUP POWDER TESTIMONIALS.

St. Leonard's Poultry Farm, Ringwood, Hants.

DEAR SIR,—Please send us, early in April, 28 lbs. of your Roup Powder, and 28 lbs. of your Poultry Powder, and if you like to make use of this you are welcome to do so. We have used your Roup Powder under the most trying circumstances possible, and have found it most efficacious.

I remain, yours faithfully, J. M. REYNVAAN, Manager.

Berwick St. James, Salisbury, August 9th.

DEAR SIR,—Please send me one box of Roup Pills for poultry. I am pleased to tell you I took first prize at our Show for a Plymouth Rock cockerel and pullet under six months old, and shown with adult birds. These were bred from a cockerel and pullet I bought from you. I have three pullets, the same age as those shown, and they all commenced laying when they were four months and three weeks old, and have continued laying ever since.

Yours truly, T. KITLEY.

Freeman Lodge, St. Peter's, Kent, January 16th.

Miss WOOD will be glad if Mr. Cook will send her 1s. tin of Roup Powder to the above address at his earliest convenience. Miss Wood has found the last tin she had of great service. Stamps enclosed for the amount.

Hillside, Ewshot, Farnham, March 6th, 1889.

DEAR SIR,—Please find stamps enclosed, value 10½d., for you to send me, early, a bottle of your Lotion for roup in short-faced tumblers, and oblige,

Yours very truly, ALFRED J. BRITTON.

P.S.—The last bottle of Lotion I received of you cured five short-faced tumblers of canker in the mouth, and very speedily. A. J. B.

57, Idmiston Road, Stratford, E.

DEAR SIR,—I am very pleased to state that the Black Minorca hen which was almost dead through diptheric roup, which I brought to you for examination, and for which you advised your Roup Powder and Lotion, is now, and has been for some time, perfectly well and in full lay again. Had it not been for your Lotion and treatment, it would have been killed; but the thought occurred to my mind, perhaps you could cure it. Thanking you very much,

I remain, yours faithfully, E. TAFFS.

Windmill Terrace, Bregstock, nr. Thrapstone.

SIR,—Please send me 5s. worth of your Roup Powders, as I find them excellent for young chickens and for hens going light. I will not be without them if I can avoid it. I remain, yours, &c., A. CROSS.

Ruthven Street, Auchterarder, N.B.

DEAR SIR,—Please send us a tin of your Roup Powder. The last we had cured every case, and some of the fowls were nearly dead with roup.

We are, yours respectfully, A. & W. GRAHAM.

W. COOK'S
ROUP & CONDITION PILLS
FOR
PIGEONS.

OWING to the great demand for Pills for pigeons for colds and roup, and to help them through their moult, or when they are drooping and a little out of sorts, these Pills have been manufactured, and are found invaluable. When a pigeon has roup, give two Pills at night; if only a little out of condition, give one Pill. Sold in 3s. 6d., 2s., 1s, and 6d. boxes; or, post free, 3s. 8d., 2s., 1s. 1½d., and 7½d.

PIGEON PILLS TESTIMONIAL.

Douglas.

SIR,—Your Pigeon Pills I have found very good. I keep a number of Homing Antwerps and Barbs, and whenever I see a bird queer I just catch it and give it one of your Pills, and if not better I keep it up, and give it two night and morning, and invariably they get better. I have not lost one through illness since using your Pills. Yours, etc., JAMES SALTER.

W. COOK'S EMBROCATION.

FOWLS are frequently affected with rheumatism and cramp in their legs and feet, especially in cold and damp weather. This Embrocation is invaluable in these cases. If it is well rubbed on their legs and feet it relieves them at once. It is also good for young chickens affected in the same way. It is a great boon to poultry-keepers, and has never been known to fail.

Sold in 6d. and 1s. bottles. Free by post for 8d. and 1s. 3d.

EMBROCATION TESTIMONIALS.

Winchester, Hants.

SIR,—I am glad to say I have found your Embrocation for cramp in the legs very good indeed. By treating the birds as you recommend they soon get all right again. Yours faithfully, EDMUND JONES.

Kilkenny, Ireland.

SIR,—The Embrocation you sent me quite cured my fowls of cramp. After a few days' treatment I was able to let them run out in the pen.

Yours, etc., JAMES McKENNA.

W. COOK'S

Price List of Meal and Corn.

Meal Bags included. Delivered free to any Goods Railway Station in London.

CASH OR P.O.O. WITH ALL ORDERS.

	1 cwt.		½-cwt.		¼-cwt	
Improved Poultry Meal	19	0	9	9	5	0
Poultry Biscuit Meal	17	0	8	10	4	8
General Poultry Meal	12	6	6	7	3	6
W. Cook's Special Poultry Meal...	15	0	7	9	4	0
Bone Meal	14	0	7	0	3	9
Granulated Meat	21	0	10	6	5	6
Ground Oyster Shells	9	0	4	6	2	6
Meat Dog Biscuits...	15	0	7	9	4	0
Groats (whole), extra quality	19	6	10	0	5	3

5 cwt. of either Meal or Dog Biscuits, or part of each, made up to that quantity, carriage paid to any Railway Station in England.

The above prices include bags, and also free delivery in Carter, Paterson's London district.

	Sack.		½-sack.		Bush.	
Wheat (best)	19	0	10	0	5	0
Buckwheat (best French)...	18	0	9	0	4	6
Barley	18	0	9	0	4	6
Maize (small round)	18	0	9	0	4	6
Dari...	18	0	9	0	4	6

Prices of Corn are subject to alteration according to Markets.

Free on Rail in London.

Sacks charged 1s 4d., 1-bushel bags, 6d. each, but allowed for if returned to London Warehouse within six days.

Carter, Paterson will bring back all empties free of charge.

THE SPECIAL MEAL.

Is the best I ever used for Poultry—either laying hens, young growing chickens, turkeys, or pheasants. It can be mixed with cold or warm water; contains bone meal, oatmeal, and a small quantity of meat and other nutritious materials. It has given the greatest satisfaction to all my customers that have tried it.

GENERAL MEAL.

THIS is a cheap and useful meal, especially where the fowls have scraps from the house. It is much relished by fowls (also by cows, horses, sheep, &c.). It will mix with cold or hot water (not boiling) without becoming sticky. It is often used with the Biscuit Meal, as it helps to bind the latter.

BISCUIT MEAL.

THIS is one of the best meals of the kind in the market, as great care is taken in the baking of it. It contains a large percentage of meat and a little oyster shell. This meal can be mixed with cold or boiling water. When mixed with cold water, it should be allowed to soak for eight or ten minutes before being given to the fowls. It is a very bulky food, and swells very much after mixing.

POULTRY FOOD TESTIMONIALS.

Arbury Road, Nuneaton, December 8th, 1888.

DEAR SIR,—At the end of August last I had 1 cwt. of your Special Poultry Meal, and some of your Powders. I then put together a pen of white pullets (half-bred White Leghorns); three were hatched end of April, and three on May 7th. Their morning meal has been alternately your Special Meal, and barley meal and sharps, with a teaspoonful of poultry powders—occasionally I have used a little roup powder. The result is, that on November 14th I had the first egg from this pen, and by the 26th November all the six laid, as on that day I had six eggs—from the 26th November to this date (13 days) 56 eggs. This to my mind is good average laying. It is very evident your food and powder are very good for bringing on young fowls to lay early. Awaiting the favour of your reply,

Yours truly, GEORGE CLAY.

Samuel Street, Woolwich.

SIR,—I am glad to tell you that your Biscuit Meal and Powders are working wonders in promoting the laying of my hens. I am very pleased indeed with the results obtained from feeding on your system. Yours truly, H. HANN.

Emmett Lodge, Chobham, Surrey,
November 13th, 1888.

DEAR SIR,—I received the meals, &c., safely, and am well pleased with them. I see a tremendous difference in my fowls already. I am sure it is due to you, for the Insect Powder, Grit, etc., *have* improved them. I will send you a cheque in a day or two. Yours faithfully, DANVERS HAMBER.

4, Montrose Villas, The Terrace, Hammersmith, W.

DEAR SIR,—I enclose postal order for 15s. and 3s. worth of stamps for buckwheat, Special Meal, and two fountains, which arrived safe, and cannot, I think, be spoken too highly of, for my fowls seem to relish and enjoy them. We cannot get them here, and the fountains are a great boon, much better than the tins I have been using. I may tell you in this I took your advice of giving the cock some of your Roup Pills; you will remember I told you I had him indoors, where we kept him for a fortnight giving him the pills. He got quite well, and now seems as strong as a lion, also a fine looking fellow; and as for the pullet, *she is a picture*, fine shape, and much larger; although she has not laid yet, I think she will not be long. We are very pleased indeed with them, so that we tell everyone we know what good birds yours are.

Believe yours, &c., GEO. CROFT.

Lurgan House, East Molesey.

Thanks to the advice you are always so willing to give, and to your book, which I find invaluable, my birds are always in good health. I feed them on your Meals, and use your Powders and sharp grit, which I find excellent for fowls kept in confinement. Yours, &c., E. FOLLETT.

Warton Grange, Carnforth.

MRS. BARTON has pleasure in saying, in reply to Mr. Cook's inquiry of the 15th, that the Poultry Food he has supplied her with has been in every way satisfactory. The Buff Cochin chickens reared with it have grown well and feathered well, which she attributes to the carefully-selected and judiciously-mixed food on which they have been fed as supplied by Mr. Cook.

Bragborough Hall, Rugby.

LADY EVELYN RIDDELL is much pleased with Mr. William Cook's Biscuit Meal, and also with his Poultry Powders, which she has found excellent, not only for fowls of all ages, but also for young pheasants.

Havering Well House, Hornchurch, Romford.

DEAR SIR,—I have great pleasure in testifying to the excellence of the Poultry Meal supplied to me by you. I consider it one of the best foods I have ever used.

MR. COOK. H. J. PIKE.

St. John's Park, Blackheath.

DEAR SIR,—I began to keep poultry here about two years ago, and I have used your Poultry Meal and Corn during the whole of that time. I have been very successful with my poultry, both in the number of eggs obtained, and in the broods of chickens reared. I attribute this in a great measure to the excellence of the food and corn which you have supplied me with, and to the directions given to me by you, which I have followed very carefully.

MR. COOK. Yours very truly, EDWARD D. DRURY.

TO MR. COOK.

SIR,—I have much pleasure in saying that I have used your General Meal now for over two years with complete success, my birds keeping always well and in fine plumage, and laying splendidly. With the addition of a very little of your Poultry Powder my birds laid all last winter, only missing six days; and, without the usual fattening process, my cockerels of this year were ready for table at five months old. I enclose my card.

Reigate.

DEAR SIR,—I have much pleasure in bearing testimony to the excellence of your Poultry Biscuit Meal and General Poultry Meal, having used them most successfully in the rearing of young chickens and as general meals for adult fowls; I only keep a few, and last year I was but twelve days without eggs, which speaks most highly of their egg-producing qualities. It gives me great pleasure to recommend your Poultry Meals to my friends.

Yours faithfully,

MR. COOK. WILLIAM E. BLACKISTON.

Elmsleigh Hall, near Leicester.

SIR,—I have much pleasure in testifying to the quality of your Poultry Foods. Please send me the same quantity of food—5 cwt. I have also found your Poultry Powders very useful. Yours truly,

MR. W. COOK, Orpington. PERCY STAFFORD.

Ringwood, Newhampton.

DEAR SIR,—Please send me another cwt. of your Biscuit Meal. I like it better than any other meal I have ever used. My hens lay better since I commenced to feed them with it, and I consider it good value for the money.

Yours truly,

MR. COOK. C. H. MUSSELWHITE,

Ivy House, Swinton.

DEAR SIR,—In reply to your note respecting your Poultry Food, I have very much pleasure in recommending it to all poultry keepers, having used it myself for the last six months with very good results.

Yours truly,

MR. COOK. PERCY H. LEIGH.

Hundreds of Letters have been received stating how useful the Journal has been.

St. Alban's, Herts.

SIR,—I am most pleased with your Monthly Journal. The Hints for the Month have been exceedingly useful to me. Yours truly, J. W. S.

Gamlingay.

SIR,—I am sure your Monthly Journal has already been a great boon to many. I look for it eagerly every month. Each number seems better than its predecessor. Yours, etc., J. MARSH.

Manchester.

SIR,—I cannot speak too highly of your Monthly Poultry Journal. It is full of sound, practical, and instructive matter, which cannot fail to be instructive to all. Yours faithfully, WILLIAM SMART.

Oldham.

SIR,—Your Monthly Journal has been a great help to me. I wish you every success. I am sure it will soon get the very large circulation it so richly deserves. Yours truly, J. JONES.

London, S.E.

SIR,—I must congratulate you on your Monthly Poultry Journal. I have found in it many useful hints, although I have kept poultry for many years. It is a most excellent paper for amateurs, as the advice is so practical. It is useful alike for amateurs and those who have had experience in poultry keeping. Yours faithfully, JOHN WILLIAMS.

SIR,—Your Poultry Journal has been very instructive to me, the chapters on crossing being most useful. It is not filled with useless show reports, but with good sound information. Yours, etc., WILLIAM SEARLE.

SIR,—I am sure your Poultry Journal will become very popular, as it is filled each month with such information as cannot fail to give instruction to all who read it, whether amateur or poultry farmer.

Yours truly, U. DANE.

W. COOK'S
POULTRY REQUISITES.

W. COOK'S POULTRY FOOD BINS.

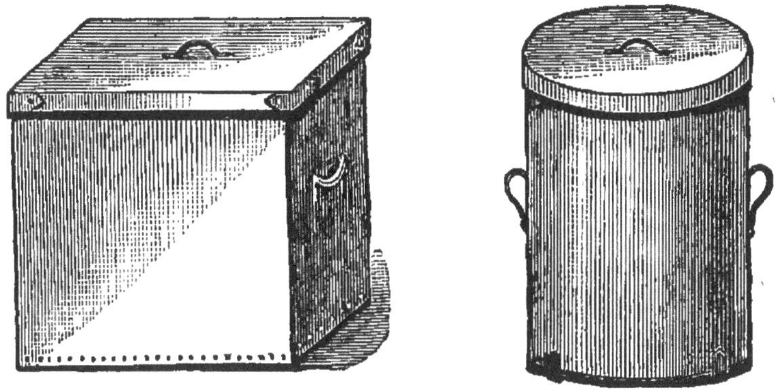

These articles supply a long-felt want amongst Poultry-keepers and fanciers. They are made of strong Wrought Iron, Galvanized. Where food is kept in bags or boxes a constant source of annoyance is caused by Vermin. By using these Bins all this is avoided. They are produced at such prices that they are within the reach of all; the outlay would soon be paid by the saving in food.

No. 1.	Round Bushel	... ...	7s. 6d.
" 2.	" "	... ...	11s. 6d.
" 4.	" "	... ...	19s. 6d.
No. 1.	Square Bushel (with Divs.)		9s 6d.
" 2.	" "	" ...	14s. 6d.
" 4.	" "	" ...	25s. 0d.

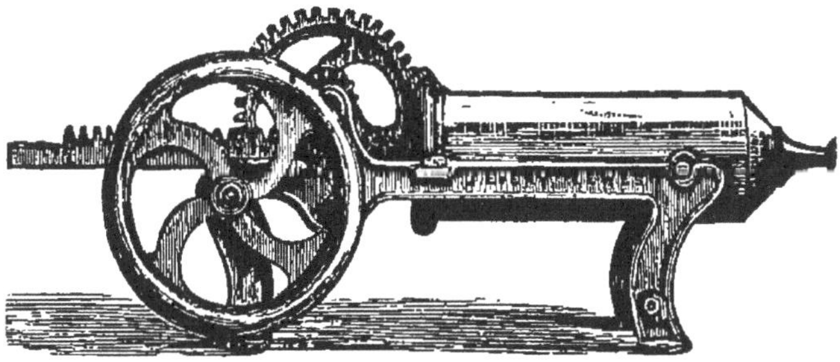

CHICKEN CRAMMING BY MACHINERY!

"IT is not generally known that the fine Fat Poultry and Capons London is supplied with are forced forward in the progress of fattening by the system called 'CRAMMING.'

"This system has been practised for many years in Surrey and Sussex. It is carried out by pushing a soft, rich barleymeal ball (well saturated and moistened with greasy buttermilk) down the throat of the chick. The bird is held between the knees, then with one hand the 'Crammer' opens its mouth, and with the other hand inserts the 'bolus,' which is pushed down the throat by stroking gently both sides of the neck.

"Crammed Poultry can be detected by the neck being always bare of feathers. This method is now improved upon by using a Gutta Percha Tube, which is attached to the Machine; the tube is thrust down the throat into the crop, and the food begins to find its way down as the wheel of the Machine is turned. By this means a great number of fowls can be fed or crammed in a little time. Two weeks' full feeding is sufficient, as they are generally in good condition when put into coops. Great weight is obtained by this mode of fattening; a couple of fowls weighing 16-lbs. is no uncommon sight when they are capons.

"It is said the fowls enjoy the tube process."—*Land and Water.*

JOHN EVERY has for several years manufactured Machines specially made for the above purpose, which are used by most of the large Poultry Farmers, to whom the same have given great satisfaction.

No. 1.—Barrel holding about 3 Quarts - - - -	**Price £2**	**15**	**6**
No. 2.— " " 6 Quarts - - - -	**" £4**	**15**	**6**
No. 3.— " " 9 Quarts - - - -	**" £6**	**15**	**6**
India Rubber Nozzles - - - - - - - - - - -		**2**	**0**

The above are strong, thoroughly well made, and have Barrels "Engine Bored."

JOHN EVERY,

PHŒNIX IRON WORKS,

LEWES.

Lightning Source UK Ltd.
Milton Keynes UK
UKOW06f1849250815

257528UK00017B/519/P

9 781313 372800